Trauma, Culture, and Metaphor

In *Trauma, Culture, and Metaphor*, John P. Wilson and Jacob D. Lindy explore the language of both individual and collective trauma in an era dominated by globalization and interconnectedness. Through lucid, careful discussion, this important book builds a bridge between the etymology of trauma-related terms commonly used in Western cultures and those of other cultures, such as the Burundi-Rwandan *ihahamuka*. It also provides the clinician with a framework for working with trauma survivors using a cross-cultural vocabulary—one often based in metaphor—to fully address the experienced trauma and to begin work on reconnection and self-reinvention.

John P. Wilson, PhD, is professor of psychology at Cleveland State University, a Fulbright scholar, and a widely recognized expert on PTSD. He is co-founder and past president of the International Society for Traumatic Stress Studies (ISTSS), a diplomate and fellow of the American Academy of Experts in Traumatic Stress, and a fellow of the American Institute of Stress.

Jacob D. Lindy, MD, is a clinical professor in the department of psychiatry at the University of Cincinnati College of Medicine and a training and supervising analyst at the Cincinnati Psychoanalytic Institute.

ROUTLEDGE PSYCHOSOCIAL STRESS SERIES

Charles R. Figley, Ph.D., Series Editor

1. *Stress Disorders Among Vietnam Veterans*, Edited by Charles R. Figley, Ph.D.
2. *Stress and the Family Vol. 1: Coping with Normative Transitions*, Edited by Hamilton I. McCubbin, Ph.D., and Charles R. Figley, Ph.D.
3. *Stress and the Family Vol. 2: Coping with Catastrophe*, Edited by Charles R. Figley, Ph.D., and Hamilton I. McCubbin, Ph.D.
4. *Trauma and Its Wake: The Study and Treatment of Post-Traumatic Stress Disorder*, Edited by Charles R. Figley, Ph.D.
5. *Post-Traumatic Stress Disorder and the War Veteran Patient*, Edited by William E. Kelly, M.D.
6. *The Crime Victim's Book, Second Edition*, By Morton Bard, Ph.D., and Dawn Sangrey.
7. *Stress and Coping in Time of War: Generalizations from the Israeli Experience*, Edited by Norman A. Milgram, Ph.D.
8. *Trauma and Its Wake Vol. 2: Traumatic Stress Theory, Research, and Intervention*, Edited by Charles R. Figley, Ph.D.
9. *Stress and Addiction*, Edited by Edward Gottheil, M.D., Ph.D., Keith A. Druley, Ph.D., Steven Pashko, Ph.D., and Stephen P. Weinsteinn, Ph.D.
10. *Vietnam: A Casebook*, by Jacob D. Lindy, M.D., in collaboration with Bonnie L. Green, Ph.D., Mary C. Grace, M.Ed., M.S., John A. MacLeod, M.D., and Louis Spitz, M.D.
11. *Post-Traumatic Therapy and Victims of Violence*, Edited by Frank M. Ochberg, M.D.
12. *Mental Health Response to Mass Emergencies: Theory and Practice*, Edited by Mary Lystad, Ph.D.
13. *Treating Stress in Families*, Edited by Charles R. Figley, Ph.D.
14. *Trauma, Transformation, and Healing: An Integrative Approach to Theory, Research, and Post-Traumatic Therapy*, By John P. Wilson, Ph.D.
15. *Systemic Treatment of Incest: A Therapeutic Handbook*, By Terry Trepper, Ph.D., and Mary Jo Barrett, M.S.W.
16. *The Crisis of Competence: Transitional Stress and the Displaced Worker*, Edited by Carl A. Maida, Ph.D., Norma S. Gordon, M.A., and Norman L. Farberow, Ph.D.
17. *Stress Management: An Integrated Approach to Therapy*, by Dorothy H. G. Cotton, Ph.D.
18. *Trauma and the Vietnam War Generation: Report of the Findings from the National Vietnam Veterans Readjustment Study*, By Richard A. Kulka, Ph.D., William E. Schlenger, Ph.D., John A. Fairbank, Ph.D., Richard L. Hough, Ph.D., Kathleen Jordan, Ph.D., Charles R. Marmar, M.D., Daniel S. Weiss, Ph.D., and David A. Grady, Psy.D.
19. *Strangers at Home: Vietnam Veterans Since the War*, Edited by Charles R. Figley, Ph.D., and Seymour Leventman, Ph.D.
20. *The National Vietnam Veterans Readjustment Study: Tables of Findings and Technical Appendices*, By Richard A. Kulka, Ph.D., Kathleen Jordan, Ph.D., Charles R. Marmar, M.D., and Daniel S. Weiss, Ph.D.
21. *Psychological Trauma and the Adult Survivor: Theory, Therapy, and Transformation*, By I. Lisa McCann, Ph.D., and Laurie Anne Pearlman, Ph.D.
22. *Coping with Infant or Fetal Loss: The Couple's Healing Process*, By Kathleen R. Gilbert, Ph.D., and Laura S. Smart, Ph.D.
23. *Compassion Fatigue: Coping with Secondary Traumatic Stress Disorder in Those Who Treat the Traumatized*, Edited by Charles R. Figley, Ph.D.
24. *Treating Compassion Fatigue*, Edited by Charles R. Figley, Ph.D.
25. *Handbook of Stress, Trauma and the Family*, Edited by Don R. Catherall, Ph.D.
26. *The Pain of Helping: Psychological Injury of Helping Professionals*, by Patrick J. Morrissette, Ph.D., RMFT, NCC, CCC.
27. *Disaster Mental Health Services: A Primer for Practitioners*, by Diane Myers, R.N., M.S.N., and David Wee, M.S.S.W.
28. *Empathy in the Treatment of Trauma and PTSD*, by John P. Wilson, Ph.D. and Rhiannon B. Thomas, Ph.D.
29. *Family Stressors: Interventions for Stress and Trauma*, Edited by Don. R. Catherall, Ph. D.
30. *Handbook of Women, Stress and Trauma*, Edited by Kathleen Kendall-Tackett, Ph.D.
31. *Mapping Trauma and Its Wake*, Edited by Charles R. Figley, Ph.D.
32. *The Posttraumatic Self: Restoring Meaning and Wholeness to Personality*, Edited by John P. Wilson, Ph.D.
33. *Violent Death: Resilience and Intervention Beyond the Crisis*, Edited by Edward K. Rynearson, M.D.

34. *Combat Stress Injury: Theory, Research, and Management,* Edited by Charles R. Figley, Ph.D. and William P. Nash, M.D.
35. *MindBody Medicine: Foundations and Practical Applications,* by Leo W. Rotan, Ph.D. and Veronika Ospina-Kammerer, Ph.D.
36. *Understanding and Assessing Trauma in Children and Adolescents: Measures, Methods, and Youth in Context,* by Kathleen Nader, D.S.W
37. *When the Past Is Always Present: Emotional Traumatization, Causes, and Cures,* by Ronald A. Ruden, M.D., Ph.D.
38. *Families Under Fire: Systemic Therapy with Military Families,* Edited by R. Blaine Everson, Ph.D. and Charles R. Figley, Ph.D.
39. *Dissociation in Traumatized Children and Adolescents: Theory and Clinical Interventions,* Edited by Sandra Wieland, Ph.D.
40. *Transcending Trauma: Survival, Resilience and Clinical Implications in Survivor Families,* by Bea Hollander-Goldfein, Ph.D., Nancy Isserman, Ph.D., and Jennifer Goldenberg, Ph.D., L.C.S.W
41. *School Rampage Shootings and Other Youth Disturbances: Early Preventative Interventions,* by Kathleen Nader, D.S.W.
42. *The Compassion Fatigue Workbook: Creative Tools for Transforming Compassion Fatigue and Vicarious Traumatization,* by Fran_oise Mathieu, M.Ed.
43. *War Trauma and Its Wake: Expanding the Circle of Healing,* by Raymond Monsour Scurfield, D.S.W., and Katherine Theresa Platoni, Psy.D.
44. *Healing War Trauma: A Handbook of Creative Approaches,* by Raymond Monsour Scurfield, D.S.W., and Katherine Theresa Platoni, Psy.D.
45. *Helping Traumatized Families,* by Charles R. Figley, Ph.D., and Laurel Kiser, Ph.D.
46. *Treating Traumatic Stress Injuries in Military Personnel: An EMDR Practitioner's Guide,* by Mark C. Russell, Ph.D., and Charles R. Figley, Ph.D.
47. *Trauma, Culture, and Metaphor: Pathways of Transformation and Integration,* by John P. Wilson, Ph.D., and Jacob D. Lindy, M.D.

Trauma, Culture, and Metaphor

Pathways of Transformation and Integration

John P. Wilson and Jacob D. Lindy

Routledge
Taylor & Francis Group
NEW YORK AND LONDON

First published 2013
by Routledge
605 Third Avenue, New York, NY 10017
4 Park Square, Milton Park, Abingdon, Oxon OX14 4RN

Routledge is an imprint of the Taylor & Francis Group, an informa business

Library of Congress Cataloging-in-Publication Data
Wilson, John P. (John Preston)
Trauma, culture, and metaphor : pathways of transformation and integration / John P. Wilson and Jacob D. Lindy. – 1 Edition.
pages cm. – (Routledge psychosocial stress series)
Includes bibliographical references and index.
1. Psychic trauma. 2. Psychiatry, Transcultural. 3. Psychotherapy–Social aspects. 4. Globalization–Social aspects. I. Lindy, Jacob D., 1937– II. Title.
BF175.5.P75W55 2013
616.89'14–dc23 2012041966

ISBN: 978–0–415–95330–6 (hbk)
ISBN: 978–0–415–95331–3 (pbk)
ISBN: 978–0–203–89357–9 (ebk)

Typeset in Minion
by Swales & Willis Ltd, Exeter, Devon

Contents

Series Editor's Foreword

"My wife is a rock," the hardened combat medic blurted out in a video interview with him between deployments at Ft. Hood, the sprawling U.S. Army base in Texas. He was explaining that as so many people come to him for help with their medical and mental stress, his wife was his inspiration in managing the distress all around her. Though not a therapy session, the interviews with combat medics, part of a three-year study, provided a window into the emotional landscape of men and women who are expected to keep their soldiers alive and well despite being in the middle of a brutal war.

Wilson and Lindy's important book provides the groundwork to appreciate the toll of psychic trauma and its treatment by carefully summarizing the advances in our understanding of basic brain functions and psychological processes in managing the cultural complexities and norms that take the form of linguistic metaphors. The authors argue that these metaphoric expressions can be the primary pathways for clients to recover from psychic injury including PTSD.

Because a metaphor is a form of expression in which one thing is likened to something else with similar properties, they are an extraordinarily personal and specific way for the traumatized to share with the world their unique views. Because a metaphor is a figure of speech and often a play on words, it provides an opportunity for those struggling with managing the emotional energy of memories, trauma survivors can access more areas of their brain to explain their current function in just a word or two.

Practitioners will appreciate that this book includes a description of the process by which most people attempt to make sense out of their traumatic experiences as a way of mastering and managing the consequences. They help describe how clients construct and deconstruct memory and their expression in behavioral manifestations and verbal metaphors; that these expressions reveal their relevance to posttraumatic psychological existence.

Throughout the book Wilson and Lindy illustrate how these posttraumatic metaphors are lexical, real and the product of one's cognitive processing. They argue that traumatic metaphors are the verbal expressions of deep internal states rooted in the complex, cognitive-emotional processing of these very difficult life experiences.

It will become clear to the reader that the authors are proposing an approach to assessing and treating PTSD and other trauma-induced challenges that combine existing approaches to treatment, psychodynamic, cognitive-behavioral, psychological–metalinguistic analysis, that is amenable to research verification.

Rooted in linguistic analysis, Wilson and Lindy argue that metaphors are especially important in recovering from trauma; that our metaphors provide pathways to discovery, recovery and psychic integration. Thus the reader, particularly the busy mental health provider, will be able to learn to listen for and emphasize the utility of trauma metaphors as signs of health and growth, ideal guideposts for success.

Charles R. Figley, PhD, Series Editor
New Orleans

Preface

On a beautiful spring weekend in Cincinnati, in 2008, John Wilson and his new bride Silvana Turkovic visited Jack and Joanne Lindy in their home in Hyde Park. It was a respite for Silvana who was adapting to her new country and battling several medical conditions that were carry-overs from her work in African war zones. John was completing several projects involving trauma and refugees; Jack and Joanne, ten years their senior, were adjusting to their newly semi-retired lives. Particularly lovely were the bright red cardinals and yellow finches feeding at their respective feeders, their colors brightly bouncing off of those of the flowers in the garden. It was a pleasant respite for all four. Jack was moving out of the office he had occupied for the past 27 years, and with that move had brought a painting home with him. The four reflected on their reactions to the painting. The artist was the survivor of a near fatal fall in which she crashed through a glass door, a crash that severed her brachial artery, leaving her collapsed and nearly dead from blood loss on her front porch. The painting, while beautifully crafted, evoked an other-worldly tone. Barely discernible as images were the door frame, some steps, the shattered glass and the porch. On the left of the painting was the figure of a woman, dressed in a shroud with the look of death on her face. Each of us speculated at some component of the painting, its tone, its capacity to rivet the viewer, the closeness to death, the potential of life. Was the woman in the painting the survivor, registering the moment of exposure to the abyss? Jack responded that the artist had said the woman was not her. It was rather the survivor's image of her guardian angel; a visitor from the world of a heavenly afterlife who had appeared at that moment indicating to the survivor that her time had not yet come and intervening so as to see that she did not die. Jack explained that he was working on a series of cases where, in the transference, the survivor had at times seen the therapist not as a figure in the distant past but as a figure located in the spiritual world poised somewhere between life and death. Perhaps, he thought, this type of transference was unique to work with trauma survivors. John was working on a book that was looking cross-culturally at ways different peoples conceive of the near-death experience. Somewhere in the discussion that followed the word "metaphor" in its broadest sense came up, how metaphor, in this case a guardian angel, seemed to be an organizing feature of the trauma experience. As John and Silvana were about to depart, John announced, "that's our next book, trauma, culture, and metaphor."

Such a project resonated well with Jack's life review process, one that came with a rush as he turned 70. He was already scribbling notes of stories from his life that he might fashion into reminiscences for the benefit of some grandchild someday who might discover them. Now he had incentive to ponder his clinical work as well, memories of patients who had shared their trauma experiences with him over a 40-year span. What came from this was a series of 60 case vignettes where he highlighted various metaphors that came to describe the subjective nature of the trauma for these individual survivors as well as later metaphors arrived at during the recovery process that helped them gain some mastery over their trauma experiences. Meanwhile, John was reviewing his wide experience with the many cultures he had encountered as survivors faced the complex journey from trauma to return, either to their own or new communities.

A second artist enters the picture at this point. Susan Carlson is a social worker and artist whose son was killed in a fatal accident during his 21st year of life, a time when he was on the verge of great potential as a student, as a musician, and as an altruistic human being. Susan, over many months, chronicled her subjective states of grieving after the sudden death in a series of art works that she now exhibits under the title, "I Can't Imagine." She had agreed to present the collection of her art to a small audience at the Cincinnati Psychoanalytic Institute and Jack was asked to be the discussant with her.

Living with Susan's impressive body of work for several weeks Jack fixed on several pieces. Soon after the death, Susan painted a still life as a project to take her mind off the chaos of her grief. The forms in the still life consisted of some books, an old photo, an open persimmon, some dried leaves, one small vase of dried flowers and another that had fallen, but seemed have no contents, onto the cloth-covered table. The painting was dark and lifeless. The broken twisted stem of an eggplant seemed to emerge from the antique photo, some broken connection between the generations. Interesting to Jack were some of the book titles, *Things Fall Apart*, *Concepts of Space*, *Forgotten English*, conceptual schemas as it were, that seemed to organize Susan's life up until now. The broken pomegranate, Jack saw as the broken promise of life of her son, each seed a blessing for the future that would never come to light. It seemed to him that the painting captured a series of older metaphors that described life as it should be, but that simply did not do a good enough job to capture the new world of traumatic pain she felt. It was the last representational piece she did for some time, as the next works were full of black images and repetitious words about the fatal accident. For purposes of this book, that first work seemed to convey the idea that resonated with the stories of his patients: after trauma, old metaphors just do not work.

A second work that captivated nearly all who saw it was the grouping of a series of words, "there has been a fatal accident." In almost child-like printed penciled form the same words repeat themselves in line after line, smudged with tears, stretching from one end of the canvass to the other, without punctuation, one word running into the next as though there were no syntax, and hence no meaning, as if the artist is trying to absorb something that will not register. It is a painting composed of words about an unspeakable circumstance, where there are no words to express the feelings.

Much later there is a third piece, equally devastating. This time the art is a small sculpture, a human figure with a complete hole hollowed out of the abdomen. Here we have the beginning of newly found bodily metaphor for the experience of the death of her child, the absence of the product of her womb, an internal emptiness. Indeed, as with my patients there had been periods of inchoate thinking, where words lost syntax and meaning. Then there were bodily metaphors that began to capture the essence of their trauma experiences, metaphors so wrenching that most would rather turn away than listen or see.

As we begin this book we turn to the special people who have chosen to share their Abyss Experiences with us, artists like Susan and Gretchen above, and others whose only art was the creativity of their own awkward but newly discovered words and phrases. In this book we want to honor them and the tragic experiences they have endured. We also want to join with them in their and our wish that their experiences add to some greater understanding of the world of trauma and therefore to the aid of others in the future who may have to endure similar journeys.

Acknowledgments

There are many special people that we wish to thank during the writing process and production of this book. First, we wish to recognize our wives, Silvana Turkovic-Wilson and Joanne Lindy, whose steadfast love, encouragement and commitment to our lifelong collaborative work has been supported unequivocally and enthusiastically.

Next, we wish to thank Dr. Charles Figley, now of Tulane University and editor of the Routledge Psychosocial Stress Series, who has been most supportive of this book project and its heuristic role for the future! In the same vein, a special thanks to Dana Bliss, Chris Tominich and Anna Moore, senior editors at Routledge Publications in New York City, whose criticism and remarks only served to make this book richer in scope and vision.

We are grateful to the Cincinnati Psychoanalytic Institute's Research Fund, to the leadership of the Cincinnati VA Mental Health Line, Peter Kotcher, M.D. and to Kathy Cutright, Director of the Cincinnati OEF (Operation Enduring Freedom)-OIF (Operation Iraqi Freedom) clinic and to the many others who helped with this book.

On a personal note of significance, we want to acknowledge Ms. Kathy Letizio, our personal assistant for over 15 years who ensured the quality and character of the book. Time and time again she worked long hours and tirelessly to make the book "top shelf" in its brilliance and literary quality. Thank you, Kathy!

As a word of further appreciation, we extend our heartfelt love and appreciation to all of the survivors, patients, and others who have shared their trauma stories and histories with us. Their openness and disclosures enabled the 67 case histories encapsulated in this book. They gave from their pain, sorrows and struggles to inform us and the readers of this book.

Finally, we want to thank our special friends and colleagues. From Cleveland, Dr. Patrick Enders, M.D. and Dr. E. Karl Schneider, D.D.S. and his beautiful wife, Lisa Schneider, friends of constant care and support of this effort. In Chattanooga, Tennessee, Mrs. Martha Butterfield, a dear and cherished friend for four decades. Our European colleagues, from the Netherlands, Drs. Jan Persoon, M.D. and Boris Drozdek, M.D.; and from Denmark, Dr. Libby Arcel of IRCT and her husband, Lars, all special and gifted people.

1 Understanding Psychic Trauma and Metaphors in an Era of World Globalization

Introduction

In centuries and decades past, especially in the 19th and early 20th centuries, the study and scientific analysis of psychological trauma revealed that it was becoming clearer to clinical investigators and research scientists that there were universal expressions of posttraumatic and complex self- and personality states after trauma but also multiple languages and metaphors cross-culturally for understanding them (Wilson, Friedman, & Lindy, 2001).

Intellectual inquiry, extending and broadening knowledge from that critical and historically pivotal scientific turning point on psychological trauma and abuse (1895–1945), the seminal European works of Freud (1895, 1914, 1923), Janet (1889), and Oppenheim (1895), amongst others, working respectively in Austria, France, and Germany, provided astute insights, discrete and clinical informative analyses concerning psychological trauma that would eventually transform dormant medical and psychological sciences in the study of traumatic stress syndromes. However, their medical discoveries did not converge and were subject to severe criticisms by prominent researchers, such as Jean Charcot in Paris in his investigations of hysteria.

Their scientific approaches ultimately laid new psychobiological bases of posttraumatic reactive patterns. Nevertheless, their seminal works began to establish and identify a structural-conceptual platform of intrapsychic dynamic processes that would allow future investigators a clear, useful, and heuristic pathway to follow. Later, these same scientific-medical patterns of prolonged stress reactions would reveal a coherent set of posttraumatic patterns of adaptive behavior.

The basic evolutionary stage was set in place for subsequent theoretical and scientific-empirical integration. Eventually, the findings would redirect professional inquiries in a set of complex investigative discoveries that recognized posttraumatic stress disorder (PTSD) phenomena, which later became a diagnostic entity of the American Psychiatric Association (APA) in 1980. In less than a century (1850 to 1918), the long anchored history of psychic traumatic experiences became a new medical-psychological phenomenon, one that would forever transform empirical knowledge and scientific studies in the 20th century.

Moving forward, in the 20th and early 21st centuries these empirical, research, evidence-based, and clinical discoveries of traumatic stress processes created medical and scientific foundations and unique groundings that advanced psychological insights worldwide and culminated in deeper wisdom after subsequent global wars, catastrophies, and conflicts (i.e., World War I, World War II, Korea, Vietnam, Iraq, Afghanistan, etc.). In time, other events throughout the world permeated two centuries of disharmony of the most unimaginable nature, including ethnic genocides (e.g., Bosnia, Cambodia, Congo, Croatia, Liberia, Libya, Rwanda, Sierra Leone, Sudan, Syria, etc.), refocused medical, psychological, and political/humanitarian investigations and new knowledge in empirical studies. Later, within this same time period, terrorism, unbridled ruthless aggression, and, ultimately, world threats of mass destruction of the human race by nuclear holocaust, acts of terrorism, constitute to this day an omnipresent threat to peace and security on a worldwide basis.

Trauma, Culture, and Metaphor: Pathways of Transformation and Integration Through Metaphoric Expressions of the Human Condition

This book is an attempt to explore how the experience of overwhelming stressful life events, psychic trauma, *articulates within the inner and outer worlds of basic brain functions and psychological processes, cultural complexities and norms, and results in verbalized linguistic metaphors.* These metaphoric expressions include conscious and unconscious mental processes and the intrapsychic encodings of traumatic experiences and as such have illuminated the Rosetta Stone for deciphering recovery from PTSD in our times. How does this therapeutic discovery process occur?

Orientation to the Book and Chapters

This first chapter is a foundation for those that will follow, especially in the initial forward and the foundational, critical Chapters of 1–5. We attempt to identify, analyze, and pursue inquiries into the linkage between traumatic experiences, their encoding in memory, their expression in behavioral manifestations and verbal metaphors that reveal or disclose to patients, clinicians, researchers, or others their relevance to posttraumatic psychological existence. Posttraumatic metaphors are lexical, real, and the product of intrapsychic mental processes. Traumatic metaphors, simply said, are the verbal expressions of deep internal states rooted in the complex, cognitive-emotional processing of these very difficult life experiences.

In basic respects, our approach is a psychodynamic, cognitive-behavioral, psychological–metalinguistic analysis that seeks to build on empirically research-grounded scientific data (i.e., evidence-based). In brief, it is a *top down–bottom up* approach to discovery and further clinical knowledge.

Trauma and PTSD disrupt the continuous flow to internal psychological processes at many levels. In the fractured state that follows trauma, the survivor invents new language, often disturbing metaphors that we do not want to hear, but that truly convey his or her posttraumatic condition (Chapters 2 and 3). The clinician, broadened by application of the Hero myth (Chapter 4), and the cross-cultural concept of the Nurturing Guide (NG) (Chapter 5), addresses these trauma metaphors in exploratory and healing-promoting manners (Chapter 6). In the process of recovery, the nature of each survivor's trauma metaphor changes in the direction of mastery and cultural re-integration (Chapter 7).

In groups of trauma patients (in treatment), where leaders attend to trauma metaphors, there is a different quality to the depth and meaningfulness of exchanges than in groups that minimize them (Chapter 8). All this leads us to recommend some changes in how we currently teach about trauma and its recovery (Chapter 9). Finally, in Chapter 10, we chart out some considerations for future research and educational efforts that may facilitate changes and innovations in educational curriculum.

Rooted in linguistic analysis, metaphors can and do provide pathways to discovery, recovery, and psychic integration. At this point in time, however, we believe that the hypotheses-generating questions are more important than our reflective questions about diagnosis and clinical orientations. In this sense, there is no future expansive vision of these complex intrapsychic-psychobiological processes without new creative paradigms of the possible organismic complexities. How do the systems of mind–body synergize posttrauma? What is the basic connection between internal biological processes and their psychic representations in verbal metaphors and mental states?

The Historical Advent and Scientific Role of Posttraumatic Stress Disorder (PTSD): Global Impacts and Changes in Scientific Research and Clinical Directions

As a result of the historic and global-changing world and ubiquitous, traumatic events, posttraumatic stress disorder (PTSD), as a centrifugal, mostly American-Western psychological phenomenon, became an official diagnostic criteria subsumed under the rubric of Anxiety Disorders in the Diagnostic and Statistical Manual revision (DSM-III) of the American Psychiatric Association (APA, 1980). Beyond doubt, from then to the present time (2012), the study of PTSD, in all of its facets, has become center stage in scientific investigations in the behavioral sciences, medicine, neuroscience, anthropology, and other disciplines. The term PTSD is now a household word in America, Europe, and elsewhere and appears in documentaries, movies, and television talk shows and media news reports on war traumas, disasters, and acts of terrorism. In the United States, there have been many excellent documentaries on the personal realities for Iraqi and Afghani war veterans suffering from PTSD as well as TBI (traumatic brain injury). These reports concretize psychic reality.

Portals of Entry (POE) to the Inner World of Psychic Trauma

We believe that "opening our eyes" to new posttraumatic language and ideas, e.g., to trauma-specific metaphors (TSM), trauma-specific transference (TST), trauma-specific complexes (TSC), trauma-specific archetypes (TA), etc., offers a new and valid cross-cultural method to find portals of entry (POE) into the central impact of trauma to self-processes (Wilson, 2006). Looking beyond what we at first could not see, trauma in its cultural dimensions and the effects of traumatic and overwhelming experiences to the integrity of persons, no matter where they lived in the world. How, then, do we sort out the trauma–culture relationship in terms of its impact to self- and complex personality processes?

Trauma-Specific Metaphors (TSM)

The central and critical questions facing us, in our scientific journey, are ones of trauma focus. What is the relation of culture to the inner psychic understanding of traumatic experiences? In a relevant article, to quote Smith, Lin, and Mendoza (1993):

> Humans in general have an inherent need to make sense out of and explain their experiences. This is especially true when they are experiencing suffering and illness. In the process of determining whether a particular explanation and associated treatment plan will make sense to the patient. Numerous studies in medical anthropology have documented that indigenous systems, such as ours, have health beliefs and practices persist and may even flourish in societies after exposure to modern Western medicine.
>
> (p. 38)

Pathways of Metaphor in Daily Life, Social Relationships, and Psychotherapy

The Nature of Trauma-Specific Metaphors (TSM): They Are There for Everybody: Just Pay Attention

What are common trauma metaphors and how do we identify them in usual life encounters, clinical practice, research interviews, and assessment protocols? What makes them unique and so important to our understanding of psychic trauma? Moreover, how do psychological and culturally-tied metaphors express themselves in interpersonal relationships and everyday life? How, specifically, are they manifest in psychotherapy? In this regard, the definitions of trauma archetypes and trauma metaphors and archetypal traumatic experiences are provided in Tables 1.1 and 1.2, and we will explore their essential relevance in later applications and chapters in this book. These initial tables provide a foundational basis of understanding how universal, archetypal traumatic experiences become the germinal ground for trauma-specific metaphors.

The Essential Definitions of Trauma Metaphors

The critical and essential definitions of trauma metaphors defined in Table 1.2 have direct applications to all forms of psychotherapy: (1) cognitive-behavioral therapy (CBT, CPT, PE); (2) psychodynamic treatment (analytic and insight-oriented); and (2) group-oriented counseling approaches or treatments (see Wilson, Friedman, & Lindy, 2004). What are the dimensions and components of trauma metaphors in psychotherapy? And how do they relate to modern CBT, CPT, and other current clinical trials of medication and psychotherapy or other *non-traditional forms* of healing?

A critical question is how to *decode and apply trauma metaphors* to psychodynamic and other (i.e., cognitive-behavioral, CBT, CPT, or EMDR, etc.) psychotherapeutic treatment processes? How to use them in prolonged exposure (PE) treatments of CPT or CBT? Are there mythological and metaphorical pathways to undiscovered traumatic phenomena and their expressions in language? How does this assumptive reality of PTSD appear in concrete forms of psychotherapy? How to generate empirical, evidence-based

Table 1.1 Trauma Archetype (Universal Forms of Traumatic Experience)

Dimensions:

1. The Trauma Archetype is a prototypical stress response pattern present in all human cultures, universal in its effects and is manifest in overt behavioral patterns and internal intrapsychic processes, especially the Trauma Complex.
2. The Trauma Archetype evokes altered psychological states, which include changes in consciousness, memory, orientation to time, space and person and appear in the Trauma Complex.
3. The Trauma Archetype evokes allostatic changes in the organism (posttraumatic impacts, e.g., personality change, PTSD, allostatic dysregulation) which are expressed in common neurobiological pathways.
4. The Trauma Archetype contains the experience of threat to psychological and physical well-being, typically manifest in the Abyss and Inversion Experiences.
5. The Trauma Archetype involves confrontation with the fear of death.
6. The Trauma Archetype evokes the specter of self-de-integration, dissolution and soul (psychic) death (i.e., loss of identity), and is expressed in the Trauma Complex.
7. The Trauma Archetype is a manifestation of overwhelmingly stressful experience to the organization of self, identity and belief systems and appears as part of the structure of the Trauma Complex.
8. The Trauma Archetype stimulates cognitive attributions of meaning and causality for injury, suffering, loss, death (i.e., altered core beliefs) which appear in the Trauma Complex.
9. The Trauma Archetype energizes posttraumatic tasks of defense, recovery, healing and growth, which include the development of PTSD as a Trauma Complex.
10. The Trauma Archetype activates polarities of meaning attribution; the formulation of pro-social – humanitarian morality vs. abject despair and meaninglessness paradigm.
11. The Trauma Archetype may evoke spiritual transformation: individual journey / encounter with darkness: return / transformation / re-emergence, healing (J. Campbell, 1949). The evocation of a spiritual transformation is manifest in the Trauma Complex as part of the Transcendent Experience and the drive toward unification.

Source: Wilson (2013).

research on these potential hypotheses and clinical studies? For example, do patients or clinicians engaged in CBT treatment protocols assess or probe trauma metaphors? If so, how does it happen?

To be clear, we do not have answers for many of the essential and existential scientific questions we will pose in this book but they will serve heuristic purposes and generate more theoretical and clinical hypotheses for future investigators (see Chapters 8, 9, and 10). It is a rich and rewarding inquiry of its own merit.

The Nurturing Guide (NG) as a Soul Protector and Mentor for Posttraumatic Journeys: The Host to the Places of Sanctity, Respite, and Temporary Peacefulness in the Soul

The Mythical Hero/Survivor, upon return, when fortunate enough, is not alone. How alone he or she feels upon re-entry depends on the opportunity to find trusted, loving friends, anchors, nurturing guides, counselors, clergy, fellow survivors, spiritual experiences, authentic personal relationships, fellow addicts, or fortunate encounters with God

Table 1.2 Trauma Metaphors: Conceptual Definition in Terms of Psychic Trauma

TRAUMA METAPHORS: DEFINITIONS OF SUBTYPES

1. The trauma metaphor is a spontaneous verbal picture of the traumatic event and serves as a psychic organizer to rearrange the nature and meaning of the experience. It encodes in memory at unconscious levels. It reflects unmetabolized aspects of the traumatic event and its impact upon pre-existing structures of personality. It represents the self in existential moments of phenomenological trauma.
2. **The structure of the trauma metaphor: Subtypes**
    a) The trauma experience itself represents conscious and unconscious elements in the experience and its consequences. Initially, it reflects unmetabolized aspects of the traumatic event and its impact on pre-existing structures of personality, identity, self-structure as a whole and integrated parts of daily functions and ego-processes. It becomes the deep inner structural and verbal synthesis of trauma. As it represents the latent psychological meaning of trauma as encoded in memory. As a transforming metaphor it serves as psychic organizer to rearrange the nature and meaning of the experience.
    b) The trauma metaphor is an organizer of *spontaneous* verbal pictures of the traumatic event and serves as a way to rearrange the nature and meaning of the experience. It is an *ongoing* intrapsychic process of complexity, which transforms over time as confrontation with the unprocessed memories occur and present cluster states.
    c) Trauma metaphors are verbal, i.e., cognitive expressions of the soul of the person's life following significant psychic trauma.
    d) Trauma metaphors contain unspoken truths of life, the self and the personal journey endured. Sometimes they reveal more about the unsaid than the said especially in psychotherapy.
    e) Trauma metaphors are reflections of archetypal journeys, universal in nature, progression, and meaning.
    f) Trauma metaphors evolve and change in *structural* and *functional* dimensions across the stages of epigenetic development, i.e., life-course ontogenetic development and change, the process of life-span evolution.
    g) Trauma metaphors appear in dream symbolisms, parapraxes and expressions concerning PTSD symptoms themselves in multidimensional ways.
    h) Trauma metaphors reflect culturally-shaped beliefs, values, ideologies, and ways of living. There is no proper understanding of trauma metaphors without a cultural embedding framework.

or God-given kindred spirits or the Spiritually Blessed (i.e., those with *Pax Mentix* ["Peace of Mind"]). Posttraumatic Nurturing Guides (NG) guides are simply that: Agents of different protocols, styles, and appearances to shepherd and oversee a helping way and caring relationship of good benefit to others. In one anthropological perspective the Nurturing Guide (NG) is a special entity, a chosen or special one, or mythological "Yoda" guide.

In the best sense, the Hero/Survivor can be assisted by Nurturing Guides (NG) who take many forms and or wear diverse masks and uniforms and role responsibilities (see Chapters 5 and 7), using their personal experiences and wisdom to help the *re-entry processes and journey* for those fellow-survivors they encounter.

The Hero Guides' Sensory-Psychic Acuity

In a sensory-based psychic wisdom, the sense, smell, and know what is about to happen to the Hero/Survivor or what may develop in the future. They are persons of character-based compassion and personal integrity (i.e., "just basic down-to-earth everyday people"), someone with whom we want to have a coffee, pancakes, eggs and bacon, green tea, a glass of good wine or strong liquor, or play soccer and then later smoke a Cuban cigar and drink cognac. They are folks of comfort, naturalness, ease, and authority with inner strength, character, and sense of being present in the moment.

Two Directions of Soul Journey: Teaching and Loving

The Nurturing Guides (NG) represent the roles of caring, teaching, and loving, which, for the survivor, may not be evident until the stresses, challenges, horrors, and travails of their particular journey become clearer and emerge in more transparent patterns and then find a way into their life-structure of personality functions and daily living. Eventually, it typically becomes more focused in direction and rises to the necessary functions of astute consciousness between two kindred spirits; between the Good and the Bad, between the dialectic poles of self-destruction versus self-integration and healing of the organism and the soul of the survivor. Ultimately, spiritual transformation and personality integration (see Chapters 9 and 10).

When these moments of conscious posttraumatic epiphany occur, there is a God-given moment and inner sense of relief associated with new insights about uncertainty and the intrusion and travails of the unwelcomed memories of traumatic events and the life journey. There are *rare moments* of instantaneous traumatic transformation; acute life moments of change and hopeful, spiritual revelations as to a new future of a God-blessed existence. But, what if that does not happen (see Chapter 4)?

At these moments of astute, higher awareness and inner psychic tension, regarding self-consciousness and awareness, that which was previously avoided or "put on hold," emerges more fully into conscious reality in new forms, i.e., old previously unwanted traumatic or bad memories that were "unsaid," "unbidden," "unspoken," and "unwanted" because of their painful nature. When this set of intrusions from the "unwanted" past occurs, the entire posttraumatic cycle "resets" itself.

For the victim or survivor, it is the existential moment of self-confrontation and the life-pain of the worst sort due to immersion in the Abyss Experience (AE). That is, the worst of memories comes back and challenges life, once again in painful recollections.

Re-Entry: The Ongoing Journey of Trauma Recovery

How do we follow the trauma survivor's journey on the return from the Abyss Experience (AE), the darkest forces of psychic trauma? What clues might he or she give us as to the nature of their psychological posttraumatic inner-space and ability to access crucial affective states concerning experiences and movement toward recovery and return home?

A Metaphor of Surfing "Life" and Trauma Encounters

The Journey of the Trauma Survivor (JTS) is sometimes like a surfer on a good ride on magnetic, fun, desirable, and challenging ocean waves. For them, at the peak moment of joy in the ride of adrenaline and happiness, it is as if catching a top crescent wave breaking the crust of the ocean's blue-white turbulence and their ride on the wave, at that moment, is the source of life enjoyment. *It is a peak experience of psychic flow-infused mental orgasm in the moment of consciousness.* Some surfers ride the wave with ebullience, adrenaline pumping and enhanced *in-the-moment* joy of life. Others fall off their boards into the ocean.

Some board riders end up on the ocean's floor or coral reefs or, if lucky, a sandy, soft beach. And so it goes for the trauma survivor. Some ride the waves and master them. Others never do. When that happens, the ocean rules the outcome.

The Need for Nurturing Guides (NG)

Knowledge of how cultures deal with trauma can be found in the great mythologies of the world (Campbell, 1949). Mythology contains themes that converge across cultures, literary forms (e.g., epochs), style, storytelling, and oral histories (e.g., Native American myths, rituals, traditions of knowledge). The analysis of these recorded and unrecorded and unwritten myths (oral histories) are a rich source of inquiry as to the interplay between culture, traumatic events, and their transformation by facing challenges to life in a more universal sense.

These myths and traditions contain or embed accumulated and passed-on traditional wisdoms, often of an oral, verbal storytelling mode, rather than written form. They are typically passed from wise elders, shamans, and keepers of the secret knowledge known by few others.

The American linguist mythologist, Joseph Campbell (1949, 1992), researched the universality of myths in many of the world's literatures and cultures, including the myth of the Hero (i.e., survivor) who journeyed into Zones of Danger (ZD) only to emerge transformed in mind, body, and spirit (Campbell, 1949). A simplified illustration (see Figure 1.1) of this important myth includes personal encounters of trauma, disaster, war, and individual confrontations of the demonic, evil, catastrophic, or of the traumatic dimensions or elements of the Abyss of trauma (see Figure 1.1).

Myth of the Hero and 21st Century Applications of the Nurturing Guide (NG) to the Survivor

How do we elaborate and expand on Joseph Campbell's life-accumulated insights to the Hero–Survivor mythology?

- *The Life Journey (LJ)* that can begin at any point in life-span development and existence, from childhood to old age. A journey to the unknown or unexpected or traumatic experiences or personal difficulties of an extreme, upsetting nature and altering nature (e.g., unexpected death, killing children, foreign enemy, pregnant wives, etc.) to basic psychological processes and life itself (e.g., how could this happen to me?).

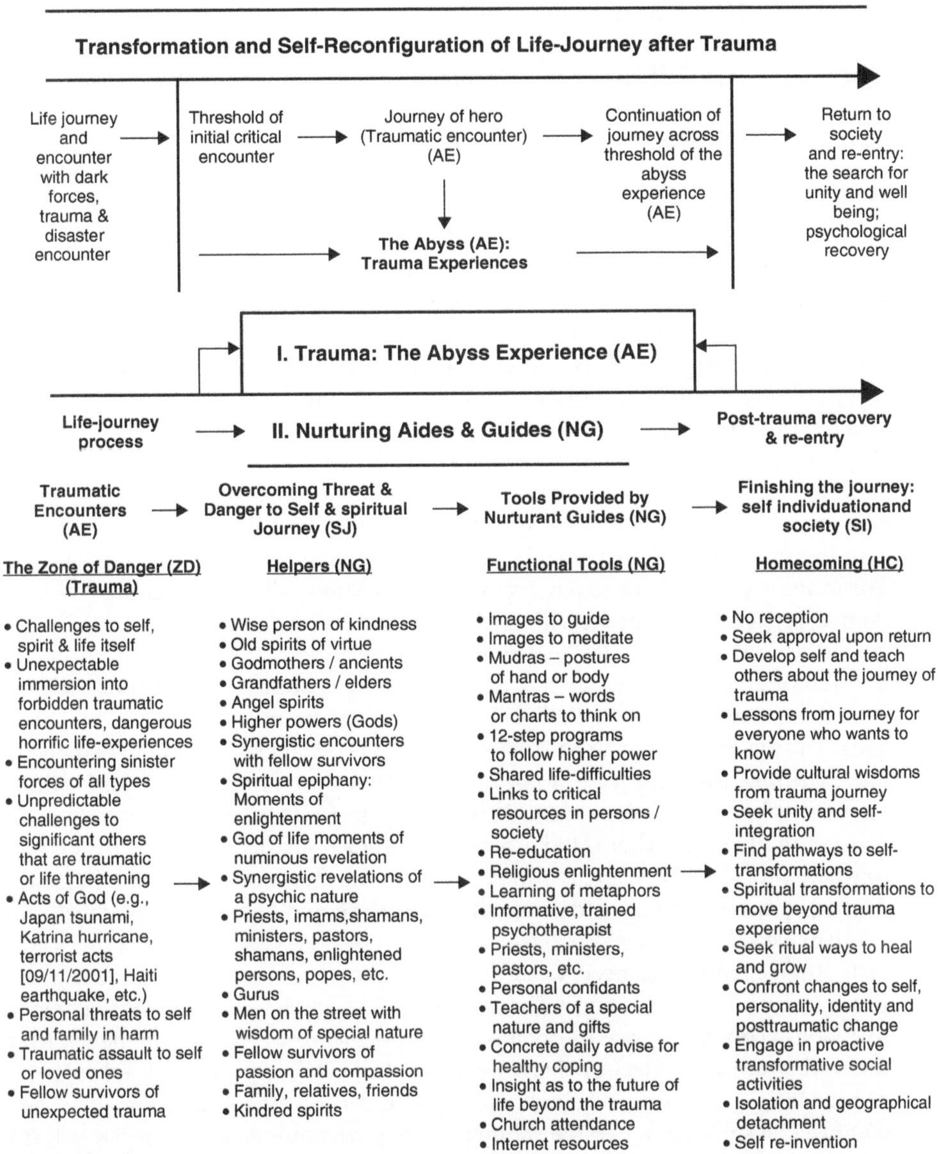

Source: Wilson, 2011

Figure 1.1 Mythology and the Journey of the Hero/Survivor: the Abyss Experience and Transformation of Psychic Trauma: The Role of the Nurturing Guide (NG)

- *The Trauma Encounter (TE)* with the trauma, abuse, death, losses, life challenges, threats, personal bereavement, and disasters that are multidimensional in nature of many types; the Zone of Danger (ZD) and all that it embraces in culturally-specific and historical realities.
- *The Zone of Danger (ZD)* to entry and exit from an existence of powerful natural or supernatural forces, which create life-altering experiences that encompass different

and overwhelming facets to one's understanding of the meaning of life itself (e.g., Why me, God, why do I have to go through this?).

- *The Four Tests* (see Chapter 5) of the human spirit to the traumatic encounter and survival of the experience and life itself.
- *Trauma and the Great Cycle of Living and Dying*: What is the life journey and one's role in it? Why does it change? Why does one have to endure these tribulations and trials of spirit? Beyond these fundamentals, what remains on re-entry?
- *The Return of the Survivor and the Task of Transformation Upon Re-entry into Society as Previously Known*: The expected and unexpected re-entry process into one's known culture, replete with disappointments, joys, and confusion. Who really cares or wants to know the truth of what one had to experience? These are among pervasive, pressing concerns and existential questions for victims and survivors. They do not go away or just disappear. What is next for the family, wives, loved ones, and their life journey?
- *The Transformation of Self and Identity in One's Culture and Nation of Origin after the Traumatic Journey*: What do these posttraumatic changes in personality and self-identity mean? How does one find the "new me" and go on? What does self-reinvention mean and how can it be achieved? How to find a pathway for the future? For example, sometimes survivors say, "I don't know where I am going." This, of course, reflects a time of searching and reformation and reinvention of the self, a period of soul-searching and questioning the meaning of life. It is often confusing and full of emotional uncertainty, anxiety, and daily somatic tensions of different sensory-somatic expressions. Who, indeed, is the posttrauma trauma person in their soul identity? How to be the Nurturing Guide (NG) or anchor person to help them?
- *A New Pathway and Ideology of Life after the Return from the Heroic Trauma-Based Journey*: What to believe in now? Where do I go from here? What was or is my mission in life now? What is the future about in its potential context? How do I get to where I want to go? There is a strange part of me that wants to go back in Iraq or Afghanistan or Vietnam and relive the adrenaline and "living on the edge." The survivor asks, "am I crazy?"
- *New Attachments*: The need to attach or detach to those who feel needed is a posttraumatic common corner. The need to find or search for an intimate partner or to establish controlled ways of isolation and/or detachment. To remove the self from memories and reminders of that which was unspeakable or too painful to say in normal life (i.e., the unspeakable) or share with trusted others and find a detached, comfortable solitude. When the trauma survivor becomes detached, separated, and distanced in personally controlled ways they end up alone and isolated. Their anxiety does not diminish, but by imposing detachment and isolation, they feel control over their tension, PTSD episodes and life-spaces (Wilson, 1980, 2006).

Travails, Pathways, and Trauma-Related Life Journeys

The Myth of the Hero (MH) concerns the travails of ordinary people through unordinary extreme experiences. In some cases, these myths characterize the life journey itself, beginning with youthful innocence, hope, vision, exuberance, and naivety and the eventual encounter with powerful forces of seemingly insurmountable dimensions, in which one feels vulnerable, if not inadequate and insecure, when confronted with such realities.

There are so many divergent, complex variations on the themes of this myth and how the individual is transformed by the nature of their life experiences. For example, young men become war-hardened combat veterans (e.g., one, two, three, or more combat tours in World War II, Korea, Vietnam, Iraq, or Afghanistan). The apprentice shaman who enters the underworld of spiritual and forceful encounters with "demonic," awful, ugly beings or entities of a hellish-sinister reality (Wilson, 1989). The knight of the king's realm challenges dragons, beasts, and the search for sacred, lost symbolic objects that have secret powers important to sovereignty and political, moral authority (see Campbell, 1949, 1992; Wilson, 1989).

In essence, the Mythological Journey of the Survivor-Hero (MH) is the journey and psychological sequelae of the trauma victim. While not immediately transparent, they are *not* the same at first look and become enormously complex in nature and psychic constellations.

The fundamental processes and comparisons are parallel and undeniable in analogies and metaphors, amongst other aspects of verbal expressions and psychological dimensions. In both scenarios, they encounter difficult, dark, extreme stress, overwhelmingly difficult life experiences, sinister, life-threatening forces at critical threshold points to cross and to re-enter normal life and society. Traumatic experiences can and do "invert" psychic realities (see Wilson, 2006, for a discussion of the Inversion Experience after trauma).

The power of life-threatening dark forces constitutes the essence and nature of the Abyss Experience (AE) (Wilson, 2005). During the Abyss Experience (AE) the individual confronts the specter of death, extreme threats and overwhelming immersion into traumatic stressors or other abnormal experiences outside the boundaries of conventional societal expectations, experiences, and moral structures. These confrontations change the meaning of life for most people in significant and powerful directions. The continuity of life past is now forever altered in directions yet to be discovered. Discontinuity in self and living now seeks a new pathway in the wake of finding renewed self-continuity. It is a difficult journey to find integration, self-peace, and comfort; it is the journey of the soul and self-identity, which may take a lifetime to create personal meaning in a self-centered, personal cosmos of meaning.

The Archetypal Journey of the Trauma Survivor Continues Unabated Into the Future

In most cases, the re-entry journey of the trauma survivor is not a simple one. *It is not* a simple, unenigmatic, uncomplicated process of going from point A to point B in a life journey. Indeed, the traumatic Abyss Experience (AE) always changes everything about life itself (see Table 1.1 for a discussion). In brief outline form, there are at least five dimensions of the Abyss Experience (AE) (Wilson, 2006) and re-entry which include: (1) the confrontation with unspeakable evil and death; (2) the experience personal and or soul death with the possibility of non-being (personal physical or soul death) and total personal annihilation; (3) a sense of abandonment by humanity; (4) ultimate existential aloneness, despairing about life itself; and (5) cosmic challenge of meaning of one's spiritual life and purpose. The survivor often experiences these dimensions and is existentially alone in their journey.

Who Is Indiana Jones? What Is His Identity as a Hero/Survivor Icon?

The fictional cinematic character, "Indiana Jones," embraces and embodies all of the positive attributes of Joseph Campbell's Mythical Hero on a life journey but always manages to overcome the travails of the Abyss Experience and live for another day of adventure. Indiana Jones is the mythical antithesis of the traumatized Hero/Survivor.

In a deeper fundamental analysis, these five dimensions correspond to basic or core posttraumatic phenomena: (1) the trauma experience: (2) identity and personality impacts; (3) loss of connection or continuity in ego-processes and a sense of self-sameness and continuity with one's culture; (4) separation and isolation experiences; and (5) spirituality and sense of the numinous and higher spiritual experiences and encounters. Upon re-entry into society and the posttraumatic world after the Abyss Experience (AE), the survivor faces the task of transformation of self and the psychic trauma metabolism of these extraordinary experiences and encounters. It is not an easy but inevitable task for trauma survivors because their worldview has often turned upside down and inverted in so many ways, subtle, overt, and beyond initial comprehension.

The Discovery of Nurturing Guides (NG): A Gift From Higher Spiritual Powers and Cultural Rituals of Transformation and Healing

The Survivor-Hero, if lucky, discovers nurturant Helper Guides (NG) who take the archetypal form of Wise Old Men (WOM) or Women (WOW), Spirit Guides (SG), deceased Elder tribal relatives as Spirit Guides (ESG), the embodiment of God, or an Angelic Persons (AP), Spiritual Persons (SP), or another survivor (i.e., kindred soul survivors, KS) who have had similar traumatic or harrowing experiences (e.g., a recovering addict, alcoholic, disaster survivor, abuse victim, war veteran, a catastrophic disaster victim, a traumatically bereaved person, cancer survivor, heart attack victims, traumatically injured individuals, accident victims, etc.), who can assist in the processing of the re-entry journey itself, having suffered an uncomfortable return experience by society in its usual ways and customs of greeting returning survivors. These kindred spirits (KS) already know about the difficult and tension-filled interface between the dark spaces of the life journey and the re-entry process (see Figure 1.1 for an overview of these roles, persons, and processes).

The Culture of Origin and Homecoming Expectations for the Returning Hero/Survivor

In general, most non-survivors in the re-entry environment expect that when the Hero (MH) returns, they will be emotionally and psychologically the same as they were before the trauma journey, i.e., the same person, and will resume normal living *as before* their journey of trials and tribulations, as if nothing happened to them in the trauma journey. In short, there will be continuity and sameness in their identity and personality, falsely assessed in almost all cases.

Posttraumatic changes in identity and self are not necessarily pathological but those in the homecoming environment may not understand these differences in functioning. Unfortunately, clinically and otherwise, this rarely occurs and the survivor senses it immediately. They don't need fortune cookies. For them, it is shocking and emotionally painful. But, in many PTSD cases, hyperarousal and hypervigilance pre-dates the return home and they are already defensively prepared for the worst, just like combat in war zones, or the hurricane or rape attack. The brain, as a computer, is rewired and pre-set (i.e., allostasis) at new program levels and dynamics. Their organismically biological state is still the same as during the trauma but with anticipated anxiety responses and a broad range of adaptative behaviors, actions, and dispositions. In a sense, an older body but newly rewired posttraumatic brain and behavioral dispositions (Wilson, Friedman, & Lindy, 2004).

The Hero's Journey Continues: Vicissitudes and Tasks of Future Life

Re-Entry: Acceptance, Rejection, Disorientation, Confusion, and Reflections

The expected, loving return for survivors rarely happens and sets in motion an intrapsychic dialectic between the survivor and his or her culture, friends, and loved ones. The dialectic acceptance encounter initiates a process of ideological and value changes as to how life should be lived on a daily basis. What matters now (i.e., post-trauma) and how to go about it, living in the present? For many survivors, the conflict is the unwanted and distressing struggle to get valued others to know their new sense of self which is nascent in form—yet to emerge (see Figure 1.1).

Pathways of Psychic Metaphoric Metabolisms of PTSD and Posttrauma States of Existence

Figure 1.2 illustrates the expected pathways of psychic metaphoric metabolism, after a traumatic event, and processes of integration that occur gradually over time.

Tabla Rosa: Ten Phases of Linguistic Transformations of Trauma Experiences: The "Big Picture" of Metaphoric Epigenesis

As Figure 1.2 illustrates, there are at least ten distinct phases to the chronological progressions of the posttraumatic metabolism of extreme stress experiences, beginning in phase I with the organismic, multi-leveled effects of trauma. As such, these are systematic organismic pathways of differential effects to psychic states and psycho-biological processes (e.g., brain functions, memory, cognition, hyperarousal states, etc.). But, in the initial phases of organic/physical transformation, they evolve and differentiate like cell metabolism.

In phase II, there are corresponding impacts to self and personality processes which we will discuss in detail in Chapter 3. These functions constitute the initial foundation of the posttraumatic self (PTS) in its complexities and structural forms. In short, the (PTS) dimensions of ego-states and identity are synergistic.

Phasic Sequence	*Posttraumatic Pathways of Psychic Vicissitudes of Metamorphic Manifestation in Consciousness and Language Metaphors*
I & II Initial traumatic impacts to body and self-process (metabolic)	**I. Traumatic Events: Stressor Effects to the Organism: Multileveled Effects of Traumatic Impacts (Embryonic Psychic Phases)** Physic Flow: Pathways to Effects to Psychic States and Psychobiological Processes (Physiological Body and Somatic Practices) **II. Impact to Personality: The Creation and Formation of the Posttraumatic Self (PTS)** Multilevel Impacts to Personality and Self-Structural Processes
III & IV Stages of metabolism and a metamorphic genesis and biopsychic emergence	**III. The Initial Process: Undifferentiated Nascent Germinal Stages of Traumatic Effects: Shapeless and Almost Wordless Forms of Expression in Metamorphic Expressions** Germinal Stages: Metamorphic Language to Describe Injury in Basic Forms of the Organism that May Be Undifferentiated and Emotionally Unclear or Confused **IV. The Core Dimensions of Personality and the Posttraumatic Self: How Trauma Creates the Genesis of Traumatic Metaphors and Beyond as Expressed in Self-Processes and Verbalized Linguistic Manifestations** Genesis of Metaphors: Psychic Metabolism and its Progression in Epigenesis of Identity
V–VIII Transformation and working through unmetabolized trauma issues and information	**V. The Conscious and Unconscious Creation of Trauma Specific Metaphors (TSM) of Traumatic Life Experiences (TLE)** Levels of Awareness of Trauma Impact to the Self and Personality: The Inner Self as an Emergent Posttraumatic Entity and Phenomena **VI. The Nature of Traumatic Metaphors as Physical or Verbal Encoding of the Trauma Experience: Impact to the Intrapsychic Structure of Internal Ego-and Self-Processes** Metamorphic Encoding: Idiosyncratic Cognitive Processes and Metabolism **VII: The Verbalization of Expression of Metaphors in Psychotherapy and Everyday Life** Verbalized and Somatic Expressions via Metaphors: theUnsaid and Said Components of Trauma: Disclosure of Importance in Therapy and Life **VIII: The Utilization and Interpretation of Trauma Metaphors in Posttraumatic Psychotherapy and Beyond: The Role of Metaphors in Treatment** Metaphors in Treatment: Interpreting Internal States Reflective of Metaphoric Expressions
IX–X Resolution, integration and synthesis	**IX. The Gradual Transformation of Trauma Metaphors and Psychic-Emotional Movement Towards Integration** Metamorphic Transformations: Therapeutic and Other (NG) Bridges to Self-Integration and Self-Individuation **X. Resolution: Insight and Understanding of Trauma Metaphors, Self-Synthesis, Integration and Personal Transformation** Integration in Self-Structure of New Configurations (PTSD): Reinvention of Self in its Relevant Dimensions: Self-Transformation After Journey; Appreciating the Nurturing Guide

Figure 1.2 Metaphors: Doors to Intrapsychic Processes in Trauma Victims

Embryonic Phases of Trauma Metaphors: Introduction to Sequencing Phases I–III

The initial phases (I and II), generatively set up (i.e., determine) phase III in which there are undifferentiated, nascent germinal (evolved embryonic) stages of traumatic effects to posttraumatic adaptive functions. In metaphorical terms, they can be construed as almost wordless and shapeless forms of embryonic posttraumatic psychic expressions, much like a nascent human embryo about to unfold and undergo fetal epigenetic development. As such, metaphoric linguistic verbalizations represent, in various ways, psychic injuries in the most basic forms, yet to be further differentiated in phases IV–X and explored and differentiated in later stages, especially in psychotherapy.

As noted by Lifton (1976), basic psychoformative processes are altered by trauma, especially massive trauma, and generate new modalities of self-experience and introspection and affect regulatory attempts connected with anxiety, anger, guilt, and fear responses. These mechanisms then become the genesis of trauma-related metaphors as they reflect assimilation of the trauma experience within existing self-schemata, i.e., representation of the self in personality processes (see Wilson, 2006, for a discussion and also Horowitz, 1982). Stated differently, how does the posttraumatic self express itself in metaphors?

Phases I–IV and Beyond

As phases I–IV unfold, emerge, develop, evolve, and become synthesized intrapsychically, they are experienced at conscious and unconscious subjective-emotional levels of awareness (see Figure 1.2). As parallel phenomena, these intrapsychic processes emerge as an active tendency, a distinct force of psychic energy, at all levels of consciousness (LCA, Wilson, 2004) to express trauma-specific metaphors (TSM) of traumatic life experience (TLE). This is a continuous process which, like the twist of a well-made kaleidoscope, changes the images' content, views, and creation of trauma metaphors in the drive toward mastery, assimilation, and integration. When this happens, it is the visual representation of trauma metaphors in the purest, symbolic sense of meaning. The clinical treatment implications of this reality become importantly transparent, i.e., the patients' verbal descriptions of internal psychic states are transformative in character, shape, image, content, and configurations and, as such, provide critical clues to emergent posttraumatic processes, personal concerns, and ego-defenses at any given point in time.

Decoding Trauma Metaphors

The empathically attuned psychotherapist learns how to decode and interpret metaphorical expressions of internally organized psychic states as they are portals of entry to critical, and often unspeakable, unsaid trauma-based experiences (see Wilson & Lindy, 1994).

In phases IV and V, metaphoric encoding tends to become more idiosyncratic, clarified in focus in terms of cognitive and defensive processes of the patients' life developmental history and individual identity processes and issues. Their idiosyncratic nature reflects individual differences in personality processes, intellectual capacity, and cognitive styles. In this sense, their personal self-differentiation becomes accelerated [like the mitosis of a cell in reproduction; epigenesis in terms of trauma specific metaphors (TSM)], this (constitutes) a psychic metabolism and differentiation which is an isomorphic process to psychobiological activities in the brain and body associated with trauma metabolism in very specific ways. As cell divisions follow a determinant biological process, psychic metaphoric posttraumatic divisions do so in isomorphic ways related to internal biological processes. Hence, they are isomorphic in structure. In essence, it is a set psychobiological isomorphism processes among systematically integrated bodily processes. Therefore, decoding trauma-specific metaphors (TSM) is directly parallel to decoding the manifest and latent content of dream imagery as described by Freud (1900).

Phases VI–VII: The Emergence of PTSD Awareness

In phase VI of Figure 1.2, the evolved and accelerated metabolic processes reflected in the previous stages becomes more crystallized in verbal and somatic metaphors. It is here, especially in terms of clinical treatment, that which is unsaid or unspeakable becomes as important as that which can be said or spoken. It is here that such issues as survivors' guilt, existential shame, guilt, and hidden secrets may emerge at different levels of consciousness and subsequently be connected to defensive forms of avoidance, denial, detachment, peri-traumatic dissociation, dissociation, isolation, repression, or purposeful or amnesic forgetting. In short, they don't want to talk about it. While all such self-protective mechanisms have a function and purpose, they will be eventually concealed or will be revealed in metaphors, then, the unspeakable, unsaid, unspoken or experiences difficult to share or disclose with therapists, loved ones, and significant trusted others, will be manifest and disclosed in raw terms. Thus, the unspeakable becomes the inevitable in psychic disclosure or a leakage. They move to center stage of treatment or not at all, especially when unrecognized (see Chapters 8 and 9).

Phasic Stage VII: Psychotherapy and Metaphors Expressed in Treatment

In phase VII, the focus of understanding doors of knowledge to intrapsychic processes through metaphors extends specifically in posttraumatic psychotherapy. When a trauma patient seeks help, it is expected that progress, if successful, will proceed through four major phasic sequences as illustrated in Figure 1.2 on the left margin: (1) initial impacts to the organism and psychobiological processes and personality; (2) the stages of psychic metabolic processes of changes in assimilation; (3) transformation and working through unmetabolized posttraumatic issues; and (4) completion, resolution, and integration processes and new internal reflective metaphors. These disclosures will emerge transparently in TSM and TST processes for the empathically attuned psychotherapist and everyday people.

In terms of an epigenetic and transformative set of organismic and intrapsychic strivings toward the eventual resolution of posttraumatic stress disorder (PTSD) or posttraumatic effects to the self-in-the-world, phases IX and X best reflect the final internal struggles, efforts, and joys toward integration, happiness, and satisfaction; completion of the inevitable journey born by an unwanted trauma and changes to self and personal identity. It is a feeling of coming home to oneself: a new inner sense of identity and selfhood.

If all goes well for the resilient-enough survivor who finds Nurturing Guides (NG) after trauma, there then emerges, slowly at first and then more comfortably and calmly with time, an inner trust in one's own integrity, a sense of personal harmony in self-reinvention. At this stage of metaphoric metabolism and integration of the trauma experience, a new sense of self can be born or also accepted, both by the survivor and their intimate or trusted friends. This, then, constitutes the essential core of self-reinvention and hope for a new future for the trauma survivor. Life is both a known (old) and new (emergent) personal identity posttrauma (Wilson, 2006).

Legend: The Myth of the Hero and the Trauma Survivor

There are commonalities in the cross-cultural mythic stories of survivors who have returned from a quest that has taken them to meet great and overwhelming difficult challenges through traumatic or stressful encounters. There are hundreds of variants on how these mythic journeys occur, many of them explored in Joseph Campbell's classic work, *The Hero with a Thousand Faces* (1949). On a more concrete level, his work is timeless and important to all who study it. As in ancient times, the disasters and traumas of our times are timeless and tragic. How did they impact the 20th and 21st centuries, persons and souls across cultures in the world? Campbell's work is a universal anchor point for those who delve into mythology and metaphors. It is a treasure chest for those interested in trauma and mythology. It is, simply, an indispensable body of knowledge at many levels of study.

There is nothing easy or simple in life about understanding how a chosen person happens to be selected and sent on an unforeseen journey that will ultimately challenge the boundaries of the meaning of life itself. More often than not it is a God-fearing encounter and life journey. Who survives it is another story in God's palm of mercy of the most complicated and difficult sort of mythical life narratives. Who wants a leg blown off in war or a traumatic brain injury? Who wants to be homeless after Hurricane Katrina or the tsunami in Japan (2011)?

Who are the examples of these Mythic Heroes (MH)? What are their life-journey pathways? What defines the circumstances of the person facing a life-changing, if not life-threatening, call to duty or the endeavor or mission or life itself? In fact, how do they re-enter society and create meaning of what they have experienced? Who will ever properly understand them? What if political-historical circumstances block or prohibit re-entry?

Are there Nurturing Guides, Helpers, Angels, Spiritual Ancestors, or encounters with Kindred Souls, Ancestral Grandmothers and Grandfathers or elders to shepherd them, walking the same pathway of trauma and survivorship? Can they be discovered by wounded souls in their search for meaning? The answer is, yes! Indeed, how does modern mental health professionals, scientific-processes discover these encoded processes? How do modern medicine and psychology-psychiatry understand the complexity of these issues in its nascent seminal form?

Cross-Cultural Universality: The Journey of the Hero/Survivor in the PTSD Experience

Inspection and study of Figure 1.2 reveals the nature of the trauma survivor's journey. As such, Figure 1.2 is a summary, modification, and oversimplification of overly difficult trauma-related but graphic visual representation of the Myth of the Hero, Joseph Campbell's groundbreaking work (1949) and later (1992) explications and clarifications, in his book *Pathways to Bliss.*

As Figure 1.2 illustrates, there is a process of transformation of the trauma encounter and a life journey that follows. The life journey has a typical flow and chronological, if sometimes disrupted, sequence with its profound difficulties and life-changing experiences. It has phases and stages, starting with entry into the Zone of Danger (ZD) and trauma, the process of overcoming experienced threats, dangers, the possibility of death or life-altering events (i.e., the Abyss Experience) to eventually, after the travails of the difficult journey itself, discovering Nurturing Guides (NG) who provides wisdom and help to self-re-integration and personal meaning after the traumatic journey (Wilson, 2006).

Some Journeys of the Mythic Hero (MH) are immediate and necessary: A call to action or duty in an urgent personal sense (e.g., responding to Hurricane Katrina (2005): the earthquake in Haiti (2008); the tsunami and nuclear proliferations in Japan (2011); or coping with situations of war or the murder or rape of loved ones). Other crises may not be so immediately pressing or transparent but ultimately may be governed by external authority and reality, historical moments of necessity, and the dictates of God. These seeming oddities are what give the Myth of the Hero (MH) its traditional psychic character and reference point in non-obvious ways and why the beautiful works of Joseph Campbell are immortal.

The Mythic Journey of the Survivor uniquely stands alone in its psychological structure. For example, how do traumatic experiences shape the person in their identity? In that limited sense, it gives them their identity and transferred trauma-shaped character structure, altered posttraumatic personality states and emotions. But what about later in life's journey? What are the traumatic vicissitudes for the self, individual identity, and personality processes in the life-cycle itself? We will devote later chapters to these critical considerations of personality and adaptations in this book.

Ordinary People and Extraordinary Experiences

As it is told in diverse cultures in the world, the mythology of the Hero/Survivor (MH) enters our story in many complex and diverse ways and consciousness. Our awareness is shaped by those trauma survivors and friends close to us. They become our teachers. In reality and mythical sense, the Myth of the Hero concerns travails of ordinary people through extraordinary circumstances as witnessed by those closest to them and ourselves.

The Trauma Mission in the Hero's/Survivor's Life Journey

In the perspective presented above, we suggest that the Mythological Journey of the Hero/Survivor is an apt metaphor for the journey and psychological sequelae of trauma survivors across cultures. Their universal human journey reveal that for which one is chosen by some known or unknown external power, fate, political, or sociocultural dissolution and involves commitment to a mission higher than one's immediate sense of self or personal control. It involves preparation, where possible, in varying degrees or forms, crossing into a dark and often sinister life-threatening and unknown spaces, combating and confronting the forces therein and later re-crossing a threshold to re-enter a defined normal life and society. The ordinary person confronts the extraordinary and returns to their world, as known, society and culture but not without profound psychic changes to self and soul, most of which they cannot express or verbalize in ways that others will understand. But, what about the survivor?

In the posttraumatic journey re-crossing the "*there and then threshold*" of re-entry may not be normal anymore and replete with unexpected challenges, personal disappointments and profound despair and accelerate the search for meaning and purpose in being a survivor. The re-entry process may be experienced as alien, disconnected, disengaged, unfamiliar, estranged, rejected personally or other worldly ways in a phenomenological sense (e.g., I don't belong here anymore, it is all different now and I don't fit anymore).

The exposure to the Dark Forces of trauma constitutes the core nature of the Abyss Experience (AE): The experience of death encounters, confrontation with evil, abandonment, despair, and the cosmic challenge of ultimate meaning (Wilson, 2004, 2006). After the Abyss Experience (AE) (i.e., traumatic life challenge) and soul taxing and wrenching journey, without everyone in the Homecoming World of the survivor (i.e., re-entry environment) opens their arms and welcomes the Hero/Survivor with understanding and love, affection and needed nurturance or acts as a guide of compassion (NG, as will be discussed in Chapter 5). This void is one of despair and rejection.

Unfortunately, for many reasons, *indifference* is as common as so-called *gratitude* and loving acceptance with authentic affection. The polarities of acceptance and welcome alternate, with indifference and superficial greetings to the wayfarer, to pretend that they do not recognize PTSD-related behavior changes is a shame of culture and governments.

The Homecoming Reception: Moving Beyond the Survivors' Journey Into the Posttraumatic Afterlife

The Initial Homecoming Process: Trepidations and Worries in the Transition Point of Re-Entry: The Past Confronts the Present

In the reception environment, many non-affected persons (i.e., non-participants in the journey) are anxious, afraid, nervous, worried, uncertain, and eager to see and reunite with the one who left their home, parents, wife, marriage, church, ethnic-clan, culture, neighborhood of safety and familiarity, and who returned transformed, not quite the same person as before their trauma (encounter) journey. They, the veterans, were changed, but who or whom would soon "get it" about their posttraumatic changes in behavior, personality, and self?

This then, becomes the transition point; the past confronts the present. For the survivor, it is a psychological point of re-entry and life-changing transition. This transition may become pivotal for future psychological well-being, health, and growth. It all depends on the quality and nature of the homecoming reception and what follows. What does psychic homecoming embrace and manifest as love?

In the recovery environment, how do we collectively approach and ask the essential question as to best welcome the wayfarant one? For the survivor or victim, this initial period of re-entry is typically experienced by the survivor as one of relief alternating with inner tension and uncertainty as how to reconnect. Later, the adjustment and adaptation processes will take on new dimensions and colorations, most filled with struggles for meaning, understanding, and a new perspective, and involve many changes in lifestyle, values, and privileges of life, especially where PTSD is a *predominant filter*. What used to be "ain't no more. It's just gone." So, where to go from here, in all directions of possibilities?

Posttraumatic Recognition in One's Culture of Origin

Contrary to popular or normative societal expectations, the returning Survivor-Hero does not always receive a glad handshake or warm-welcoming reception from those left behind during their traumatic journey, or, for that matter, society at large, although many well-meaning persons offer superficial "lips of gratitude" service to appear proper and caring (e.g., thank you for serving in Vietnam, Iraq, or Afghanistan, but don't tell me what you actually did there, or how you survived Hurricane Katrina in New Orleans or the 2011 tsunami in Japan, Sri Lanka (2005) or Thailand, or being abused and raped). The cheapest verbal expression to most combat war veterans is simply, "I'm glad you survived and thanks for serving."

Memory and Metaphors

In Chapter 2, we explore the language of trauma. Metaphors are universal in linguistic expressions throughout cultures of the world and as such represent forms of human experiences of all types, both positive and negative (Lakoff & Johnson, 1980) (see Table 2.1).

Empirical Investigations: Discovering Latent Meanings of Intrapsychic States Through Trauma Metaphors

Traumatic metaphors directly concern and define latent meaning. In this way, their verbal and linguistic expressions embrace a broad, critical, and informative range of well-known expressions that span the domain of possibilities such as, for example: (1) verbal connotations, (2) deep structural meanings, (3) the power and intensity of underlying or latent meanings and revelations; or (4) the simple or complex disclosure of latent or more unconscious mental processes. Trauma metaphors always embody all of these important dimensions. So, what about trauma metaphors and their intrapsychic roles? They are always present in PTSD clinical presentations.

Portals of Entry (POE) to the Posttraumatic Self-Constellations

In later chapters, we explore metaphors and the posttraumatic self. Language is a portal to the inner world of the speaker and metaphors are clues to that world in the ultimate, phenomenological, individually created world of meaning (Lakoff & Johnson, 1980). In Chapters 3, 4, 5, 8, and 9 we will examine trauma's impact on the posttraumatic self and changes in personality, identity, and ego-processes (see Wilson, 2006, for background).

The Unsaid, Unspoken, Indescribable, and Unspeakable: Secrets, Dark Closets, Lies, and Deceptions: What Do Metaphors Reveal?

To focus, how do words possibly disclose, contain, tame, reveal, or hide the unsaid or unspeakable or fabricated lies of truths or falsehoods? What do metaphors tell us about the internal configurations of PTSD and posttraumatic states? What is factually real or not? How is their discovery a clue to effective treatments for PTSD? How do traumatized patients express trauma metaphors? What words do they use and reveal? How many dimensions and variations are there for trauma metaphors? Clinically, do they have parallels in dream work and symbolism, the creation of literary works, everyday language, artistic creations and distort, hide and meaning? What if they lie and fabricate the historical truth of their alleged abuse experiences? What if they are concealing their inner realities of trauma? How to decode them through metaphors? What is the ultimate truth about the traumatic metaphors and how to understand and employ them in psychotherapy, research, and beyond?

The Spectrum of Avoidance Processes: Denial, Self-Deception, Repression, and Suppression of the Unsaid, Unspeakable, Horrific, and Unapproachable Aspects of Trauma Experiences

In a clinical sense, how does the trauma patient avoid telling their therapist of hidden secrets and layers of emotional concerns? After all, the patients are in emotional pain and seeking help. Do there exist metaphors of deception as avoidance, denial, repression, suppression, or concealment of the unspeakable or unsaid? What are their individual uniquely constituted/created metaphors of the unsaid, unapproachable, and the unspeakable? What is their linguistic and metaphoric form? How to clinically and empirically validate the real from fake? Clearly, these are empirically testable questions, especially to evidence-based research efforts.

Among critical concerns, these questions are among the central ones in this chapter on the need for ethical-clinical-scientific-empirical approaches to the discovery of PTSD in its most complex forms and how metaphors may be the critical portals of entry into the PTSD pyramids of hidden secrets and psychic configurations that are trauma-related complexes.

Trauma Metaphors: Applications, Definitions and Permutations in Symptom Expressions in Therapy and Everyday Life

As noted earlier, Table 1.1 presents our definitions of trauma metaphors and where we can see and use their significance to psychosocial functioning and posttraumatic behaviors. These definitions rely, in part, on the work of Lakoff and Johnson (1980) and others whose linguistic analysis of metaphors are astute and informative in their deconstruction of the structure and function of metaphors. The deconstruction of trauma linguistics, including building on the serminal research of Lakoff and Johnson (1980), we have identified at least two meaningful conceptual definitions and their dimensions of psychic trauma, PTSD, and expressions in adaptive behavior and efforts. We consider these as seminal operational definitions for future research investigations (see Table 1.1). Many empirical studies (e.g., RCT) could be forged from these ideas and symptoms analyses (i.e., scientifically investigative of the language of trauma history to trauma metaphor genesis).

Decoding Trauma Metaphors and Their Relation to PTSD Expressions in Behavioral Adaptations: Projections of Internal States

The trauma metaphor expresses a conscious or unconscious snapshot or larger photo or image presentation or projection of the inner world of trauma survivors. It is here that decoding and understanding the significance of metaphorical expressions takes on clinical significance of profound importance in scientific research and treatment, i.e., decoding internal states.

For example: What is happening in the metaphor? What do the created images, memories, or photos show? What do the memory snapshots reveal? Are they clear enough to visualize and decipher? Are they blurred, obscured, incomplete sources of information and memories? How do the images inform us as to unconscious mechanisms of cognitive processing and meaning of trauma? How do we discern the difference between "clear" and "blurred" images of trauma images? How do psychotherapists, medical practitioners, and others learn how to identify and use trauma metaphors (TSM) in aiding persons who suffer from PTSD and complex allied and co-morbid conditions (e.g., major depressive disorders, substance abuse, and existential despair) (see Chapter 9)?

Metaphors and Life-Span Transformational Self-Processes in Survivors: How Do Trauma Memories Change Over Time, Space, and Aging?

The metabolism of psychological trauma is a complex and dynamic process of integration and occurs incrementally at different rates of psychic integration over time (Wilson, 2006). *There are phases, levels, and processes of trauma metabolism that happen in short, variable, or long cycles, across life-span epigenetic manifestations in aging and that can be intensified by posttraumatic challenges to successful life adaptations (e.g., other stressful life experiences to oneself, family, children, and others)* (see Chapters 2, 3, 4, and 7).

Traumatic metaphors evolve and have functional dimensions across the stages of epigenetic development and they articulate with existing current or past life crises and sources of personal stress or helpful resources (Wilson, 2006) (see also Chapter 3).

To focus on trauma metaphors, they can "feed" on each other in complicated and "interactive ways" with many feedback-informational loops in cognitive and emotional activities. When this occurs, PTSD becomes enormously complex in its dynamics with multiple levels of psychic processes interacting at different levels of consciousness and significance, i.e., the motivational directions of daily life at stratified dimensions of personality processes and individual consciousness (see Wilson, 2006, for a discussion).

The Past in the Present and Future in Metaphoric Expressions

Traumatic memories encoded in posttraumatic states articulate with pre-traumatic personality dynamics and histories in the most complex psychosocial developmental ways. The therapist or experimental researcher needs to find clinical fact, methodological ways for sorting out these intersecting dynamics. They are a metaphorical ball of intertwined string.

A traumatic metaphor (TSM) can and does articulate intrapsychically with traumatic issues from earlier stages of life-course development as well as current concerns, life stressors, and personality dynamics (see Wilson, 2006, for a complex analysis). In simple terms, it is a matrix of self-processes in which trauma realities may take center stage and dominate internal personality processes at all levels of awareness (see Chapters 3 and 4).

The issue of how pre-existing personality characteristics, including personality disorders (i.e., DSM-IV or V, Axis II diagnoses) influence trauma metaphors is an important consideration, as always. Nevertheless, how to assign psychological "weights" or determinants to symptom configurations? How to assess trauma-induced changes in personality to pre-existing personality traits, self-dimensions, and personal identity and their expressions in trauma metaphors? We will discuss these considerations later in the book.

Trauma Metaphors, Trauma Complexes, and Trauma Archetypes: The Role of the Nurturing Guide (NG) as a Tapestry Weaver of Healing

Trauma metaphors have their unique constellations and magnetic attractions to all sorts of archetypes and trauma complexes (Wilson, 2006). Trauma metaphors express themes that are not consciously articulated but dynamically overlap with archetypal images and realities but with the purity of the inner symbols of the Archetype of trauma itself (Wilson, 2006). The patient may not have conscious awareness of these internal processes but, at some level, out of the drive for self-unification, health, and self-realization, the Trauma Archetypes reverberate in consciousness and emerge in related metaphors of clinical and personal importance.

Trauma metaphors represent the potential totality of posttraumatic psychic functioning as represented in Table 1.1. Traumatic memories, PTSD effects, and associated processes of mental and psychobiological determinants, impact the entire integrated human body as an organismic system (see Wilson, 2006, for a discussion). As far as we can discern, as have other investigators (Eitinger & Strom, 1973), no systems of the human body are unaffected following extreme and traumatic stress and more recent research evidence supports these findings (Schnurr & Green, 2004). These and other studies show that Vietnam War combat veterans and other victims of chronic PTSD disorders (i.e., Holocaust survivors, sexual abuse victims, etc.) have higher risk factors for medical-pathological systems of the body (e.g., diabetes, heart disease, hypertension, etc.) that are significantly associated or correlated with a history of trauma. In short, trauma and persistent PTSD seems to make the person vulnerable to biological system-wide dysfunctions, wear and tear on the body, and illness at different points of post-trauma adaptation and ages and stages in epigenesis, i.e., ontogenetic life-span development itself (Wilson, 2006).

Language Metaphors as Psychic Portals of Entry (POE) to the Inner World of Trauma Space

To approach a comprehensive analysis of trauma and PTSD requires a well calibrated, integrated theoretical and clinical framework, which includes metaphoric analysis. The blend of clinical wisdom and theoretical deductions of scientific empirically-based knowledge serve to sketch out the larger picture of the nature of complex and complicated psychodynamic processes after trauma. The many varied posttraumatic presentations are as complex as the intricate structure of personality itself (Wilson, 2006). As such, it is a rich earth to be tilled for research and study for future generations.

Posttraumatic Self-Constellations and Posttraumatic Identity Configurations Associated With TSM and Traumatic Stress Syndromes

How many unique constellations of PTSD exist? How to describe and classify them? We have described elsewhere 11 posttraumatic personality profiles or personality configurations (Wilson, 2006) but suspect that there may be other configurations of posttraumatic manifestations than that which is presented in the DSM-IV-TR diagnostic criteria (Wilson, Friedman, & Lindy, 2004). Later, we will discuss the linkage between the posttraumatic self and configurations of metaphors. Traumatic metaphors appear in self-presentations without internal brakes or controls of internal states.

Patients in psychotherapy treatment for trauma treatment and PTSD reveal their inner distress and concerns about changes in relevant aspects of functioning in ways that are not always transparent, expectable, conventional, or obvious.

The trauma survivors search for meaning and understanding of why they had to endure what they did and how to make sense of its place in life's journey. It is usually, if not always, a search for ultimate meaning of sacrifice, pain, and survivorship. Why me God? Why did I have to endure this pain and suffering? Why am I doing what I am doing now, after all this time? Why did I go on this trauma journey?

Metaphors and the Links to the Inner Psychic World of Traumatic Experiences

When attempting to wed theoretical, clinical, and empirical-research sources of data regarding trauma, culture, and metaphor, the task necessitates a collaborative merger of relevant perspectives to achieve a heuristically rich heritage for future scientific research and clinical programs. It is our belief that in the absence of clinical–empirical conceptual synergy, the necessary insights and hypotheses will be significantly limited, or worse, remain unexplored.

The Existential Meaning of Trauma: The Appearance of Metaphors in Daily Life, Dream States, Fantasy, and Imagination

What does psychological trauma mean at an existential, personological level (i.e., totally devoid of DSM-IV-TR or DSM-V diagnostic criteria of symptoms)? At the level of being in daily existence, how do trauma metaphors reflect being in the world?

Memory and the Complex Vicissitudes of the Trauma Experience

How do the vicissitudes of PTSD symptoms and patterns become manifest in trauma metaphors? Indeed, this is the essential question of the book. What are the possible variant patterns of posttraumatic adaptations? This question, in particular, addresses the phenomena of the lucidity, accuracy, and veracity of memories of traumatic experiences. Some trauma survivors have amazing, graphic details of what they had to endure whereas others have vague, incomplete, obfuscated memories of their experiences. As has been recognized previously, it is possible that a range of cognitive mechanisms may be at work in the processing of trauma (e.g., repression, denial, traumatic brain injuries (TBI), dissociative processes, etc.) that mediate the peri-traumatic and posttraumatic processing of traumatic situations (Marmar et al., 2006; Wilson, 1989).

A Case Illustration: The World War II (1941) Japanese Attack at Pearl Harbor, Hawaii, Oahu Island

To illustrate the lucidity and importance of traumatic memories and metaphors, a study of American survivors from the Japanese attack in 1941 at Pearl Harbor, on the Hawaiian island of Oahu, was conducted by our research team in in 1986 at the 45th reunion of the Pearl Harbor Survivors Association (PHSA), in Honolulu Hawaii, Oahu (Wilson, 1989).

The Day of Infamy, as President Roosevelt spoke of it in a national radio broadcast on December 7, 1941, initiated the United States of America's full engagement in World War II, despite previous, repeated requests for assistance from Great Britain and Sir Winston Churchill after Hitler attacked the United Kingdom (1939) and Europe, itself.

Once the war started, it changed American society and later, when Japan formally surrendered, on September 2, 1945 onboard the USS Missouri, the entire political configuration of world powers and the anticipated "Cold War" foreseeable future. On that historically fateful day, the Cold War actually then began between the United States and USSR and then realigned with second and third world powers and American policymakers turned their attention to Southeast Asia, Vietnam, Korea, Germany, and elsewhere in the world.

Pearl Harbor Survivors and Their Metaphors

Among the multitude of interesting findings from our 1986 clinical interviews (bolstered by standardized questionnaire data) was that the then 19-year-old naval and military personnel (i.e., Navy, Army, Army Air Corps, Marines, doctors, nurses, and others) had vivid, crystalline memories of what happened on that prophetic day on a beautiful tropical Sunday morning between 7:00 a.m. and 10:00 a.m. on the Hawaiian island of Oahu, itself like a soft, beautiful, sensuous Polynesian moment with a lover of unimagined beauty with tropical breezes blowing inward from the ocean as a loving message from earth-born care.

The Japanese planes attacked early in the morning only to destroy majestic, personal moments of beauty and relaxation and begin a global war for years to come (i.e., 1941–1945). In the clear, azure, sunny, reflective, inviting, brilliantly clear waters, the tropical, warm, sensual, welcoming majesty of Hawaii became a burial tomb for more than 2,200 and many more service personnel and civilians in a few hours. And more dead laid arrest on Oahu, itself, in hospitals and places of war attack, including the Northern parts of Oahu near the USMC base, Kaneohe, where a Japanese mini-submarine was captured. So began World War II for Americans and what was to follow.

To survivors, Pearl Harbor remains steadfast in memory, a tribute to the dead and living who had no idea of what was about to happen on that historical, world-changing day a few weeks before Christmas in 1941. In a few hours and days, the United States and the entire world had changed. Nor did they know what the future would bring them in the South Pacific warfare of horrible encounters with Japanese forces. As bad as the Pearl Harbor attack was, to everyone, the worst was yet to come for U.S. Marines and Admiral Nimitz' naval fleets (e.g., the battle of Midway and Coral Sea), the infantry conquest of Japanese-held South Pacific Islands (e.g., Iwo Jima, Tarawa, Guadalcanal, Okinawa) and the Philippines.

When our research team spoke with the Pearl Harbor survivors, there were detailed, profound, vivid, and disturbing recollections and memories (e.g., seeing the faces of enemy pilots and details of Japanese "Zero" attack (i.e., red ball insignias of Japan) airplanes). There were clear, emotional memories of friends, shipmates, and specific persons and how actions of a heroic nature occurred (e.g., rescuing injured and burned comrades), the tragedies and the endurance of the raw horrors of attack planes, torpedoes, fires, naval ships ablaze and explosions (e.g., the desperate screams of helplessness and needs for assistance, those trapped and desperate in flooded ship compartments, etc.), and struggles for survival amongst the many burning vessels virtually everywhere in Pearl Harbor.

Simply said, Pearl Harbor was almost destroyed by Japanese forces, but as fate had it, the two aircraft carriers were not there: the USS Hornet and USS Enterprise, which would later assist in the total destruction of Admiral Yamomota's naval forces in the South Pacific.

To the survivors and our research team it was as if the Japanese attack had happened yesterday and not nearly a half-century before our research and clinical investigations.

Background on the Pearl Harbor Study

In 1941, in the United States, Depression-era (1929–1939) men and women were strong, youthful, proud, and dedicated while processing grief and joy at being survivors of the 1941 attack. The survivors, as they told their stories, "stood tall" for their courage and remained so throughout their lives and elder years, as the few remaining survivors still do today. The Day of Infamy, beyond doubt, was indelibly imprinted in memory and consciousness. They always have, and will undoubtedly continue to take, these profound life-changing memories to their final resting place, perhaps as sacred, haunting but treasured moments of their psychic life-heroic journey in a historical moment of a national and world emergency that they did not know was about to happen at that time. Did historical destiny shape their identity and life-course development as 19-year-old persons in 1941? Yes, beyond a doubt, forever.

The accounts of Pearl Harbor survivors raise many other questions about the phenomenology of trauma exposure, PTSD, and psychic survival and its relation to metaphors born from traumatic experiences. During our 1986 interviews with the members of the Pearl Harbor Survivors Association (PHSA), it became increasingly evident that there were transformations over time in their memories and perspectives of December 7, 1941. In describing their reactions to the surprise Sunday morning sunrise attack, there were statements such as: "We were crushed like sleeping dogs"; "It was just chaos and confusion with nowhere to go"; "We were numb, violated, and the fear of annihilation was palpable." However, after Japan surrendered in August 1945 after the atomic bomb at Hiroshima and then formally, in September 1945 on the USS Missouri to U.S. Army Commander, General Douglas McArthur, the end of World War II was completed. The survivors expressed *transformed metaphors*: "We went from being victims to victors; We won the big one (i.e., World War II itself)." For the survivors of Pearl Harbor, the surrender of Japanese authorities, especially Emperor Hirohito, was just the beginning of a new, joyous life for America and themselves. They became the Heroes of Joseph Campbell's Mythical Hero. *They had a thousand faces of the Hero.* Emperor Hirohito died. They, the Pearl Harbor survivors, lived on and had families and good lives. Their legacies persist today, but as of 2012, there will be no more reunions of the PHSA as their living numbers are small and the end is very near for almost all of the men and women who served with valor. They do not want any more reunions, but to die in peace.

Portals of Entry (POE) Into the World of PTSD Trauma Victims

The intrapsychic memory of trauma encoding is among the most critical issues in the discovery of PTSD and its psychodynamic dimensions invoking trauma metaphors and their multiple pathways of verbal expressions. How do traumatic experiences get encoded in the brain? Where in neurological structures and how? What are the internal psychological processes of memory and learning? How is trauma encoded in linguistic forms and stored in memory?

In this realm of discovery, what are the *universal portals of entry* to the intrapsychic spaces of psychic trauma? How do therapists find or discover them? What do they consist of and how to identify them? What are the clues to the therapist and researchers as to trauma-related metaphors? How are they connected to transference and countertransference dynamics in treatment (i.e., TST, CTS, and more)? We will explore these issues later in this chapter and book.

Archaeological Metaphors: The Egyptian Pyramids as Clues to Internal Self-Configurations of Traumatic Afterlife

How did late 20th century archaeologists (i.e., the late 1880s and early 1900s) find the portals of entry into the ancient Egyptian pyramids and burial tombs for pharaoh royalty, the Valley of Kings and Queens, and much more? What are the facts of how British researcher Howard Carter discovered King Tutankhamun's tomb?

Our basic psychological research question is this: Are there *structural parallels between ancient archaeological structures designed for the afterlife of pharaoh kings and queens and the intrapsychic structures for imperial tombs and spaces where the PTSD unsaid or unspeakable trauma memories might reside*? What is contained in the sacred burial chambers and spaces and what does it teach us about their lives? What is contained in the unconscious of the trauma patient?

The empathically attuned mental health therapist entering the world of PTSD patients and traumatic metaphors is not unlike the anthropologist entering the ancient burial tombs of Egyptian pharaohs which contained multiple chambers of entry adorned with hieroglyphical symbols, special artifacts of importance for their afterlife and carefully constructed rooms for nobility and servants for a rich and proper, regal post-life reality in the next afterlife godly realm that was to be theirs alone. So it is the same for the trauma survivor? The trauma experience is theirs alone until shared with a Nurturing Guide (NG), but not necessarily a regal burial tomb, as we will further illuminate and discuss in later chapters of this book.

Portals of Entry (POE) to the Secret Inner World of Trauma Survivors and the World of Pharaohs

Based on verified, documented archeological findings, there are descriptions of a discrete number of portals of entry (POE) into the ancient pyramidal structures. Each portal is interesting in its purposeful architectural composition and desire for total artistic, architectural completion and function and of ultimate ancient cosmological importance for the next worldly kingdom. We have to ask, "Why and what do they reveal, however, of mythological importance to the psyche of the designers and creators?" Or, finding the secret, most hidden portals of entry? Maybe they reveal a great deal of their worldly cosmology, or, perhaps next to nothing from grandiose rulers (i.e., pharaohs, kings, and nobility). This is, in essence, the myth of ancient realities of the pyramids of Egypt and also Mayans in Mexico in a psychological perspective. How do we understand the connection of the inner visions to external realizations in material, architectural, and astrological forms?

False and Hidden Portals of Entry Into Sacred Spaces

The Egyptian tombs are extraordinary, mysterious structures and ancient realities full of mythology and symbolism. And to this day, for almost two centuries, as yet undiscovered hidden meaning or archaeological composite studies of ancient structures. *Of particular interest is that some of the portals of entry to the inner sanctums were purposely built as false or hidden entry passages to the royal sarcophagus and the burial chambers with its riches and splendors, whereas others, usually more difficult to locate, permitted discovery and a strictly limited, discrete, if any, access to the sacred inner places of royal chambers.* However, as part of archaeological investigations, anomalies were discovered on the sides of the geometric pyramids and burial sites that led to the discovery of genuine, false, or fake portals of entry. Why were they created in the first place by the planners?

Is the same phenomenon, especially for discovering through trauma metaphors (TSM), the portals of entry into intrapsychic traumatic states? How do trauma metaphors allow us to enter the Kingdom of Trauma space? Metaphors are keys to a different kind of Kingdom of Posttraumatic Existences; they illuminate the pathways of discovery. Deciphering the hieroglyphics of the pyramids may be a profound view to the intrapsychic realities of the pharaohs and their post-life aspirations. Did their inscriptions reveal metaphors of their life journey? Egyptologists affirm this reality and knowledge base and continue to decipher encryptions of the hieroglyphics to this day.

Posttraumatic Inner Spaces and False Portals of Entry: Why?

The posttraumatic stress disorder inner space is not a royal, pretty, glamorous, or desired chamber of wonder for the traumatic afterlife. Rather, in the worst metaphorical, linguistic instances, it is a basement structure full of the hidden, unspeakable, unsaid, undesired, unmetabolized, rejected, painful set of life memories. In a metaphoric sense, it is a basement of Hell.

Posttraumatic Hell: The Basement Metaphor of Ugly, Horrible, and Smelly Hidden Material

The "posttraumatic basement" of "stored or hidden stuff is a garbage dump of discarded psychic trash." It is ugly and despicable. It stinks and smells bad. It is a secret vault of memory of that which cannot be expressed or disclosed out of fear and enormous anxiety. It generates shame, depression, suicidal thoughts or threats of reprisal from the return to life from memory, reality, and the afterlife, if any seem viable in the initial re-entry process.

In the most painful sense, it is the unspeakable trash dump in the most emotionally painful, unspeakable memories. For many, it is a Psychic Hell. The Psychic Hell is unspeakable and hidden from oneself and others. To hide these sordid realities is *avoidance in the service of survival.* In short, a repository of PTSD "shit" that is nothing but awful but contained in *encapsulated inner-spaces of the mind.*

Metaphoric Transformations of PTSD Intrapsychic States

What is the intrapsychic afterlife of the trauma survivor and its transformation into metamorphic forms? Elsewhere, we have written of the five portals of entry into the intrapsychic organization of traumatic memories and PTSD symptom clusters (Wilson, Friedman, & Lindy, 2004). Our five categories were: (1) traumatic memories and re-experiencing phenomena; (2) avoidance, coping strategies, and ego-defensive processes; (3) psychobiological hyperarousal processes reflecting allostatic posttraumatic changes in neurohormonal processes not present before the trauma; (4) discernible post-traumatic changes in personality processes, identity, and the self-structural components not present before the traumatic event; and (5) alterations in attachment processes, intimacy capacities, and interpersonal relationships not present before the traumatic event (Erikson, 1968; Wilson, Friedman, & Lindy, 2004). We will elaborate in detail on these issues and symptom clusters later in the book.

Whether entry into ancient pyramids and portals of the pharaohs' tombs or the inner world of states of psychologically traumatized survivors and their generative personal metaphors, the task is the same: To discover the purpose of structural organization and the functional meaning of symptoms and their future implications for ego-synthesis, posttraumatic adaptation, and potential for success in psychotherapy.

In specific and ancient regard, hieroglyphics, symbolic objects for the afterlife, are of ultimate importance and relevance to our comparative analysis. What do they ultimately mean? What was their functional purpose for living or existing in the after-world?

In a parallel way, how does the trauma survivor find their intrapsychic space in the pyramid of PTSD phenomena and determine their personal construction of a posttraumatic world? What does the posttraumatic life consist of in intrapsychic and behavioral adaptations? How do traumatic experiences get organized into posttraumatic mental life, existence itself, and cosmological order? How to transform the five portals of entry or just how to find a proper portal to exist vis-à-vis a Nurturing Guide (NG)? This, in essence, is a task of self-reformation and challenge of reinvention (Wilson, 2006).

The Patients' "Walk" Into the Unconscious Realm of Trauma Experiences Through Memory, Metaphors, and Recovered Consciousness

The historic journeys into the ancient pyramids were processes of discovery over a long period of thousands of years starting in groundbreaking forays by British archaeologists in the 1920s. Similarly, a psycho-anthropological journey into PTSD psychic inner space through portals of entry is a journey of unparalleled dimensions and opportunities. It is a scientific portal of almost unimagined clinical potentiality and scientific knowledge.

A walk into the unconscious vault of the unknown of the trauma survivor is a walk of uncertainty and the discovery of the Abyss Constellation and Trauma Complex (Wilson, 2006). As such, it can be disturbing, distressing, and have profound psychological impacts to medical professionals, treatment providers, or healing professionals, shamans, counselors, scientific researchers, or Nurturing Guides (NG). *In this sense, it is a virtual reality parallel to walking back into the actual life-stressing journey of the Hero/Survivor. The authentically grounded Nurturing Guide (NG) enters the virtual reality of the survivor through empathy. They walk with them in past time and space to trauma memories of the then and there as if it were now.*

In this specific sense, a sensitive psychotherapist for PTSD patients is similar to a dedicated, passionate archaeologist or anthropologist: To discover the undiscovered and be prepared for the unprepared but with a desire to find the truth of what existed and happened at a given point in time and place in life experiences to find the undiscovered realities; the hidden structures of what exists and what they may mean in ancient or current social context. To discover that unsaid, secret, horrible, or just plain unspeakable. That is the essence of the psychotherapist's task who ventures to encounter PTSD.

The portals of entry into ancient pyramids and the portals of entry into inner psychic space of trauma survivors result in different outcomes as to what they reveal. The burial tombs of pharaohs and queens of Egypt were magnificent spaces of opulence, wealth, gold-gilded statues and coffins, artisanal objects, artifacts, and much more for the journey to the afterlife. As such, they reflected the glory, power, status, and recognition of royalty and deity; the glory and adulation they were going to take with them to the afterlife.

To the trauma survivor, there is no analogy of Godness possible. It is only the journey to the metaphoric slopes of survival and an uphill journey, which can last a lifetime or eternity.

The Trauma Inner Psychic Space for the Afterlife

The inner-spaces for trauma survivors are often dark, foreboding, anxiety-generating places, repositories of overwhelmingly difficult life-experiences that tax the body, spirit, and soul of the person for that of what is left of the posttraumatic life as they know it.

This reality sets up internal dialects that require metaphors for synthesis, integration, and transformation.

Trauma transformation can be a life-long and difficult journey. Metaphors also contain clues as to the chambers of the nexus of trauma complexes (Wilson, 2006). What is contained in the secret posttraumatic chamber? For example, there are many possibilities, like a storage of lockers in New York City, NY, or Cleveland, OH, basement apartment rental units. In bold contrast, trauma survivors struggle with ancient icons of what they endured or left behind. In this sense, they are indelible images, memories, and emotions of universal (archetypal) experiences of human existence, which ultimately appear in verbal metaphoric and artistic expressions, often in sculptures and free-paintings. Indeed, one cannot suppress traumatic creativity as it has its own life in the humanities and literature. The therapeutic, artistic-creative question is simply: How to unleash it?

Posttraumatic Healing Challenges After the Survivor's Journey

After the Abyss Experience (AE), the trauma survivor faces the arduous and painful task of re-entry where he or she is met with additional stressors and psychic burdens, often unexpected and disappointing in nature, for the quality of life on a daily basis. As previously noted, contrary to expectations, the survivor does not typically receive a warm, knowledgeable, and informed welcome from those left behind who were not part of the traumatic journey (see Figure 1.1). The contradictions and discrepancies in expectation and reality are painful and difficult to endure and figure out (see Chapters 4 and 5).

Joseph Campbell (1949) notes that there are three prototypical patterns of re-entering society after the Heroic/Survivor journey: (1) no reception; (2) the search for approval, validation and confirmation of one's journey, travails, and suffering; and (3) the need to share their story of survival and teach others in generative (wisdom sharing) ways in due and proper time, i.e., to perhaps eventually become a Nurturing Guide (NG) and teacher to others and share wisdom for their journey.

The trauma survivor, upon re-entry into the culture of origin, like the Mythical Hero, encounters some or all of the following reactions to their Heroic journey and life-transforming experiences.

The Delineation of the Hero-Trauma-Survivor's Life-Journey

(See Figure 1.1.)

1. The need to understand the journey itself: The lack of appreciation for the traumatic journey, sacrifices endured, and why it had to happen:
    - The absence of recognition of the true nature of suffering, sacrifice, and survival about the Hero-Survivor's journey and its psychic consequences to well-being (e.g., PTSD, depression, physical healing, personality changes, addiction, compulsion, anxiety, marital conflicts, etc.).
2. Alienation upon return: The lack of recognition of traumatic stressors and perils endured: The blunt untarnished reality of what happened.

- The absence of recognition of the actual perils endured, or indifference from significant others that was unexpected, disappointing, depressing, anger-producing or alienating.

3 Insufficient knowledge of sacrifices of the journey: The non-recognition and understanding of sacrifices by others:
   - The absence of appreciation for personal injuries and changes to body and soul; the avoidance to acknowledge or talk about such injuries by significant others.

4 Absence of needed resources: The lack of appropriate medical care and psychological treatments and other forms of assistance upon re-entry:
   - The absence of treatments, forms of psychotherapy, health care, or opportunities to engage in traditional healing rituals that would facilitate recovery; or the absence of needed current medical or psychological care.

5 The need for a Nurturing Guide (NG): The reality of existential transformation of trauma as a task:
   - The emergent realization that personal meaning must be created out of the trauma experience itself; absent recognition or acceptance from others who matter, and a new understanding of personal acceptance of responsibility for recovery and finding ways to restore wholeness to self.

Trauma Myths and New Metaphorical Directions

According to Campbell (1949), mythology suggests that the Heroic survivor seeks to find pathways to healing, i.e., there is a search for inner unity and integration of the self. Based on this insight, as well as others (Wilson & Tang, 2007), we can identify six consequences of healing pathways within the diversity of cultures: (1) to restore harmony in mind, body, and spirit; (2) restore vital physical and mental energy; (3) promote well-being through mindfulness and psychic integration; (4) empower personal energy for life-course development; (5) access and utilize useful treatments available in the culture; and (6) develop healing practices that promote resilience and a life-sense of well-being and hopefulness.

Campbell (1949) outlines the four functions of mythology in terms of mental activity as follows: (1) spiritual-mystical; (2) cosmological; (3) sociological; and (4) psychological. Each of these functions is revealed within mythology and has direct parallels to the nature of psychological requirements in dealing with the impact of trauma to self and a sense of well-being. For example, traumatic life-experiences form a reconciliation with unconsciousness and the meaning of life. This issue directly concerns the mythology of one's own life and the role and stress trauma has played in it. For example, novels and autobiographies of former combat soldiers typically characterize the horrific war encounter with death, the existential questioning of the purpose of war and how such experiences subsequently shape life-course trajectory. Traumatic experiences often force a self-effacing look at personal identity, consciousness, and the search for existential meaning. Trauma serves to put the individual in touch with their unconscious processes, including the disavowed, dark, or "shadowy" side of personality (e.g., Jung's Shadow Archetype, Wilson, 2006).

For example, to be a combat soldier fighting an enemy involves killing and "you or me" paradigms of life and death encounters. How do such life and death encounters get sorted out? How does the therapist even begin to understand the you or me metaphor of war veterans or similar existential confrontation?

What Is Undone Is Done: Decoding and Confronting the Trauma Past in the Present and in the Future

By carefully analyzing the functions of mythology within a cultural perspective we can identify how it is that cultures shape posttraumatic adaptation, growth, and the challenges of self-transformation for its members. These mythological and culturally-based themes emerge spontaneously in metaphors of trauma survivors and their residue in unmetabolized cognitive processes and emotional manifestations. They remain psychically unconscious with unmetabolized energy. What is undone is undone and awaits the reopening of the fold in time and moments of psychic integration with an empathic helper at the right time and place at any stage of life (NG). Indeed, it could be immediate or much later in one's life or in episode sequences along the way. It is the journey of life itself, unyielding and pressing.

It is a truism that sensitive and seasoned psychotherapists feel and know these therapeutic moments at the right time and critical therapeutic situations and/or healing moments. When this happens, it is the kernel of empathic resonance and genuine connectedness of two people. It is at this point that the importance and significance of metaphors emerge amongst treatment-seeking patients or in the everyday lives of trauma survivors or just ordinary people that we all know and love in everyday life.

The trauma survivor comes to the treatment milieu with open wounds that are expressed in metaphors at different levels of consciousness and mental integration and at different points in time. Trauma-based metaphors (TSM), while changing and transforming over time, remain critical portals of entry to the inner space of psychic trauma.

Trauma metaphors always reflect intrapsychic processes, inner vulnerabilities, and profound unconscious processes trying to confront the unspeakable, unsaid, horrific and undesired, unpleasant memories. Simply spoken, they are mirrors to their soul. Or, maybe not, depending on the level of defensiveness and avoidance of a diminished, numbed, and closed-off survivor whose soul feels lost, gone, abandoned, dead, numb, or no longer there in their previous inner soul of personal identity.

The Ultimate Importance of Trauma-Specific Metaphors (TSM) and Trauma-Specific Transference Processes (TST)

Over time, especially with the building of a therapeutic relationship, survivors may abandon their negative transference to the Nurturing Guide (e.g., psychotherapist, social worker, etc.) and reveal the portals of entry into the PTSD pyramid of secret or hidden chambers and much more, including the significance of pre-traumatic personality development and how it articulates with posttraumatic patters of adaptation (Wilson, 2006).

How does the psychotherapist or clinician-medical doctor "get there" and find the critical transfer roots of it? This is among the basic tasks of the Nurturing Guide (NG) who facilitates ways of healing and discovery of the newly formed nascent, posttraumatic self after the journey they endured. An unspoken reality now exists. To the trauma survivor, when this moment occurs, it is often experienced as a God-given moment or spiritual connection and hope for the future. They know that this person can or will be their guide and helper (NG) to moving on and personal change. If this hopeful moment does not occur, as it often doesn't, then despair anchored in the effects of trauma take hold of the ego and daily functioning and generate an agenda of profound struggle.

Rebirth: Transformation and Integration

When this essential and existential moment exists, it may constitute an epiphany of life-altering reconnections to a higher power of being and an immediate sense of grounding to a new potential sense of self-in-the-world. It is experienced, for the survivor, as an emergent, hopeful sense of optimism for a new and better future in life.

The evolutionary eyes of life go immediately to a fresh, new horizon after any form of trauma. In time, life starts to feel good again and joy returns to daily life in the recovery process, if only episodically. This is, then, the existential moment of epiphany, a moment of rebirth of personality in the life-cycle. A new transformation of self-reinvention is possible and begins to happen. Life is reborn at all levels at this moment.

The Freedom of Spirit has returned; life-eternal and grounded if only in the present moment. Traumatic experiences teach us that wisdom when we feel it and begin to understand its complexities. But to feel the gift of wisdom is to know the intrapsychic world of the survivor. To understand this survivor world is a gift of the God-given moments and then some. At such moments, the survivor feels spiritually connected to the Nurturing Guide (NG) himself and, maybe, God. The survivor's journey continues in time and space in a new self-configuration. Where it will evolve remains to be understood in terms of identity and self-redefinition. But, for sure, it is a life-source of energy and further differentiation of the self and one's identity as a person of integrity. The task of transforming and integrating trauma is life-long and ever-changing in its nature.

2 The Language of Trauma in Metaphors

Trauma Language and Narrative: Etymology of Key Trauma-Associated Words and Linguistic Expressions; History of the Language of Trauma

Trauma, from the dawn of historical record, challenges the survivor to speak the unspeakable, to say the unsaid but desired truth. How do survivors invent or unconsciously manifest the language to express their extraordinary experiences? How do these newly discovered words and phrases act to organize and represent these traumatic experiences? What are their cognitive, mnemonic origins?

In this chapter we examine how language itself, particularly *bodily centered metaphors*, becomes the psychological scaffolding to carry forward these complex, cognitive, executive functions for adaptive behaviors. They are words in the form of understandable narrative that eventually becomes the container holding the survivor's experiences and making the journey home possible. It is a transformative process of complexity and challenge over time, space, and identity integration.

The Historical, Etymological Roots of Psychic Trauma

To begin our exploration, let us turn to the language those involved with trauma studies and clinical work use, such as: disaster, trauma, shock, and Holocaust. What are their origins? Each of these terms began as combinations of newly created metaphors, capturing the essence of something people knew and felt, and yet, rearranging them in novel ways to approximate something fresh, inventing, unconsciously or partially consciously, words to express their events that otherwise would have remained beyond the survivors' capacity to describe. In other words, trauma survivors tend to remain silent but when they talk of their extreme stress experiences, they often speak in trauma-associated metaphors (TSM).

Trauma, of course, has a metaphoric etymology and historical origin and history. We use it both medically to relate to violent sudden injury to the body, and psychologically to refer to mental states of having been shaken and profoundly distressed by an experience. Thus, trauma forms injury to the body and the mind, inter-related but discretely different in nature.

The Greek, Sanskrit, and Persian origin of *tere*, to which the word trauma is related, goes back to 1500 BC and refers to an "*open hole*," as in a nostril, or by extension any hole in the body, while another meaning of the term captures the sense of passing through or changing from a state without the hole to a state with the hole. Hence, a transformation from one bodily organismic state to another, reflected in language and metaphors.

Contemporary textbooks have been written on its medical-psychological-traumatic consequences, and volumes by contemporary PTSD experts and many others on its psychological implications, the word (*tere*) itself derives from ancient trauma metaphors that capture the image of a sudden change in state where the body now has a break in its integrity, a "hole" in it, a change in wholeness of bodily and spiritual being.

Disasters

Disaster is another word dating back to approximately 1200 BC in Greek history, meaning "*against the stars*," a metaphor itself. It describes a state in the universe, which is out of order, against the orderly arrangement of heavenly bodies. Indeed, "*Dis*" represents a Greek god of the underworld, so that an additional meaning is implied, namely that this *disordered universe* is the doing of some underground, unforeseen, and unpredictable chaotic forces. Were we to invent a word three millennia later that conveys our notion of a posttraumatically altered worldview any more directly and forcefully, we could do no better than disaster, catastrophe, and trauma.

Disaster, Catastrophe, and Trauma

In the 19th century, European and American physicians and research scientists began to use the term shock to apply to the physiological and psychological effects of trauma. In its general usage, we still use shock as a synonym for trauma. We say, referring to an apparently dazed mental state, that the survivor was "in shock" after the tornado. But medicine and psychology have gone in slightly different directions with this term, so that today, medical shock is a *specific set of physiological consequences to a sudden dangerous fall in blood pressure or other vital signs.* Psychologically, we have tended to retain the word as it is employed in general usage. *The bodily centered metaphoric derivation is clear.* Shock is derived from the state of having been suddenly shaken as after receiving a blow. Implicit in this usage is the sense of psychological disorganization and disruptions in higher-order cognitive functions. Thus, we have a most precise word, derived metaphorically from a familiar bodily state that we all have some awareness of, the state of being "shaken," "shocked," or suddenly "disrupted." In this same set of logic, posttraumatic stress as a prolonged organismic set of reactions are a specific set of psychological sequela.

Holocaust and Genocide

In the 20th century, another term came to be used in man-made genocides and with special reference to the murder of six million Jews as well as gypsies, homosexuals, communists, mentally retarded children, and regime-perceived non-Aryan political enemies by the Nazi regime in World War II, namely Holocaust. This was Nazi Germany between 1941 and 1945. Holocaust meant destruction of human life by "gas, fire, bullets and electrocution."

In Hebrew, "*Ola*" means to "*go into thin air*" and the *root cause*, means to be totally "*consumed by fire*." The word captures a *visual* and even *olfactory* representation of death by fire, the burning of humans in Nazi crematoria and their disappearing into thin air. Its medieval roots indicate that the word is connected with *religious sacrifice.* Such images and connotations both describe the events in *body-related terms* and elevate their murderous incineration to an existentially profound level.

Historically, we have a term with ancient derivation, medieval connotations, and yet fresh meaning in the 21st century. While the term, Holocaust, was first used five years *after* the genocidal events of World War II, it was 15 years before it gained general usage in medical and psychiatric reports. How is this situation possible scientifically? Where were the sufficient and necessary medical-psychiatric-psychological investigations of discovery? While Holocaust represents a combination of ancient Hebrew words, it took Western civilization many years before it could digest the traumatic events sufficiently to arrive at an organizing, metaphorically based, and, in a sense, newly formed term for a contemporary trauma legacy.

Trauma and disaster, shock and Holocaust, four familiar terms, derive etymologically from historically older metaphors that capture a malevolently altered ancient universe. They have particular bodily-based images such as death by fire, a state of being shaken, and a body with a hole in it, or disintegration by death and destruction.

The words we use to describe the *indescribable emerge spontaneously through metaphor*. They do so when prior words capture images that serve as metaphors when applied in creative ways to express new experiences more clearly. The origins of these trauma metaphors are *bodily-based* and "*experience-near*" (i.e., experienced in close spatial and temporal proximity to the event itself). They require time from the onset of the event to the general usage of the word, trauma metaphors of linguistic guides to significant places, time, and experiences. In a sense they are latent summary memories of overwhelming, fearful dimensions and elements and Abyss Experiences (AE).

Ihahamuka—A New Trauma-Related Word After Genocide in Rwanda, Africa

Do survivors continue to invent new words to describe the effects of trauma? Yes! In recent decades, following the Rwandan genocide, survivors rearranged several root words to describe the bodily condition that so many were experiencing: "*ihahamuka*."

The term combines African *root words* that indicate the absence of inhaling or a state of not breathing. In particular, the Kinyarwandan root, like the English approximate synonym, inspiring, carries the connotation of both inhaling and bringing hope (Hagengimana, 1992). By adding a prefix that negates, Rwandans formed a word that describes a physical state in which the action of moving air in and out of the lungs through the diaphragm fails to bring about a sense of being alive or having any hope. The Rwandan survivors, with the brutal death of loved ones all around them, and the total destruction of their community fabric, found a way, in their own language, to vocalize their state of numbing depression and loss. One might say that they invented a metaphor for how they were feeling after genocidal warfare, the state of no inhaling, no inspiring, no hoping, no breathing room. A state of post-genocidal despair about life itself.

Western-trained mental health workers trying to conduct research after the genocide in the late 1980s found that their words, posttraumatic stress disorder (PTSD), anxiety, intrusive images, and hyperarousal, held little or no currency among the survivors of these survivors and their personal experiences.

Conceptualizing and Categorizing PTSD in Psychiatric Diagnoses

How did posttraumatic stress disorder (PTSD) come to be named PTSD? In contrast to the spontaneous emergence of a word like "ihahamuka," born organically from the ethnic existential soil of genocide itself, let us consider the term posttraumatic stress disorder (PTSD), a grouping of words coined by committee between 1977 and 1979. The term PTSD appeared with the February publication of the DSM-III (1980) in an effort to identify a generic stress response syndrome with a common cluster of symptom groups, classified within the province of science and medicine in hopes of further research and clinical application. However, not dissimilar to the Rwandan term "ihahamuka," the 1980 inclusion of PTSD as a diagnostic category originated from clinicians, researchers, and trauma survivors themselves, including: Holocaust survivors; World War II, Korean and Vietnam war veterans; rape victims; child abuse victims; battered women and survivors of natural disasters. Their posttrauma syndromes shared more commonalities than differences and therefore reflected a core set of psychobiological posttraumatic processes.

The term posttraumatic stress disorder (PTSD) itself relies upon Latin (post or following), Greek (traumatic, see above), Middle English (stress), and a semi-correct designation for mental illness, disorder. The word stress is central and has connotations related to force in physics and engineering, which, by being excessive, sets further actions of physical structures in motion. It refers to the elaboration of these ideas in physiology where a flight or fight response occurs in the presence of strain or danger, an HPA brain response.

As to PTSD as a distinct diagnostic entity, many positive features, reflective of the committee's intents regarding the potential for future study, are imbedded in these four name-parts in the cluster of criterion (A–D). In the 30+ years of study that followed the 1980 inclusion of PTSD in the diagnostic manual the study of stress responses led to neuroanatomical (brain patterns), neurophysiological, and pharmacologic findings (Wilson, Friedman, & Lindy, 2004). The study of posttrauma phenomena helped clarify acute, latent, and chronic forms of illness, and promoted a search for a specific threshold range of traumatic stressors and their consequences to psychic functioning and behavioral adaptation.

In retrospect, we can see all too clearly some disadvantages of the committee's choice of words for the 1980 DSM-III diagnostic criteria. Nowhere does the PTSD diagnostic name convey the central organizing changes in personality processes, self-character, the paralyzing effect of discontinuity in self and identity, the pernicious effect on worldview and sense of future. The name PTSD ignores the *existential despair at the core of the survivor* who suffers with the condition induced by psychic trauma. Indeed, PTSD, as a word phrase, casts a softer shadow when compared to *ihahamuka* (the inability to breathe or inspire) or the original Sanskrit *tere* that leaves a hole in the body. Why should any clinicians, research scientists, therapists *not* awaken to trauma-specific research?

Repositioning Posttraumatic States Within the World of Language and Narrative

How do we reconcile the two characteristic ways in which various linguistic terms have emerged in the field of traumatic stress? We have, at least, two traditions in the words we use as trauma clinicians: (1) one grows from the bodily experiences of survivors; (2) the other from our scientific interest in codifying, generalizing, measuring, and demonstrating empirically valid interventions and psychobiological mechanisms.

While both are central for our field, we attempt to re-equilibrate the balance between the two. While the clinician must assess and treat, he must also listen deeply, so that his or her care for the survivor touches those humanistic issues that are at the core of trauma pathology and recovery.

If we are to reposition our understanding of the core psychological states that follow trauma, we must strive to understand the central *organizing role of words in speaking the unspeakable.* We must broaden our brush stroke beyond definitions derived by medicine, psychology, and neuroscience. We reach out to the world of language itself, especially how it is formed within the context of existential despair. Recovering from trauma requires narrative, and narrative requires the central role of fresh organizing words and phrases. Trauma study requires that we expand our knowledge base to include contributions from the companion fields of developmental linguistics, literature and literary criticism, anthropology, and in particular their ways of using metaphor and metonymy as key tools in understanding trauma language.

In order to do this, we ask what are the central elements in language? What kinds of word phrases are most important? In the terms of poetics and rhetoric, should we focus on figures of speech, idioms, aphorisms, idiometric expressions, proverbs, parables, similes, symbols, synecdoche, metonymy, metaphor, or others? Fortunately, contemporary linguists help us to focus on only two: metaphor and metonymy, the others being conceptually subsumed under these major categories but not inclusive for PTSD and trauma.

George Lakoff: The Study of Cognitive Metaphor Linguistics

Following the lead of Lakoff and Johnson (1980) we begin with metaphor. Metaphor is the linking through similarity of an earlier experience with a current one. It is how we first develop the words that describe our experience. Metaphors help us explain how we feel and organize those experiences that we find fulfilling. They help us remember those things we should avoid. They provide ways of organizing what we do to face challenges so that we are more likely to be successful. Groups of metaphors begin to describe our sense of self, our personality, and our identity. Still other metaphors characterize our view of the world around us, and how we expect it to behave.

We learned of warmth through the tactile comfort and temperature when our mothers held us in soothing ways. Later we refer to the warmth of a dear friendship, for example. When we have exerted ourselves strenuously we lie down for a restful sleep, and awaken refreshed. As adults we speak of someone's comments as representing a refreshing perspective. As we learn to walk upright we associate our mastery with pride and advantaged viewpoints. Later we feel up and a sense of well-being when things are going in positive directions.

Metaphor organizes what we should avoid and understand. We learned that hot stoves will burn you. In adulthood we say after a stinging rebuke "that burned."

Metaphors describe characteristic coping strategies. We might take each day as a "new beginning," keep on our toes to take advantage of opportunities, approach problems one step at a time, deal with others by sharing, and in turn, expect that our exertions are met with sweet reward. Because these approaches have been successful in the past, the phrases that convey them are like organizers for how we ordinarily cope with the world.

Groups of metaphors or aphorisms tend to complement each other and, together, organize our beliefs about the world as well. We may have been taught, for example, that teachers and others in authority, like our parents, have our best interests at heart, an attitude that describes how we think of basic trust. We learned in childhood that if we stop, look, and listen, we ought to be safe crossing the road. We have been taught that what we say and do to others has consequences for which we are responsible, an attitude that affects how we think of the impact of our power. We are taught that keeping things in "ship-shape" order means we are prepared. The "buck stops here" implies that we are in control of much of our world. The phrase, "when we smile, the world smiles back," implies an ongoing sense of positive self-esteem. Love is its own reward implies a high value on intimacy. Such groups of proverbs define our unconscious beliefs about crucial values such as trust, safety, power, control, self-esteem, and intimacy.

New problems create a torrent of metaphors explaining how we should cope, each implying a theory of cause and a potential method of repair. With the financial crisis of the last decade (i.e., 2008–present), politicians were falling over themselves with similes such as the economy is in gridlock; our markets are frozen; the whole banking system is a sinking ship. Each metaphor implied a different mechanism of action for the crisis and a response that fit the metaphor. Gridlock called for external control of market traffic. Frozen markets simply required a thaw. A sinking ship called for a bail-out. Cognitive linguists maintain that we use language, particularly metaphors, to come to know and understand the world. It is in this context that metaphor takes on its special significance, standing in place of all formal language elements that accomplish the end of applicable building units for growth of knowledge.

For Lakoff, therefore, metaphor is much more than a category of speech. It is an *image schema* that provides meaning and organization to thoughts, actions, and language. It is an active process of thinking. It is the way we find to perceive and organize something new, or more complex (a target), in terms of more readily known images drawn from prior experience (a source). Thus, trauma metaphors are also image schemes with meaning and specific organizational functions.

In the common expression "time flies," the apparently rapid passage of time is the target to be described. The phrase, "flew by," an experience familiar to any of us who have watched birds fly rapidly from one position to another, is the source.

The fundamental role of metaphor is to project inference patterns from the source domain (an experience in the past) to the target domain (an experience in the present).

Primary metaphors link our subjective experience and judgments to our sensory-motor experience. These primary metaphors supply the logic, the imagery, and the qualitative feel of sensory-motor experience to abstract concepts. We all acquire these metaphoric modes of thought automatically and unconsciously (Lakoff & Johnson, 1999).

Psychobiologic Centrality in Psychic States

What are the very first set of experiences that act as sources for further metaphor formation? Where do they begin and end in the process of epigenesis in life?

Lakoff begins his discussion of metaphor with the common bodily and life experiences that we all become aware of as we grow and attain language. We see, we feel, we touch, we hear, we sense, we taste. We breathe, eat and digest food, exert ourselves, move, are awake, and fall asleep. These psychobiological categories apply universally across cultures in that we share these bodily attributes universally with all others. We first come to know the world through our senses and bodily sensations. It is words that derive from these common human forms of perception that form our first metaphors, our first learning tools once language develops.

Such metaphors are prominent in the language we choose to describe our feelings. We have already come upon the common phrases of feeling warm and from these simple illustrations flow the eventual complexity of metaphoric transformations.

Primary metaphors have as their source their derivation from our earliest activities and experiences as well as perceptions. Primary metaphors are bodily centered. The categories that cognitive linguists use to organize such primary metaphors begin with the sensory list above but expand to include other groups of common human experience early in life, placing the self in its relationship to everyday living. When frightened it is reassuring to be able to find mother and have her hold us. Often we are rewarded after performing well with something sweet. To explore something new and curious we must move from here to a new destination. And as we grasp and name objects we learn something about their properties, such as they are bounded in space, different parts fit together, or they have or do not have support. Indeed, the act of grasping something as in grasping the meaning of a concept.

These *named sensory-motor experiences* and the associations we have with them are building-blocks of learning, we use them in order to explore and master more complex matters in our universe, to open our eyes that we might grasp something new. We tend to use old words as metaphors as we learn to apply combinations of them to the new situations.

In the accompanying table we see some of Lakoff's original building blocks of language, with examples from the everyday world of adulthood in which we use them unconsciously in our language to describe our feelings in the present.

Metaphors After Traumatic Experiences

What happens when, in a single moment, trauma disrupts? The metaphors we live by, demonstrating ever so clearly that their assumptions have proven to be untrue. For example, after officials at a nuclear facility misled neighbors about the risk of radioactive contamination, and after a young lieutenant risks his men by charging an untakeable hill in Vietnam, the idea that superiors have one's best interests at heart hardly appears true. After a random mortar round kills the most fastidious soldier in the platoon, the idea that keeping things ship-shape will keep you alive loses its impact. After watching one new soldier after the other being maimed or killed, the idea of investing love in others hardly seems a virtue. The destruction of building blocks from the past through trauma creates doubt where there was certainty, a void where there were answers, and therefore, gradually, a search for new metaphors.

To put issues in a larger perspective, if trauma is, by definition, an unformed and incomplete wordless state of psychobiological processes (see Chapter 1, Figure 1.1), and, if it is significantly unique from any previous experience in life, then to describe the event externally and internally and to break it down into workable elements, the survivor will need to build a new language to express these words and phrases in narrative forms.

The linguistic process search is a fundamental characteristic of the language of trauma and its aftermath. What we now access regarding our bodily awareness is a new truth, based not in the extension of mastery experiences of childhood but in the physiology of the overwhelming trauma experience itself. However, the new language must reference the same categories or sensory-motor domains.

Just as the physician listens for symptoms in the many physical areas of the body, the trauma therapist listens to the way his patient's language reflects areas of biological functioning that may have been powerfully affected during the trauma itself.

In Table 2.1 we note that, following trauma, bodily metaphors of everyday life change as a result of sensory-motor experiences during the trauma itself.

As we see in Tables 2.1–2.3, with trauma there is a fundamental shift in language. The old building blocks to mastery via familiar metaphor are broken and no longer work. A new language comes into being that is consistent with the *altered sensory-motor experience* within the trauma situation. It is just this change in language that captures the attention of the trauma therapist. Sensory experiences are common carriers of trauma-related phenomena. They describe the affective mood in the present and something true about the trauma itself. Helen, an incest survivor, felt broken like the broken boundaries of her body. For the war veteran Abram a heavy weight sits on his shoulder just as it did after a firefight. For Chris, a civilian fire survivor, life's problems and hassles became too hot to handle just as the wall felt hot before the fire. In linguistic terms these survivors have unconsciously turned the senory-motor experience of the trauma, such as pain, pressure, and temperature, into source experiences that they will be applying to new targets, a form of learning that will unfortunately get them into trouble once they have left the trauma scene.

Returning to Lakoff and Johnson's systems of classifying metaphors, what happens as we extend outward from the body to include activities at a further level of abstraction? For Lakoff there is a larger range of sources for embodiment metaphors, all of which have relevance to trauma.

While still bodily centered, we find that linguistically we expand what we know about our bodies, our drives, our ways of thinking as humans, and our key relationship to others to express more abstract thoughts and feelings. These human ways of organizing ideas have great impact on how we see ourselves and our world at any given moment. There are linguistic groupings of metaphors that follow from our experience of hunger and satiation like empty–full and blockage, from our gathering in with our hands like collecting, containing, from our position vis-à-vis others like near–far, from our perception of size like object, mass, and scale, and from our experience of interactions between objects and between humans like contact, attraction, and repulsion. Finally there are groupings of metaphors that work because they capture something of how our minds work: we match, split, process, substitute part for whole and whole for part.

We see in Table 2.3 how metaphors expand beyond the primary senses themselves. Once more, trauma changes metaphoric language from mastered building-blocks to recurrent moments of doubt and the threat of being overwhelmed. The survivor may feel empty inside, or getting close to him is the kiss of death, or split in two different selves.

The new metaphors outlined in Table 2.3 become the verbal organizers of the changed space that the survivor finds himself occupying. No one can get close to me. I'm speechless. A crowded space can kill you.

Listening for Traumatic Changes in Mental Processes Through Metaphor

Trauma metaphor is often so striking that it is almost impossible for the listener to avoid: feeling like bashing a head against the wall, a shiver down my spine, totally blank and

Table 2.1 Common Primary Metaphors Based in Biologic Functioning Compared with Posttrauma Metaphors Set Off by Trauma Triggers

Biologic Categories	*Ordinary Language*	*Posttrauma Trigger*	*Somatic Metaphor*
Respiration	The beauty took my breath away.	Reminder of loss.	Deep sigh or weeping "Ihahamuka."
Cardiac	My heart skipped a beat.	Reminder of danger.	Heart is racing.
Proprioceptive	It was dark but I could feel him there.	Danger on the periphery.	Crowds make me queasy, agoraphobia.
Alimentary	I couldn't stomach that.	Reminder of severed body parts.	Nausea.
Movement	I flew past him.	Altered traffic pattern.	About to explode.
CNS Autonomic	I am excited.	I am wired.	Let's roll!
Erythema	She blushed when he looked.	Wish to avenge by killing.	Pattern of erythema over unremembered wound.
Arousal	My nerves are on edge.	Anticipate trauma reminder.	On guard.
Sight	Can you see the problem ahead?	Tree line.	Keep low profile.
Sound	That doesn't sound right to me.	Click.	Death is around the corner.
Touch	His comment touched me deeply.	Sweat, tension.	Danger walking point.
Taste	It was a sweet victory.	Ashes.	Bitter.
Smell	He burned rubber with his sports car.	Aroma of barbeque.	Can't stomach it.
Musculoskeletal	Pain in the neck.	Decapitation.	Relentless somatic symptom.
Sleep	Sleep like a baby.	Insomnia.	Keeping watch and hyperarousal.

black. Other times it is similar to common somatic language, can't stomach that, gives me a headache, or hurts me in the chest. Sometimes the novelty of the word choice grabs the listener, as I feel like assassinating someone; other times the words appear almost like clichés, outside looking in, drained of energy, or down. Exploring the multiple levels of understanding of trauma metaphors is the subject of future chapters. Our goal in this chapter is to grasp how they form within the context of the trauma itself, and how the clinician might listen for them, for they approximate a new truth, the truth of the trauma situation.

Just as the search for the pharaohs' most precious holdings begins with clues from the outer surface of the pyramid, so spontaneous metaphors of trauma survivors are clues

Table 2.2 Typical Metaphor Construction Based on Universal Early Childhood Body Experiences and Posttrauma Metaphor Equivalents

PRIMARY SENSORY-MOTOR METAPHORS:

Sensory-motor Domain	*Ordinary Example*	*Trauma Example*
Temperature	They greeted me warmly.	It was too hot to handle.
Bodily Orientation	I'm feeling up today.	I've been down and out for a long time.
Size	Tomorrow is a big day.	It always makes me feel kind of small when thinking about it.
Being Physically Close	We've been close for years.	My old friends are distant and gone.
Muscular Exertion	That task was easy.	There's a heavy weight on my shoulder; I'm squeezed.
Vertical Orientation	I'm up for the occasion.	I feel upside down and whirling.
Motion	John's intelligence goes beyond Bill's.	I'm not moving anywhere in my life now; I'm nothing and have nowhere to go.
Experience of Physical Objects	How does it make sense?	My beliefs are broken into pieces.
Physical Support	Support your local community agency.	I'm not feeling much support from anyone.
Bounded in Space	Sam is in the group.	I'm outside looking in.
Reaching a Destination	We are nearly home with this journey.	I'll never get back.

on the outer surface of the effects of trauma within. Here, by identifying primary metaphors, we have direct access to the bodily sensations that have encoded the trauma itself. By examining secondary metaphors, particularly those that form families of meaning, we can discern how the survivor has come to see himself as damaged by the trauma. By following the spontaneous creation of new and transforming metaphors, we can see how the survivor's own mapping operations work to provide new ways to encode the traumatic circumstances and synthesize new meaning in the future.

While primary metaphors are universal, secondary metaphors may be culture-specific, such that a Western individual may find a way to compare his difficult situation to the working or damaged parts of an automobile while a non-Western individual might compare his difficult situation to a growing plant that is not progressing healthfully. A Western trauma survivor may describe himself as stalled like an engine that is unable to get into gear. The non-Western trauma survivor may say he is covered with blight.

Families of secondary metaphors tend to overlap with one another, creating the opportunity for the source figures of speech to map onto the target in multiple ways. Such inter-related or complex metaphors create an extensive landscape upon which a number of seemingly different ideas become compatible.

Table 2.3 Source Categories for Extended Embodiment Metaphor and Change After Trauma

SOURCE CATEGORIES FOR PRIMARY METAPHORS:

Linguistic Category	*Use in Ordinary Language*	*Trauma-Related Metaphor*
Attraction	She turns me on.	I repel women.
Center–periphery	He thinks he's king of his world.	I am outside looking in.
Contact	We stayed in touch by telephone.	No one can get close to me.
Cycle	He's in the autumn of his years.	(The natural course of) my life is broken.
Iteration	His word was law.	I'm speechless.
Matching	His socks matched his sweater.	There's nothing like what happened.
Object	He tabled the motion.	A crowded space can kill you.
Process	The legislation grinds away.	My mind has closed down.
Splitting	He deserves his share of the glory.	I am half angel; half whore.
Balance	She's so busy it is a balancing act.	I've lost balance.
Collection	Michael collects girlfriends.	My mind collects garbage.
Container	I don't know how much vocabulary I can stuff in my brain.	I'm empty inside.
Enablement	Jim's interception won the game.	I'm the kiss of death.
Link	Past is prologue.	The past no longer links to the future.
Merging	Blue and yellow make green.	On a hot day I'm in Vietnam.
Part—Whole	The green berets are the best units.	My boots tell it all.
Restraint—Remove	I can't keep him from his views.	I try to push the memories away.
Superimposition	His head blocked my view.	My guilt weighs on me.
Blockage	The traffic is in gridlock.	I'm stuck.
Compulsion	It drove him to drink.	I have to get back to that peak.
Counterforce	He stood against the amendment.	90% goes into holding it back; 10% into living.
Full—Empty	He's full of himself.	I'm running on empty.
Mass—Count	Obama's first 100 days were heavy.	Too heavy a load to carry.
Near—Far	Doing it once is a step toward mastery.	Can't see the end of it.
Path	I'm on the way to getting my life in order.	I've lost my footing.
Scale	His mood was lighter after the gift.	I have more low days than high ones.
Surface	I can't touch his level of skill.	Too hot to handle.

To illustrate, Lakoff (2004), always interested in the practical application of linguistics to our larger social-political environment, presented the view after the 2004 election in the United States that a political party (the target) tends to be seen like a parent (the source) and, in particular at that time, to be Republican is to favor the father-dominated household: respect male authority, to be forceful, clear-minded, responsible, and tough while to be Democratic was to value the maternal home: seeking consensus, compassionate toward the less fortunate, and supportive of growth for all. As such, there are unconscious families of secondary metaphors that hold together in more complex ways offering new possibilities for comparison, for reasoning, and for problem-solving. In these families of related metaphors, the source (various aspects of a parent) maps onto the target (a political party) in ever more complex and interrelated manners. And they do so outside the arena of conscious rational thought and language.

Unconscious Determinants of Metaphors

How much are all of us influenced by the unconscious metaphors we choose? What families of metaphors do those of us who work in the area of trauma studies use? When we think about trauma and recovery as the target domain, what are the sources for the metaphoric language we apply? Trauma metaphors are just that: verbalized expressions of overwhelming traumatic experiences (TSM).

Different groups of workers in the field apply different families of metaphor thereby molding how we think by the source of images or ideas for our discourse. For example, medical trauma clinicians may use a biological source, so that we speak of neurophysiologic feedback loops, medication, homeostasis, and allostasis.

Using the myths of the anthropologist as our source, we might think of the trauma survivor's ordeal as a journey from the abyss, requiring exposure to peril, commitment to an ideal greater than the self, and a difficult return home.

Alternatively we may approach the task of helping the trauma survivor from a schooling perspective, finding terms such as A, B, Cs, workbooks, homework, stuck points, over-generalization, and jumping to conclusions useful.

Yet again our family of overlapping metaphors might consider trauma as a business with terms such as consumers, clients, percentages, real and manufactured feelings. We shall explore in Chapter 8 ways in which different families of metaphors limit and expand the way we think about the trauma survivor and the ways we think about helping him.

Linguistic Theory and Metonymy: Roman Jakobson's Work

Are there other elements in language that occupy a place of comparable status to metaphor? For Jakobson, a linguist and literary critic, metonymy parallels metaphor as the key rhetorical element in language (1956). He therefore suggests metonymy as the second major rhetorical element that requires our attention.

While Lakoff has his eye on the development of language from childhood on, Jakobson is concerned with how memory links one object or feeling with another, not so much by their similarity as by their contiguity in space or time.

Metonymy refers to words or phrases that are adjacent to each other, such as an event and a thought or feeling. Metonymy organizes language by *setting context*, by linking through contiguity, by clarifying what stands next. Here are a few examples from normal experience.

"A clown makes me laugh." Here, the narrator has placed the emotion of laughter next to the activity of watching a clown. A linguistic pathway is established that links the two by metonymy. Consider the phrase: he's being a clown.

"A child running through the park makes me feel young at heart." Here the narrator has placed the activity of a child's running in a public space with the feeling state of being young at heart. Consider the phrase: "just seeing the child cheered me up." The two phenomena become linked in memory by metonymy.

"A walk in the woods makes me pensive." Consider the path not taken.

"An intimate gesture from my partner makes me feel romantic." Consider the phrase, the touch of love.

"A bright brisk September day makes me happy and energetic." Consider the phrase, it's a bright day.

All of the above connections develop linguistic pathways so that when one remembers one part of the metonymy the other part easily comes to mind. One activity or physical state becomes the context for a companion feeling.

What other functions does metonymy serve? (see Chapter 7, Figure 7.1 for further insight). Metonymy is what provides sequence and continuity. One event follows another with predictability. For example, at night, after a hard day, I easily fall asleep. Or, when I become angry, I focus on the problem and do something both determined and constructive about it. Or, I can leave a task for tomorrow and not worry about it.

Does metonymy help us to generalize from likely sequences? In that we tend to expect certain activities to be universally associated with their companion situations, metonymy also provides rules or axioms for living. For example, when I am careful crossing the street I am in no danger. When I react spontaneously it is usually with good results. Unless a stranger acts menacingly, I am apt to trust him. When a person has earned a role above me, I look to him with respect.

How broadly may we think of the principles of contiguity or metonymy?

For Jakobson, metonymy, in its largest sense, is integrated syntax. Syntax is the orderly placement of words and phrases into grammatical sentences that another person can easily understand. It is the structure that sorts words into subjects, objects, verbs, and modifiers, a universal property of all language, something learned as a child, and available as the scaffold for any narrative.

For Jakobson, deeply interested in how writers express their stories, metonymy, like metaphor, is available for experimenting on the literary artist's canvas. For example, Hemingway might be seen as an author who suggests much by the simple placement of words next to each other. Joyce might be seen as an author who experiments with syntax, and the sequence by which different aspects of a narrative are linked together.

For Jakobson, these artists remember and add poignancy not only by symbolic similarity but by metonymy, emphasizing what is next to a more powerful experience that may be omitted. Metonymy plays a similar creative role in film, where, for example, the screenwriter connects scenes by panning in or out on a detail that stands next to the event, a lamp turning off next to a romantic couple indicating that the next omitted scene is an intimate one.

Since he is so interested in how a story is being told, Jakobson also includes metonymy when he speaks of the point of view or perspective of the writer. It is, for him, the place next to the subject of the narrative that the author occupies that is central for establishing the voice of the author. For example, William Faulkner, in *The Sound and the Fury*, exposes his reader to narratives of the same events as seen by a deaf mute, a young person, and an older person.

Why is a discussion of perspective important for the trauma survivor? Clearly, for our purposes, all of these characteristics of metonymy have a bearing on the survivor's effort to establish a narrative for his traumatic experiences. In a language world following trauma, where habitual memory connections are broken, usual sequence is disrupted, organizational structure breaks down, meaning is in disarray, and perspective is lost, the task of telling a comprehensible story about what happened is difficult if not impossible. For the clinician the task of listening under these circumstances requires patience, empathy, and intuition.[1, 2]

Summarizing, Jakobson considers metonymy to occupy a central role in the elements of language. We consciously use metonymy to help us retrieve memory. More importantly, we unconsciously rely on metonymy to make associations that provide context for what we say and do. Further our narratives follow a sequence that makes them comprehensible. Finally, we rely on metonymy, in the sense of syntax, to give order to the narrative we wish to tell. Metonymy represents the sequential nature of language, the ordering of words so that narrative can be understood, or the very structure of words that make coherent thoughts or syntax.

Metonymy After Trauma

What happens to metonymy when trauma intervenes? Memory connections are broken and replaced with new traumatic ones. An otherwise pleasant expectable sequence, a child running in a public place leading the observer to feel young at heart, turned out not to be true, rather the consequences were disastrous. The child, carrying concealed explosives on his back, was blown apart, and buddies killed. Not only has the metonymy changed, but the neurological character of the memory that holds the metonymy has changed. After trauma what stands next to or connects two newly linked experiences is now etched in long-term memory.

Trauma-Related Forms of Metonomy and Their Connection to Metaphors

A. Broken Connections

How are old memory links broken after trauma? A Vietnam veteran is trying to tell the story, "we were walking single file in jungle when the mine exploded and Mike lost his leg." As he does so, he must disregard the older metonymy that linked memory traces of walking in the woods with pensiveness.

Another is trying to say, "Last night my wife brushed against me in my sleep and I awoke trying to strangle her." Having lived with the danger of being overrun at night in "Nam," unexpected touch, now laid down as long-term memory, could only mean threat to life. The older metonymy placing intimate touch with romantic feelings is ripped apart.

A survivor of 9/11 observes that, since that day, "a bright September day has brought a sinking feeling in my stomach." Her new traumatic experience now unexpectedly connects a beautiful September day with tragedy. The older metonymy that placed pleasant weather with happiness is broken.

1 *Altered Sequence*
How does trauma affect sequence and chronology? The veteran described above wants to say, "I won't go into public places because I might see a child carrying a bomb on his back." The new thought replaces the older metonymy where a running child stood next to happy feelings. The traumatic metonymy turns a child running in a public space into a fatally dangerous situation. The survivor struggles not to remember the actual trauma experience. In that conflicted state of mind, narrative becomes fragmented, the more painful elements being hidden consciously or unconsciously. Interrupted narrative that has lost its contiguity or metonymy is narrative that has lost its ability to be understood.

2 *Broken Axioms*
In the trauma sequence above, new tragic sequences, registered traumatically in long-term memory, now take precedence over older benevolent metonymies. They attack the presuppositions mentioned earlier relating to assumptions about safety, trust, responsibility, self-esteem, and intimacy. The rules have changed.

3 *Altered Responsibility*
Now, let us assume, as was the case with Lee in Vietnam, that the survivor was able to anticipate the danger, by spotting the child and the explosives quickly. In order to prevent tragedy, he must fire his weapon from a distance, killing the child and forcing the explosion to occur where fewer people, especially American military, will be killed. What are the consequences for the hero? In this case, Lee changed, from a person who prided himself on being the protective big brother, always looking out for the helpless, to seeing himself as the kiss of death. If someone dared coming close to him emotionally it was at the risk of death to the other.

B. Discontinuity in Narrative

The story of the child strapped with explosives may become disjointed with its precipitant, seeing the child running in a public place, getting cut off from the weapon's firing, the explosion and grotesque images, sound, and danger. Instead, the story may contain just the first fragment, followed by silence, or a change in topic.

Linkage: Metonymy, Dissociation, and Disavowal

Because the new tragic sequence was so overwhelming at the time, the content of the trauma itself is often blotted out from later attempts to tell the narrative. In order to cope with overwhelming trauma we speak psychologically of the need of the survivor to dissociate the self from the actual experience. He may narrate events without affective connections, or express intense affect without clear connections to the trauma events; action may be repeated without understanding its meaning. We speak of dissociation as the emergency psychological mechanism that protects the survivor of trauma from being fully overwhelmed by the experience at one time. From a linguistic perspective it is to just such a place, the relatively safe place of dissociation, that the survivor fled in order to endure the trauma.

Helen, a survivor of incest, dissociated, imagining herself fixed against the flowers on the wallpaper of the bedroom rather than being penetrated by her father. When memory of the trauma broke through in her therapist's office, she literally ran to the opposite wall, stretching her body to blend in with the wallpaper. Bennett, a radio operator in Iraq, remained fixed on the dials of the instrument panel in front of him, so he could block out rather than register the news of his buddy's death, the same buddy whose movements he earlier instructed and whose death he monitored electronically. Staring distractedly at the instrument panel provided the dissociated protected space to hide from the full impact of trauma.

For Kohut and Seitz (1978), such separation of action from its internal meaning is the work of the vertical split in the ego, and is understood as the mechanism of disavowal. As we listen, linguistically, what we find is broken metonymy. That is, contiguity has been split off from the meaning of the trauma event itself. Disavowal permits the trauma memory to remain consciously separated from the ordinary behavior it is affecting. Indeed, some of the affect of the trauma is buried within the events that preceded it, and surfaces as traumatic metonymy as in the following example.

Spike's Turning Around the Tables in Therapy: "It's Your Turn, Doc"

Spike jostled with his therapist at the beginning of each session, insisting that it was "your turn to start the session." The therapist, guided by traditional technique, was determined to keep the beginning of the sessions open for the patient's initiative. The insistent, nearly combative, repetition of this interpersonal behavior at the start of each session became more and more intense, so much so that the therapist, sitting on the edge of his chair, waiting for Spike to say "it's your turn," felt as if something might explode. The therapist thought that the phrase "it's your turn" somehow stood next to something unspeakable. By noting calmly that something terrible happened in Vietnam when it was someone else's turn, the therapist helped Spike narrate the circumstances that immediately preceded the traumatic episode in war in which his friend, who was jostling with him in the rear of a 2.5-ton truck saying, "it's your turn," was suddenly shot from behind and killed by a sniper, his face disappearing before Spike at that moment. Spike's therapist had intuited that the phrase had preceded a trauma. Indeed the tension at the beginning of the session was a clear illustration of metonymy as the reservoir and condensation of traumatic memory.

Forgetting in Trauma Narratives

We pause at the moment of forgetting. Even after some suitable words return, the survivor is faced linguistically with a paradox. First, like the patient with aphasia, the survivor cannot remember; he unconsciously forgets. That is, in order to avoid unmetabolizable painful memory, the survivor cannot remember exactly what happened. Yet unlike the patient with aphasia, the survivor struggles with just the opposite problem: even when he remembers and wants to convey what happened, he realizes he does not possess the right words or phrases to utter the unutterable. Worded differently, he has not yet found metaphors that capture the truth of his traumatic experiences as they stretch beyond his current worldview or even imagination. Keeping both of these perspectives in mind, the survivor goes through two linguistic processes: he unconsciously forgets, that is to say disavows in the hopes of adapting to the present, until such time as the affective and narrative pieces of the trauma are capable of being connected and metabolized. At the same moment, he searches to invent new words and phrases, metaphors if you will, that might bring his traumatic experiences into the realm of the organizable and metabolizable.

The clinician, listening to the opposing aims in these intense expressions, dissociation and its split off half, disavowal and disclosure, forgetting and remembering, metonymy and metaphor, must make careful judgments regarding when and how to decode that which is out of the range of conscious memory, assessing the safety, trust, and relative readiness of the survivor to confront his own creative language.

Broken Meaning

What patterns of speech suggest that trauma has broken the chain of meaning in the survivor's life? How does "lexical leakage" provide clues to these broken chains of meaning? Spence and Breznitz's (1983) research demonstrated that "lexical leakage" revealed unconscious knowledge of disease processes, such as cancer.

Wordless States

The survivor has experienced a biological and psychological assault to his nervous system and to his capacity to retrieve and to generate language. Breakdown in language, following trauma, begins with the absence of suitable words to describe what happened. Not only is there no immediately available metaphor that maps onto the new trauma experience meaningful images from the past, there may be no words at all.

In its initial form a survivor's silence represents a lack of the words to express either the overwhelmed state when thinking of the disaster, or when words do come, a lack of sequential order to the extraordinary experience that they went through.

Affect-less States

Alternatively, a survivor may recount some aspect of the experience repetitively without integration, that is, words occur but they remain fixed and concrete, for example Sarah, a mother whose 19-year-old son suddenly died, simply repeated the words "your son has been involved in a fatal accident" over and over with rhythmic precision and no change in intonation or comprehension.

In this instance, no similar experience comes to mind. She speaks of herself in the second person. Words are strung together as though they are coherent thoughts, but their repetition in the absence of affect and the absence of punctuation indicate that a psychological wall protects the survivor from the meaning of the words which she cannot yet endure. The words describe an event yet remain static, disconnected from meaning.

Loss of Syntax

Another form of fragmented narrative, one that keeps the story from being comprehended or communicated, is fragments "standing" willy-nilly next to each other with no easily discernible continuity.

According to Jakobson (1956), metonymy, i.e. connection between words by virtue of their contiguity, includes, in its most basic form, the very structure of language or syntax that allow us as listeners to understand the meaning of the words others are saying. In this instance, following trauma, there are words, but they are fragmentary. The words are not placed sequentially so that the speaker explains to another what occurred in the trauma experience. Rather words, connected by their proximity to the trauma situation, tumble out without recognizable order.

Vince began his treatment more than ten years after Vietnam combat with a melange of fragmented word phrases, alluding simultaneously to combat, post-combat, and childhood trauma situations, one thought linked without syntax to the next. His was language, but literally without syntax or connection. In Vince's case, this state of words without meaningful connection carried the impression of an ongoing firefight in which confusing, contradictory imperatives and thoughts were coming in, without being processed, making useful and coordinated response impossible. Loss of syntax is the trauma-specific metaphorical meaning of his projective verbalizations.

Vince's confused, non-sequential mental states were often expressed in garbled, mixed-up phrases reflecting different periods of his life experiences. "Alex sent me . . . memories coming back . . . furious . . . Friday she wouldn't get out of bed . . . grabbed my arm . . . don't touch me . . . I killed this guy . . . went for a knife . . . if a stranger touches me I lash out . . . with her for five years . . . very helpful . . . an argument with a lady in the building . . . I stuck a gun in her face . . . I wanted to get even . . . she said, 'don't be so perfect' . . . stuck her fingernails in me . . . a guy grabbed me . . . drinking . . . I can't remember hitting him . . . only heard about it at the trial . . . he stabbed me it was self-defense . . . feel like I'm in Vietnam . . . I killed a man and a woman . . . she reached for her pistol . . . I was squad leader . . . nine of ten guys died."

One can infer the traumatic nature of the events by the intensity of the tone of voice, yet neither the narrator nor the listener is able to discern a coherent story of trauma. Such breakdown in formal word structure is another manifestation of trauma's effect on metonymy and underlying metaphoric processes.

Listening to Metonymy as a Condensation and Displacement

Despite the fact that a portion of the trauma story is missing, the part that is present, that which is contiguous, carries extraordinary psychic valence, a fact that the careful listener surmises immediately but *the survivor comprehends only when he is ready to grasp the connection between the present* and *the missing part.* In the case of Spike, above, the phrase "it's your turn," while explaining little about the trauma itself, indicated through its intensity to both Spike and his therapist that it stood next to traumatic memory. The sequence, for Jakobson, parallels the use of fading out in cinema before a scene that is too upsetting for the viewer to see.

Metonymy and Recovery From Traumatic Experiences: Fertile Ground for Clinical Discovery

The Effort to Find a Safe Place From Which to Tell the Story

While breaks in metonymy characterize various forms of loss of meaning for the survivor, they may, paradoxically, announce the beginning step in recognizing the survivor's search for a new language, one that is truthful to, that no longer tries to hide, the trauma experience.

Three years after Bennett's dissociation at the time his buddies were killed in Iraq, he re-enacted the scene, with friends from home. He was worried about their drinking too much and getting into trouble so he waited in his car for them to return from their mission outside the bar as designated driver. He stared at the instrument panel of his car but lost conscious awareness for six hours. This time he and his therapist found this numb state to be a beginning point to find words. While wordless in itself, it was the point that stood next to the trauma in Iraq where his buddies had been killed. From here he began to describe not the events of their death but rather the details of his own dissociated space at the time, a kernel of authentic experience from which to gain a new point of view. It originated not in an objective description of traumatic events, but rather it was the view from inside the self, the perspective, the authentic view from which meaningful reflective language post-trauma began haltingly to flow.

Helen, the incest survivor who literally flattened herself against the therapist's wall in a re-enactment of her dissociation during childhood trauma, blending into the wallpaper rather than experiencing incestuous penetration, was also taking the first non-verbal step in trying to put to words her survival of events she wanted to but was not yet quite ready to tell. Finding words to describe the experience of silently disappearing into the wallpaper was the beginning of Helen's narrative, because it is where she stood in metonymy with the trauma. The narrative would take form as trust with the therapist grew, and with it a safe enough space.

Changes in Metonymy During Recovery From Trauma

In the post-modern sense, metonymy is that place from which the narrator of our story places himself in order to tell it. Insofar as metonymy represents a space next to but not immersed in the subject of the narrative, it is crucial for survivors as well as artists. The survivor tries, unsuccessfully at first, and then haltingly and from gradually more distant perspective, to find words until an understandable narrative emerges. Metonymy gives us yet one more useful way to appreciate this narrative journey. The survivor moves from a voiceless position immersed in the trauma itself, one in which only disjointed and traumatic concrete fragments of the trauma experience can be articulated, to a more distant position at the edge of the trauma from which he ultimately finds his comprehensive and comprehensible voice.

The linguistic movement in ordinary people, from concrete detail, unspeakable in its traumatic impact, to metaphors formed at the edge of or next to the trauma, metaphors capable of metabolizing trauma and reconnecting the survivor to his culture, is the story of this book.

Some data from our own trauma studies may be useful here: children at Buffalo Creek who were unable to metabolize their trauma continue, decades later, to draw pictures of the event as though they were still in the midst of it, for example the black water being over their heads, while others having made better adjustments now picture the event as bounded, and seen from a more distant perspective taking in many of the variables that contributed to the flood.

Also children in danger of a school sniper attack, in which a number of children were injured and killed, positioned themselves just beyond the edge of danger, the site from which to tell the story.

What we shall be tracing throughout the book is how individuals move from the wordless states that repeat trauma, over time, to new posttrauma states transforming trauma through metaphor and metonymy into a creative process culminating in the acquisition of language to tell the narrative of their experiences. In this way they seek to comprehend, express, and heal from their highly personal encounters with trauma (see Chapter 1 for a discussion). For the most part, these are ongoing and pre-conscious processes.

As Western mental health professionals, awareness of trauma metaphor and traumatically broken metonymy allows us to more wisely discern and facilitate our patient's recovery path; to become partners in their word journeys. We learn about trauma from our own and other cultures and other languages, where bodily-based and experience-near metaphors provide windows into understanding levels of meaning that otherwise might remain closed to the surface observer. Listening to the survivor's metaphoric words is vitally important.

To review, individuals and cultures struggle at first with almost wordless ways, to understand and characterize disasters and trauma. Individuals and cultures are at first refractory to the application of older words and metaphors. In this state, newly applicable bodily-centered metaphors that were central to the trauma experience take on metaphoric importance. In a way similar to our original building of language by using metaphor units from earlier experience, the survivor applies trauma specific sensory-motor experience as metaphoric underpinning of a new language. As trauma survivors recover they gradually expand and extend the primary metaphors of trauma (see Chapter 1, Figure 1.1). More complex metaphors arise as the initial phase gives way to one of evolution (see Chapter 1).

In this way, we find tools to re-individualize trauma, arise and enable us to move from the generic back to the specific; to refine our focus on the task of one survivor trying to narrate, contain, master, and integrate his or her unique experience with the Abyss Experience (Wilson, 2006).

Schools of Psychotherapy and Elements of Language

Psychoanalytically oriented writers and teachers have long taught students to attend to special words images or phrases of their patients. Sigmund Freud (1905) discovered how jokes hinged on double meanings and overlapping metaphors, slips of the tongue captured disavowed condensations and displacements, and dreams turned figures of speech into pictures. Ella Sharpe (1949) likened dream language to the private poetry of the patient pointing out how they utilize metaphor, figures of speech, metonymy, and synecdoche. Sharpe also pointed out that specific dream images, like a rock or a rose, applied to specific memory traces from the dreamer, located in the past. This notion is similar to our position that trauma metaphors link to specific details of the trauma situation. Later, work by Siegelman (1990), Barker (1985), and Ingram (1996) applied formal principles of semantics, of signs and signals, to affect, empathy, nuances of psychoanalytic ideas of transference and counter-transference, defense, and the working alliance.

Words or phrases that seem multi-layered, symbolic or condensed, idiosyncratic, emotionally charged by tone or gesture, or metaphorically compelling are likely to point to deeper latent meanings of otherwise surface thoughts and feelings and actions. Indeed, one of the crucial aspects of listening with the third ear or free-floating attention has been appreciation of metaphor as a means of communicating that which is beneath the surface of a given communication, i.e., its latent linguistic contextual meaning. Freud likened the patient in psychoanalysis to the passenger in the window seat of a moving train, describing the scene outside to his analyst, a blind geologist, sitting in the aisle seat. By paying special attention to the unusual surface irregularities the analyst is able to discern the veins and rock formations underneath. Individually constructed metaphor is one of those landmarks he was looking for, in order to explore more deeply.

Carl Jung (1965) explored symbols and archetypes that characterize universal aspects of human dilemmas. Gestalt psychology acknowledges this central role of metaphor and includes elaborating and pursuing spontaneous metaphors in their armamentarium of techniques. Cognitive behavioral therapists recommend metaphoric phrases as teaching devices to help reframe blocks or stuck points to create a more manageable context for mastery. So, the various schools of psychotherapy are no strangers to poetics.

Indeed, we could extend this connection between schools of psychotherapy and poetics by including metonymy as the central linguistic thread in the work of the current school of close process psychoanalytic therapy championed by Paul Gray (1994) and Fred Busch (1996) where the central point of focus of the therapist is the moment of discontinuity between one expressed thought or feeling and the next.

We present this book about the language of the survivor to trauma clinicians representing diverse schools of psychotherapy in the hope that better listening will lead to better therapy. We present the book now because metaphor and other elements of language have not yet been applied to understanding the language of the trauma survivor, and because developments in the field of cognitive linguistics and literary criticism offer new insights into how we might listen more effectively. All this is the more urgent as trends toward protocol interventions in PTSD reduce the student's exposure to traditional methods of listening deeply.

Metamorphic Development and Change: Vicissitudes in Metonomy and Metaphors

Monitoring the move of the trauma narrator from the center of chaos to a safe position near its edge provides the careful listener with a frame of reference for inferring gradual change toward recovery.

Similarly, monitoring how the survivor forms metaphor, and for what purpose, helps the listener register other aspects of the same recovery process. Early metaphors reference the sensory-motor status of the survivor at the time of trauma; they employ the concrete details of the trauma experience, undigested. Later metaphors are actual figures of speech that, unlike so many others, actually turned out to be useful in breaking down complex trauma into manageable pieces. Third-level metaphor once more connects the survivor to his larger society through broadly based symbols linking the survivor to hero myths within his culture.

Review: Metonymy and Metaphor in the New Language of Trauma

To review, in the aftermath of trauma, following the breakdown of metaphor and the discontinuity of metonymy, the survivor is more likely to gain access to his subjective state (i.e., the state of his own limbic system and the unconscious coping with that state at the time of the trauma) than the events of the trauma itself. At first this is a semiwordless state. But, as he is confronted daily with repetitions of this state, he unconsciously reflects in words its bodily- and motoric-centered dimensions. Thus one perspective on the initially wordless state is from the space where the survivor was standing physically and psychologically as the event occurred. This position, next to the trauma itself, is a point of contiguity with the trauma, or in linguistic terms a metonymy. It is the very place from which new language must emerge, words and phrases that capture something unique and subjectively authentic rooted alongside the trauma experience itself. In this regard, the first verbal expression of the trauma has a sensory-motor descriptive form. It is metonymic with the trauma in that it expresses the viewpoint of the participant observer. Such metonymic expressions direct themselves to the question, "What was it like for you when the trauma occurred?"

Over time, the sensory-motor expression (words that stood next to the trauma) take on a metaphoric function, in that they now map onto the everyday non-traumatic world, as though they were the necessary accompaniments to cope with everyday living.

The reason that the phrase develops this metaphoric power is because the trauma has replaced early childhood experience as the organizer of personality, rearranging the components of psychic structure in very profound ways. We continue the discussion of decoding first-level trauma metaphors, this crucial first step in developing posttraumatic language, in Chapter 3, where we elaborate the many ways trauma affects psychic structure, and offer many clinical illustrations.

Trauma invalidates most old metaphors. Trauma initiates the search for new metaphors. Trauma relocates intensity of emotion from the unspeakable and unremembered trauma itself to the otherwise neutral experience that precedes it, stands next to it, or in metonymy with it.

After trauma the survivor begins the linguistic journey to express a new truth based on the bodily sensations that accompanied the experience, and recorded in long-term memory by new contiguous neural connections. Before trauma struck it was metaphor that provided the themes of our narrative, subtly integrating through similar words, past and present experiences and views of self and the world. Before trauma struck, it was metonymy that provided the order to our narrative, the sequence of events, thoughts, and feelings, the structure of language that allowed the story to be heard. Metaphor portrays narrative's content; metonymy provides narrative's process, linguistic evolutionary. Trauma devastates both by catapulting a new truth into the center of the survivor's experience.

From the survivor's perspective the task at hand is to understand how that new truth gets expressed in actions, sensations, and words that often surprise and alarm both the survivor and those who care about him, and how that new truth metaphorically organizes the survivor's posttraumatic present.

From the clinician's perspective the task at hand is to note how language offers clues to posttraumatic change, and how clinical judgment is needed as to when and how to decode this new language.

The theoretical forays into linguistics and literary criticism in this chapter give us tools to examine the spoken language of trauma survivors more precisely. With an eye on trauma metaphor and metonymy, we return to our consultation rooms, better armed to consider the many clinical features these elements of language highlight. Metaphor and metonymy become, for us clinicians, additional portals of entry to the clinical condition of our patients. We pause to consider the patient's striking metaphor, wondering together with the patient what deeper layers of meaning it might convey. And we direct our interest to those moments in the session that are discontinuous, where thoughts become interrupted, disconnected, or no longer understandable. Our task is not to lump these observations into the symptom baskets of PTSD, but to see them as portals of entry for a deepening of our understanding of the person who has experienced trauma. In Chapter 3 we shall explore how the new language of trauma metaphor portrays damage to the basic elements of psychological functioning, to sensations, adaptations, identity, and self.

Of course, not all metaphors that survivors choose are physiological expressions of what it was like to undergo the trauma. There are metaphors that reflect where the survivor is located subjectively along the journey home (see Chapter 1, Figure 1.2). There are metaphors that condense how values have changed. There are metaphors that describe new and dangerous relations with important others. There are metaphors that capture the ongoing existential dilemmas of those who survive while others perish.

Future chapters will take up these concepts in more detail, but for now we should mention the following.

Metaphor and the Hero's Journey

Metaphors place the survivor at different locations along the road from the abyss to recovery. Damon was stalled. Otis lost his footing. Mickey felt upside-down. John was nearly home.

Metaphor and Object Relations

Trauma metaphors place the survivor in particular relationship to those who might endanger them, or with whom they might lose control. Judd was certain the hand-offs were the source of tragedy. Tom found lethal danger in musical chairs.

Metaphor and Self-Configuration

Trauma metaphors describe highly personal views of internal or self states. Helen felt paralyzed. Luke was wiped out. Lee was haunted.

Metaphor and Existential Issues

Survivors describe their most intimate states of mind, ones that they fear will never give way and that have re-formed their identity in terms of metaphor. Michael thought his yielding during his torture had forever changed who he was. Eva thought her position outside, looking in on life, was a permanent state of disconnection from ever again feeling alive. Chris believed his only future after the trauma was to anticipate yet another crash.

Metonymy and the Unsaid

Survivors narrate their stories haltingly, with interruption and with disconnection between the spoken word and affect. Each of these poignant moments in the hour is a movement in space to and from safety, towards danger and back again. Behind the silence is meaning we patiently await to hear.[3]

Body, Spirit, Soul, and the Role of Nurturing Guides

As therapists listen to and pursue metaphors, as they respect yet to be narrated space, they find that the nature of their bond to the survivor far exceeds the usual bond between patient and clinician. The therapist is called on to do more than monitor symptoms, prescribe medication, or engage in Socratic debate. Rather they more importantly bear witness to unspeakable truths, stretch empathy beyond their previous limits (Wilson & Lindy, 1994), and seek to redefine the crucial sustaining relationship with the patient. In doing so the clinician feels a camaraderie with those who help trauma survivors in other cultures, a kinship with a cross-cultural commonality, an idea we shall develop in Chapter 5, concerning the role and functions of the Nurturing Guide (NG) in the therapeutic context of transformation and integration.

Notes

1 Jakobson (1956) develops an interesting argument for his position. He approaches this in the reverse order, examining conditions of aphasia, or situations where we fail to remember. Through an examination of two types of aphasia, he reasons that memory itself is laid down following two fundamentally different linguistic (and neurologic) pathways. In the first pathway, what is remembered stands for something similar to something currently in mind. This is the pathway of similarity or metaphor that we have been discussing above. Trying to remember the name for the timepiece on her bureau, the older adult with early aphasia asks her husband to look for her wrist watch but cannot retrieve the words. She thinks of its function, recalls the word clock and moments later finally retrieves the words "wrist watch" (reasoning from similarity or metaphor). The husband of the woman above knows what she is referring to but also blocking on the word wrist watch, thinks, "you mean the thing standing next to the picture on the bureau." In the second pathway, the husband tried to remember by metonymy, starting with that which stands next to or is contiguous with the unremembered object as the connecting link. The second method of retrieval is contiguity rather than similarity.

2 Working a crossword puzzle illustrates the point. The clue for item 21 across in the crossword puzzle is "salted cucumber," a rough synonym or connection by similarity to the word pickle. We enter "P" in the box marked 21. The clue for item 21 down might be "pied", a word that is linked sequentially or next to the word "piper" forming the phrase "pied piper." Here the link is by contiguity or metonymy. Thus "P" also works as the first letter for the second word.

3 In trauma narrative, metaphor also taps deeper streams of cultural meaning, of hidden history waiting to become testimony. Under the right circumstances, uncovering these cultural links are part of the crucial other's witness, allowing disconnected trauma to reconnect with time, to fold frozen moments back into the continuous flow of the history of his and the therapist's times (Davoine & Gaudilliere, 2004). Suffice it to say the survivor has found a creative use of language, on a par, as it were, with poetry. The survivor has found previously unused words, close to his sensory-motor experience, to describe a mood state that otherwise does not fit with past experiences.

3 Metaphor and Disturbed Internal Posttraumatic Psychic Structures

Trauma survivors and their Nurturing Guides (NG) are astrological Geminis, fraternal twins, in a locked journey of fate, history, and unpredictable circumstances. Therefore, we have seen that listening carefully to the trauma survivor's choice of words or his or her hesitations and intonations, coetaneous and simultaneous somatic reactions (e.g., a complaint, facial grimaces, burps, tongue clicks, distortions and emotional facial changes or other unusual, weird, or unsaid expressions) often provides the clinician with a typical somatic and anomalous phrase, a set of subtle trauma-cues that has made its way from an actual sensory-motor experience [within or near the trauma event(s)] to a description of the survivor's current phenomenological world. As we will illustrate, being curious about these colorful and unique, rich expressions has important diagnostic value.

What, in fact, are they and what do they reveal? Trauma metaphors give insights for the clinician in assessing posttraumatic ego-processes, self-states, identity configurations, moral judgments, cognitive processes, and object-relations. These are *internal elements* in the survivor's current mental state that function as portals of entry (POE) for the clinician with important implications for the nature and content of developing a therapeutic alliance of critical significance.

Curiosity regarding these seemingly odd expressions, sensations, or movements may lead suddenly and surprisingly, or slowly and inevitably, to their origins in the traumatic event itself; like lemmings returning home to their origin in the sea. When heard in this way, such bodily expressions may be thought of as a "shadow of the trauma" falling on the circumstances of the present life, a sensory-motor-cognitive metaphor where the survivor is unconsciously organizing the present on the basis of some fragment from the trauma experience itself. The "Shadow of Metaphors" is unconscious reality, unspoken and unverbalized but present as a driving force.

Exploring the many transformations that these metaphors mean and express over time is a psychological process we will explore more completely in later chapters. But, for now, we wish to emphasize how these phrases and linguistic images give immediate insight into personality processes, ego-states, and self-processes. In terms of clinical psychotherapeutic treatment approaches, self-states of the survivor are essential and *critical diagnostic points* in order to build an alliance on solid ground for empathic connections of the most important kind for successful treatment. Proper empathic attunement is among the royal roads to the trauma survivor's inner world.

When highlighted, metaphoric words and phrases, portals of entry (POE) into the inner world of the trauma survivor, like the unconsciously creative content of dreams, becomes a metaphorical window by which to understand the trauma survivor. We described, in Chapter 2, the way trauma metaphors transferred and displaced something from the experience of the trauma onto the present in such a way as to organize the present adaptational processes. In this chapter we emphasize how these same metaphoric phrases offer clues to the specific ways in which trauma has damaged psychic structures, distorted ego-processes and altered the self-structure and its functional capabilities. Trauma and disturbed internal posttraumatic psychic structures then become a critical focal point in understanding posttraumatic adaptations.

It is the struggle with these altered self-functions that disturbs the survivor, erodes self-confidence, and discourages and frightens the victim-survivor, sometimes to the point of fearing he or she is losing their mind or to the point of considering suicide. It is these aspects of the posttraumatic self that the clinician must first assess and address (Wilson, 2006).

Traumatic Life Events and Expressions in Posttraumatic Metaphors: From Raw Experiences to Words to Visual Images and Verbalized Expressions

In this chapter, we explore the important relationship between personality processes and trauma-related metaphoric dimensions in the way of summary case illustrations.

Conceptual Schematic Overview

To begin, Figure 3.1 presents intrapsychic posttraumatic psychic constellations. Roman numerals I–IV on the left side of the figure classify conceptually both *horizontal* (H) and *vertical* (V) dynamics of personality and trauma related processes. For example, in (H–I), horizontal processes, it can be seen that traumatic experiences influence the configuration and structure of personality processes and individual, idiosyncratic responses in ego-processes.

Figure 3.1 illustrates that the three dimensions of (H–I) directly impact categorical dimensions of the self-structure, positive and negative aspects of self-dimensions and ego-agentic active or passive processes. In this specific way (H–I–II) and (V–I–II) merge and lead to a resultant set of critically important posttraumatic configurations in the structure (H–IV), i.e., impacts to the totality of self and personality. We will expand on the elements in Figure 3.1 later in the chapter.

Trauma Related Changes in Personality and Self-Processes

The posttraumatic changes in personality and self-processes are further delineated in Tables 3.1–3.3. These tables were constructed based on the 67 clinical case examples presented in this book. They are *evidence-based empirical data* of how traumatic experiences give rise to metaphoric expressions in language at different levels of conscious representations in individual awareness. Previously experimental investigations have explored such hypotheses (Spence & Breznitz, 1983) and found confirmations that cancer patients, for example, through "lexical leakage," prematurely disclose hopelessness and despair prior to formal illness diagnosis. It is as if they knew they were ill but did not consciously acknowledge it but the reality was expressed in words and metaphors. What

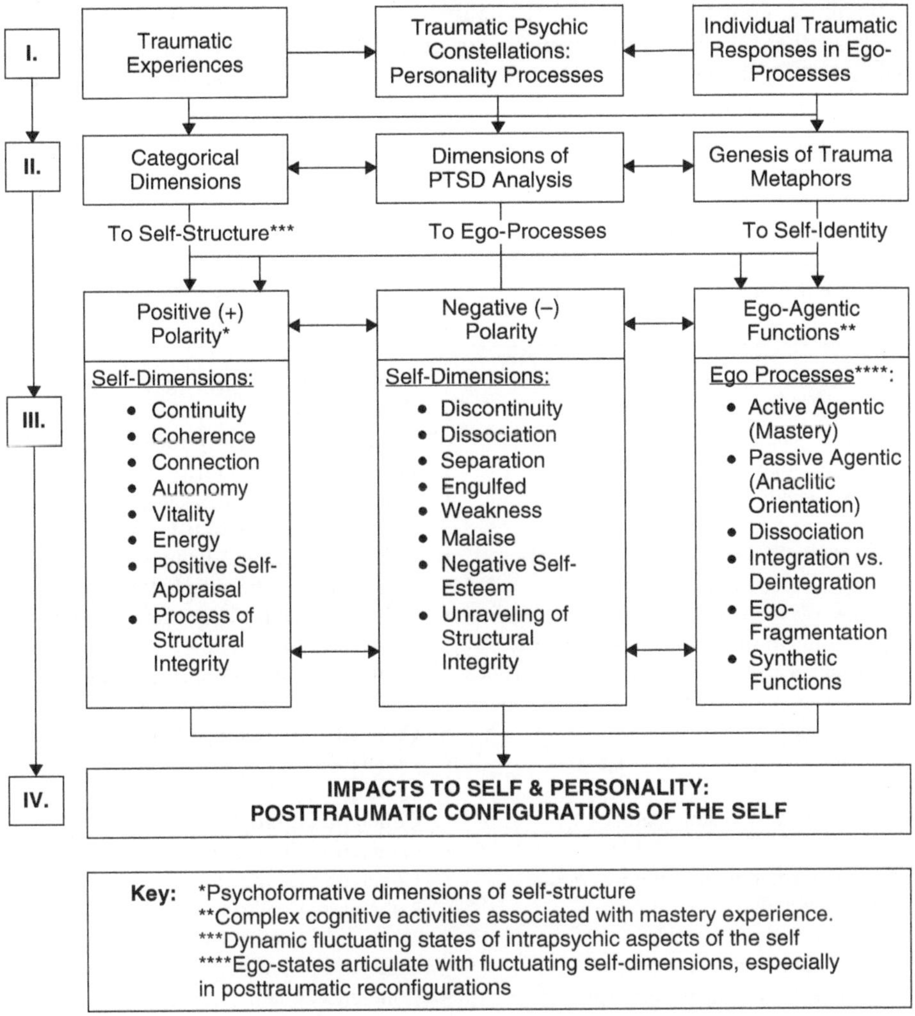

Figure 3.1 Posttraumatic Psychic Constellations

we are proposing is that trauma-specific metaphors (TSM) are a "Golden Pathway" of revelation and insight as portals of entry (POE) to inner posttraumatic states of existence. Trauma-specific metaphors (TSM) are quite similar linguistic processes to "lexical leakage," they reveal unconscious intrapsychic processes of unprocessed traumatic memories, images, and affective states. Unmetabolized psychic trauma "leaks out" in all sorts of ways, including parapraxes, dreams, metaphors, and linguistic lexical leakage.

Common Posttraumatic Metaphors

In our framework, Tables 3.1–3.3 illustrate common posttraumatic trauma metaphors and their relationship to the six major dimensions of the self, as detailed by Wilson (2006;

i.e., coherence, continuity, autonomy, vitality, energy, connection) and provide illustrations of their changed posttraumatic structural dimensions. In conceptual, theoretical, and clinical concerns, Table 3.1 is scientifically significant because it shows how trauma can impact the pre-existing structure of personality and alter it in profound ways. Stated simply, how the pre- versus post-personality structure changes its dynamic functioning and multiple levels of psychological functioning (see Wilson, 2006).

Table 3.1 Metaphorical Expressions Verbalized in Psychotherapy by Trauma Patients with PTSD

Common Posttraumatic Trauma Metaphors	*Primary Posttraumatic Self-Structural Dimensions in Metaphors*
• I am numb; I don't feel any more.	• Vitality, Coherence, Energy
• I am not the same as I was before.	• Continuity, Coherence
• I am dead inside.	• Coherence, Continuity, Vitality, Energy
• I am empty, depressed and lost.	• Coherence, Vitality, Energy
• I am overwhelmed by memories.	• Autonomy, Continuity, Coherence
• I am disconnected; "Where did I go?"	• Continuity, Connection, Coherence
• I am a shell of myself and nothing more.	• Coherence, Energy, Vitality
• I am an overused product, ravaged.	• Coherence, Continuity, Vitality
• I am a war veteran, killer of human beings.	• Coherence, Vitality, Continuity, Energy
• I am drifting in space and going nowhere.	• Continuity, Connection
• I am trapped and do not know how to escape.	• Continuity, Connection, Coherence
• I am hopeless.	• Continuity
• I am a lost soul.	• Coherence, Autonomy, Connection
• I am a morphed, weird character	• Coherence
• I am stuck.	• Continuity, Coherence, Vitality
• I am blown apart, disintegrated.	• Coherence, Continuity
• I lost my soul.	• Coherence, Continuity
• I am afloat, adrift in an unknown ocean.	• Coherence, Connection
• I am deflated, angry veteran	• Coherence, Vitality
• I am a ship without a rudder.	• Continuity, Coherence, Vitality
• I am an ugly galley of my mind.	• Coherence, Continuity
• I have no energy to focus for future.	• Coherence, Vitality, Energy
• I am dissolved.	• Vitality, Energy
• I am run-down; I am done.	• Vitality, Energy
• I am discharged shit—I stink of stench.	• Vitality, Energy
• I am worthless; what did I do?	• Vitality, Energy, Coherence
• I am gone, away from life.	• Coherence, Continuity, Connection, Vitality
• I am fragmented like the IED.	• Coherence, Connection
• I am an empty hole with nothing inside.	• Coherence, Connection, Vitality
• I am smaller, diminished, confused.	• Coherence
• I am disconnected and numb.	• Coherence, Continuity, Energy
• I am rubble	• Discontinuity, Coherence, Connection
• I am down and desolate; what did I do?	• Coherence, Vitality, Connection
• I am not free any more; fuck 'em.	• Autonomy, Coherence, Vitality, Energy
• I am lost between then and now.	• Coherence, Continuity

Note: Metaphors are complex and contain identity references, symbols, and projected mythical themes.

Metaphoric Categories of Psychic Symbolism and Constellations

Table 3.2 presents a summary illustration of two essentially related dimensions of traumatic life events and metaphors in language. First, the left-hand side of Table 3.2 lists a typology of traumatic life experiences that are empirically validated by the various databases (e.g. P.I.L.O.T.S for PTSD–NC-PTSD). These common life events are archetypal and universal in nature (Wilson, 2006). However, as noted, when a trauma produces its consequences, there are common, symbolic representations in mental states. In this sense, verbal or linguistic expressions are the clues to the unconscious vault of stored memories.

Table 3.2 Metaphoric Categories of Psychic Symbolism

Typology of Traumatic Life Experience Categories	*Traumatic Metaphoric Symbolism: Examples in Psychic States, Dreams and Language*
• Life / Survival (war, oppressive forces) • Death / Birth / Rebirth • Sexuality / Passion / Love • Survival / Existence • Hunger / Fear / Arousal • Safety / Security / Protection • Love and Belongingness • Integrity / Stability / Boundaries • Relationship with Others • Family and Kinship • Life-changes and Hardship (disaster) • Anxiety / Depression / Fears • Illness / Life / Struggle • Future Orientation and Meaning • Sense of Wellness, Health, Aliveness and Self-Actualization • Esteem / Well-Being • Life—Transitions and Future Orientation • Self-Reinvention • Transformation • Cultural Changes and Loss of Society's Fabric • Specter of Annihilation • Abyss Experiences and Confrontation • Bodily Integrity, Rape, Harm, Death	• I am dead, gone, absent, "still there" • I arose to a new life; I overcame! I died in Vietnam • I am violated, ravaged, violated; abused, used • It was the Abyss of death and near death • It was the "edge" of existence itself; I was dying • God help me, I am scared and anxious • My love and community was lost; I am empty • Life for me changed forever; what really functions • Buddies in combat are beyond wives, "bud of bros" • What was needed was lost • No way to explain what ended or happened • Why continue? • Why me, God? • Everything has changed; Is there a future? • Life is anew—reinvented, open to possibilities • What has been lost may recover, someday • Everything is in flux and changing • I can recreate myself • The old self can become a new self • The past is gone, what's ahead? • Everything seems destroyed—what's left? • Darkness prevails, I'm afraid; I want to die • What's left of me now? I want to be whole again

Internal States and Altered Dimensions of Self-Processes: Metaphor Genesis

Table 3.3 expands how posttraumatic internal states articulate with the genesis of altered self-dimensions and the production of trauma metaphors in speech and daily life. As Table 3.3 shows, there are three vertical columns that contain information regarding: (1) thematic dimensional analysis; (2) primary self-structural analysis of the self-dimensions; and (3) specific expressions in metaphoric language. For purposes of analysis and heuristic value, there are 20 categories of thematic dimensional analysis and, in a correlated manner, corresponding primary self-structural dimensions affected by traumatic life events and their trauma-associated metaphors.

Posttraumatic Personality, Self-Structure and Ego-Processes: How They Are Manifest in Metaphors: Part I

We think of the ego as the complex, higher order, cognitive executive brain activities modulating the structure of the mind, the set of functions that filters and prioritizes perceptions of the external world, that, in turn, modulates affective signals in the direction of problem-solving that both carries out and compromises with the demands of the moral consciousness and exploits and inhibits the drives of physiological health necessities aggression and sexuality in the service of mastery, adaptation, and growth. Damage to any of the regulatory functions of the ego and its programmatic structure is often implicitly present in trauma metaphors. When properly interpreted this helps the clinician understand the damaged self.

In reference to disturbed internal psychological, complex self-structures, which aspects of personality are specifically affected by traumatic impacts? Trauma metaphors (TSM) offer clues, especially to those adaptive ego-defenses employed on an emergency or necessary basis in order to cope with the trauma but which have remained actively in force. These protective mechanisms include dissociation, somatization, reversal in fantasy, and identification with the aggressor states of mind, among many other mental states. It is often the understanding of how these necessary defenses work that permits decoding of a trauma metaphor so that a tentative reconstruction of the actual subjective traumatic experience or special configuration of the traumatic event can be scientifically determined.

By examining the primary sensory-motor metaphors as fundamental linguistic building blocks for a new posttrauma language, we have already been introduced to how perceptual distortions in sight, sound, touch, smell, and taste find their way into trauma metaphors. In the context of ego malfunctions, we have only to add that feeling "blind," "bitter," non-physiological pain illustrate a sensory modality for metaphors and an altered set of ego-functions, somatoform metaphors of intrapsychic configurations of posttraumatic states.

Table 3.3 Internal States and Altered Dimensions of the Self: Metaphoric Genesis

Thematic Dimensional Analysis	*Primary Self-Structural Dimension Affected**	*Trauma Metaphors Examples*
1. Helpless, Hopeless, Despair	• Coherence, autonomy, vitality	• I am nothing; I am gone
2. Active vs. Passive Agentic Ego Function	• Separation, continuity	• I'm divided / split inside
3. Injured, Damaged or Healthy Self	• Coherence, energy	• I am broken; I am a toilet
4. Future Oriented: Uncertain vs. Purposeful	• Continuity, vitality, energy	• I am without a future; I am without vision
5. Sense of Self-orientation; State of Confusion vs. Clarity	• Coherence, continuity, energy	• I am confused and foggy; I am in a cloud
6. Posttraumatic Shame and Guilt; Existential Meaning	• Coherence, vitality, energy	• I am disgraced and guilty
7. Configured Images of Being a Survivor	• Coherence, connection, energy	• I am "twisted steel"; am broken apart
8. Moral Compass: Past Trauma Experience and Future Outlook	• Integrity, continuity, coherence	• I am not the same as before; nothing left
9. Continuity vs. Discontinuity	• Integrity, continuity, energy	• It (war) destroyed me
10. Sense of Stasis vs. Growth	• Continuity, energy	• Nothing of me left of value
11. Sense of Separation vs. Connection	• Connection, coherence	• The past does not exist
12. Sense of Integrity vs. Despair	• Integrity, autonomy	• I am out of control
13. Dissociative, Unintegrated Personality Processes	• Coherence, continuity	• I am crap and no longer whole
14. Loss of Sense of Being Centered, Grounded, and Whole	• Coherence, autonomy	• I am unglued and lost
15. Keeper of Secrets and Feared Disclosure	• Coherence, continuity, energy	• I am ashamed; I am hidden, alone, no energy
16. Sense of Self-disclosure	• Coherence, continuity, energy	• I am alone, fearful & uncertain
17. Disruption of Understanding of Life's Journey	• Continuity, coherence, energy	• I am without any place; I am lost
18. Life-trajectory and Traumatic Role in Epigenesis	• Continuity (all)	• I am lost, alone but still going, but anxious
19. Animated; Sense of Vitality; Aliveness vs. Numbing; Constitution	• Vitality, energy	• I am exhausted; I am depleted but trying to survive
20. Self-transcendent vs. Self-resignation to External Forces	• All dimensions	• Life is empty, gone
		• Life seems gone, but I'm ok, sometimes

Source: Wilson (2006).
Note: *Metaphors can reflect either positive or negative polarities of the self- and ego-processes.

Trauma Related Changes in Psychoformative Processes: Case Examples as an Introduction to Self-Alterations in Complex Personality States

I Sensory-Motor Physiologic Changes in the Self Expressed in Trauma Metaphors

a Distorted Perception

The first area of psychic structure altered by trauma is the *perceptual apparatus* of the cognitive processing. At the moment of trauma, various sensory modalities are stimulated in an overwhelming manner, overloading neural circuits in the absence of resolution or problem-solving assimilation. These unresolved stimuli return in the form of repetitions that affect perception in the posttraumatic state. These altered sensory states may then begin to characterize the long-term experience of the survivor. They act as metaphors in that the trauma-based perceptual sensations become a distorted way of perceiving and experiencing reality. It returns to memory and cognition in encoded complex ideas. Language expresses the unsaid, unspoken, and unspeakable aspects of traumatic memories in metaphors. As such, these expressions in language reflect unconscious mental processes rooted in the trauma experience.

b Distortions of Vision and PTSD Hallucinations

Dante, a recent veteran of the war in Iraq, noted with an expression of terror crossing his face that: "I'm afraid to look in the mirror." On the surface, this reference was a visual metaphor for being uncomfortable, i.e., seeing himself as he was. It was also more specific. Each time Dante looked at himself, he actually saw the distorted images of two Iraqi men whom he killed at point blank range (i.e., immediately in front of his weapon) and whom he delusionally feared would retaliate against him (now or in the afterlife). The PTSD-based hallucinations frightened him. He thought of it as evidence he was losing his mind and going crazy. His PTSD symptoms were constant and disturbing, upsetting his sense of psychic balance, harmony, and inner peace. And the more disturbing the intrusive imagery, the worse was his state of combat-related hyperarousal, which did not abate upon return to the United States after the war.

In a different clinical case, it was the absence of sight or the sense of being blind that formed Iraq veteran Rex's metaphor: "I am just blind; I can't see a future." He was dejected and saw no tangible future.

Rex was describing his inability to foresee obvious consequences of actions he was currently facing in his life. In Iraq he had failed to anticipate his proximity to an RPG (rocket propelled grenade) explosion that killed several in his unit and led to loss of consciousness and his own temporary blindness. It was an overwhelming and confusing traumatic experience. He made himself avoidantly blind to the posttraumatic memory of these experiences. Hence, the somatoform loss of vision, a phenomena noted extensively in World War I associated with shell-shock symptoms.

c Distortions of Sound

Sound is another source of primary sensory metaphor. For Otis who survived the dam collapse and flood at Buffalo Creek, Pittson Coal Mine, in West Virginia (WVA, 1972), a phrase developed: "Not good, it's rainin' too much." Indeed the sound of seemingly incessant rain on a rooftop was an omen of disaster to come, as it was this condition that preceded their catastrophe on February 28, 1972, in Logan County, WVA, USA.

d Clicks: M-16s, AK-47s, RPGs, and Automatic Weapons: Triggers for Trauma-Specific Cues, Trauma-Specific Metaphors and Trauma-Specific Transference Reactions and Hyperarousal States

In another case, there was an ominous twist in Derrick's facial expression as he found himself making a "click-like" percussive sound with his tongue slapping from his palate against the floor of his mouth. He did this in situations in which people were doing something he considered dangerous and had instructed them to stop under the rules of engagement of war in Iraq. They were frightened of his potential anger by such an odd demeanor in a warzone.

Derrick explained that the click was the sound that one hears in Iraq or elsewhere prior to a rocket propelled grenade (RPG) being discharged and marks the setting of an explosive device. Clicks also extend not only to RPGs but to other automatic rifles, AK-47s, M-16s, etc. In it he turns his hyperalertness in situations of danger from one of being killed into the reverse role of the combat warrior setting his instrument of death on the enemy. To him the click means death and potentially the murder of innocent civilians.

e Distortions of Smell and Synergy of Senses: Flashbacks to Critical Traumatic Events

Olfactory sensations are another group that find their way into posttrauma metaphors. For example, survivors of the Beverly Hills Supper Club fire (1977) used the phrase that they lost (their) taste for BBQ cooking, reflecting a general loss of interest in social gatherings but also referencing dread as the smell of burning meat was associated with the grotesque experience of the many burned bodies of the fire at the Kentucky entertainment supper club. Similar metaphoric descriptions have been reported to us by firefighters who encounter burned bodies in homes, especially when deceased children are recovered but basically charred and disfigured.

A Cleveland, Ohio, senior-level firefighter told of his personal trauma of recovering a young four-year-old girl from a lethal house fire. As he searched the house in smoke and confusion, on the second floor, he found the girl lying on a bedroom floor, dead from smoke inhalation with a shocked look on her face, eyes fixed (dead) and wide open. When he attempted to remove her, the burnt skin and clothing on her back peeled off. After this critical incident, he was unable to attend family cook outs, summer gatherings, eat BBQ or tolerate the smell of smoked and grilled meat. He could not stand to see a grilled salmon, fish scales or a charcoal file that would "peel" off once cooked. So, he avoided all outdoor events of BBQ and grilling meats, etc.

Similarly many Vietnam veterans are hypersensitive to the fetid, rotten, gaseous smell of decomposing organic matter, especially in warm weather. One veteran took to bed and refused to leave the house, because there was an "ill wind" outside. At first, this was a vague reference to something ominous but later he referenced the specific similar smell of decomposing bodies during a jungle war. For others, there are many other metaphoric references by Vietnam veterans to the trauma-specific cues (TSC) of decomposing human remains. For example, "I can't stand the smell of cat food; I can't stand the smell of rotten cabbage; I can't stand the smell of degraded earthy materials (e.g., old grass, weeds, flower debris, etc.) in compost piles."

An Iraq war veteran, in an odd seemingly paradoxical reaction, refused to "break bread" with strangers. He found himself offended by the ordinarily pleasant sensations and smells of baking bread. Then, he remembered the smell of one household in Iraq which his squad entered, searched and killed insurgents, while mothers and children were baking bread. The metaphor encapsulates the reality of breaking bread with friendly persons with breaking life itself. Hence, the connection between killing, death, and the pleasant smell of fresh-made bread. In essence, the symbolic juxtaposition of life and death, which is indelible and intrusive, a haunting painful intrusive memory.

f Distortions of Taste: Why Can't I Stand the Taste and Smell of Ash?

Taste is another primary sensation cable of being incorporated into posttraumatic metaphors and complex ego-states. As metaphorically applied to posttraumatic ego-states, what does the trauma experience taste like?

Richard, a 40-year-old business executive and survivor of the September 11, 2001 terrorist attacks, was describing his general attitude toward the world after the 9/11 trauma. He escaped from the first of the twin towers, but lost numerous co-workers who stayed behind. The taste of the "ash debris" from the towers he remembered as particularly bitter. Ash is bitter in taste and few American foods embody that specific flavor of acridness, which is not the case in other cultures in which ash-tasting meals are prized (e.g., Africa, Australia, Morocco, Mongolia, etc.). For him, ash represents death and unpleasant distressing memories of 9/11. This is another example for trauma-specific metaphors (TSM) expressed in sensory-perceptual modalities.

g Distortions of Touch: I've Been Lying on His Grave

Touch is another modality from which, especially in childhood trauma, metaphors are formed. For example, Sarah, a depressed grieving mother, startled her therapist by describing her activities to her doctor with the phrase, "I've been laying on his grave." In fact, her adolescent son committed suicide. She was preoccupied with the mental and physical image of laying on her son's grave. She found the tactile elements enlivening, as through it she recaptured a sense of connection to him. The metaphor of death spoke to the only part of herself that she now felt was alive. Resting on his grave was importantly associated with her self-structural dimension of proximate and ultimate connections (Lifton, 1976).

h Angela's Story: I Am Covered by a 'Wet Blanket'

Angela, a child survivor of the Buffalo Creek, West Virginia dam collapse and flood (1972) was spared from a grotesque image by her grandmother who covered her eyes with a blanket so she would not see a mutilated, truncated mud-covered baby nearby. Years later, she referred to the quality of her life by the unusual tactile phrase, covered by a wet blanket (i.e., as was the dead baby in the dam disaster).

Trauma survivors and their families are often startled by distorted and hypersensitive perceptions. Survivors themselves are distressed to learn that they cannot always rely on their senses to provide accurate information about reality and perceptions of situations.

When understood as trauma metaphors, these phenomena are less frightening and more readily understandable to practitioners, in particular, as well as significant others. They are comprehensible within the context of the trauma and important windows to what is underneath the unsaid and unspeakable phenomenology and knowledge of posttraumatic states. As such the survivor and the clinician see the individual problem as having a particular connection to un-worked-through aspects of the trauma experience. As such, they are psychic forces of energy that permeate consciousness, perception, and cognitive processes, i.e., the organismic energy infuses the being of the trauma survivor.

II Hyperarousal States, Affect Modulations, and Disturbances in Emotions

The second major ego-function frequently damaged in posttraumatic states and fundamental to treatment is the failure of affect regulation, hyperarousal states, and associated adaptational problems. Posttraumatic, allostatic disregulations and adaptive processes are at work at all levels of mental functioning (Wilson, Friedman, & Lindy, 2001). They are complex and inter-related organismic processes. They are synergistic and interactive at all levels of the organism.

a Eli, about to Explode in Flames

Eli, a returning U.S. Army Iraq sergeant, enraged by his Iraqi war experiences and chagrined, explained that he had yelled at his wife when she lowered the window of their car while on a busy street. His words were sharp, military-like commands and frightened her by their intensity and directness. When asked how he felt during that therapeutic moment, he said, "I felt I was about to explode."

The phrase captured his sense of imminent loss of control of anger. By exploring the details of the circumstances of lowering the window the therapist learned that in Baghdad during the insurgency, lowering bulletproof glass on a Humvee military vehicle was an invitation to be target for an improvised explosive device (IED) which could explode glass and metal. As a sergeant, it was his duty to prevent such explosions. In a clinical context his fear that he would explode was both a figure of speech regarding loss of inhibitory control of intense affect and a war-related memory stimulus (TSC).

b Disturbances in Impulse Control, Frustration Tolerance, and Allostatic Processes

In essence, allostasis is a level of conscious awareness (LCA) by the survivor of what they have endured and experienced and knowledge that they are not the same as before, i.e., there is a new baseline level of functioning, awareness, and cognition (Wilson, Friedman, & Lindy, 2001).

c I'm Going to Crash and Die

Chris, a survivor of the Beverly Hills Supper Club fire (1977) outside Cincinnati, Ohio, just across state lines in Kentucky, dreamed that he was in an aircraft that was going fast and was out of control, too close to the ground. The metaphor "I'm going to crash" captured the sense of his loss of control and referred overtly to his current life situation where he was losing job after job through abrupt maladaptive behaviors and might lose his wife as well. The crash metaphor, however, not only referred to a current state of damaged psychological processing, it also referred to an actual event; the death of his brother in a motorcycle crash before the trauma of the fire, an event adding one trauma onto another. PTSD can be multi-layered in its psychic configuration.

Trauma Induced Changes and Psychoformative Processes: Conceptual and Clinical Summary Perspectives

The clinical case illustrations at the beginning of the chapter serve to demonstrate how trauma experiences can and do disrupt and alter changes in ego-processes, personality characteristics, and the self-structure including the functional structure of personal identity. These are complex specific structural and self-structural changes to the internal organization of the self and its components. To return to the central question: How is the self-structure and personality affected by trauma? Figure 3.1 presents an overview of these potential traumatic effects, both negative and positive in nature, and provide a useful visual schematic analysis.

Posttraumatic Psychic Constellations

As Figure 3.1 illustrates, trauma can and does significantly influence the dimensions and organization of the self (both positive [+] and negative [-]) and associated ego-processes and personality processes, thus setting up other dimensions for critical clinical post-trauma analysis and psychotherapy implications.

Critical-clinical posttraumatic analyses are important to bring conceptual clarity to the pathways by which traumatic experiences influence the survivors' adaptational processes. Figure 3.1 is an overly-simplified but extremely useful schematic-figural representation of how trauma impacts personality and self-processes. In other writings, we have detailed these complex processes (Wilson, 2006; Wilson, Friedman, & Lindy, 2004). For purposes of this book, these theoretical and empirical considerations are cast in a somewhat different light. For example, how is trauma related to complex personality processes and the generation of trauma metaphors? This question makes Figure 3.1 immediately intelligible and critically useful to psychotherapy considerations, especially diagnostic assessment procedures.

Trauma always impacts the entire organism as a holistic system of integrated psychobiological processes (see Miller, 1978; Wilson, 2006). Trauma "hits" at all levels of organismic functioning. Every system of the human body is potentially affected by the impacts of prolonged stress and psychic trauma (see the discussion of allostasis by Wilson, Friedman, & Lindy, 2004).

By careful examination of the positive polarity of the self represented in Figure 3.1, or the negative polarity of the self-structure as such, it can be seen that many of the self-structural dimensions shown in Figure 3.1 can be adversely impacted. In terms of negative polarity effects, the following dimensions of negative polarities will be manifested, as illustrated in all of our case examples. However, to simply highlight and list the self-dimensions in the negative self-structural polarities, see Table 3.4.

The traumatic impacts influence all of the following psychological processes: (1) psychoformative processes; (2) cognitive processes of executive functions of intelligence; (3) personality and self-processes; (4) personal identity; and (5) concurrent ego-processes, etc. As such, trauma metaphors reflect and illuminate these changes to the inner world of the trauma survivor. Figure 3.1 summarizes the complex, intricate interplay between the following: (1) traumatic experiences and the formation of posttraumatic constellations and individual traumatic responses in daily occurring ego-processes; (2) the interactional effects of these dimensions to categorical dimensions; the

Table 3.4 Positive and Negative Polarities of the Self

SELF-STRUCTURAL DIMENSIONS: HEALTHY FUNCTIONAL POSITIVE (+) POLARITIES	*TRAUMA INDUCED ALTERATIONS: NEGATIVE (−) POLARITIES*
1) Continuity	Discontinuity
2) Coherence	Dissociation / Splitting
3) Connection	Separation / Detachment
4) Autonomy	Constriction
5) Vitality	Weakness
6) Energy	Malaise
7) Self-Esteem	Self-Esteem: Shame
8) Structure Integrity	Structural Disintegration
9) Identity Integration	Identity Diffusion

specific dimensions of PTSD analysis and the genesis of metaphors; (3) these subsequent processes have direct impacts to all aspects of self and personality processes, which result in alterations; and (4) psychoformative processes and internal psychic mechanisms of adaptation.

Trauma, Posttraumatic Self-Processes, and Metaphors: Lexical Meaning and Portals of Entry (POE) to the PTSD Phenomenological World

The Comprehensive Overview of Trauma, Personality Processes, and Metaphor Genesis: Assessing Complexity

Tables 3.5 and 3.6 present an expanded version of Figure 3.1, a more detailed and inclusive conceptual analysis of how posttraumatic self and personality processes are associated with metaphoric processes.

For purposes of clarity and simplicity, there are columns in Table 3.5 that contain specific summary content information as identified by the title of the column. In this way, by crossing the six self-dimensions with the other content categories, 42 separate sources of data are identified directly relevant to metaphor genesis and their intrapsychic connections to internal posttraumatic processes. In the way of summary, the columns include: (1) the six self-structural dimensions; (2) key reference linguistic words; (3) nouns; (4) verbs; (5) epigenetic stage-specific modes; (6) core trauma metaphors; (7) transforming metaphors; and (8) portals of entry (POE) into PTSD phenomenology.

Trauma Disclosures in Psychotherapy

Figure 3.2 presents a condensed summary of traumatic stress impacts to structural components of the self and personality variables based on the Five-Factor personality dimensions (FFM): (1) neuroticism; (2) extraversion; (3) openness; (4) agreeableness; and (5) conscientiousness. Analysis of Figure 3.2 shows from left to right the six core

Table 3.5 Trauma, the Posttraumatic Self (PTS), and Metaphors: Lexical Meanings and Portals of Entrance to PTSD Phenomenology

Posttraumatic Self-Dimensions and Associated Metaphorical Processes to PTSD:

Self-Dimensions	*Key Word*	*Noun*	*Verb*	*Psychological Reference*	*Core Trauma Metaphor*	*Transforming Metaphor*	*Portals of Entry (POE) to PTSD**
I. **Continuity**	Continuance	Continue, Resume	Sustain	Identity Stability	I am not the same.	I am moving on.	SP, B
II. **Coherence**	Cohesion	Wholeness	Make Clear	Self-Sameness	I am broken.	I am back together.	SP, B
III. **Connection**	Union	Linkage	Interconnect	Ego-States	I am disconnected.	I am reconnected.	IP,C
IV. **Autonomy**	Control	Independence	Be Free	Ego-Dexterity	I am not in control.	I am fine and in control.	SP, IP, C
V. **Vitality**	Potency	Strength	Exert Mastery	Sense of Strength	I am lifeless.	I am alive again.	SP, B
VI. **Energy**	Vigor	Potency/Drive/ Animation	Dynamic Self-Regulation	Sense of Well Being	I am run down, fatigued.	I am energetic.	SP, D

Note: *POE (Wilson, Friedman, & Lindy, 2004), Five POE's: PTSD Clusters (B, C, D), Interpersonal (IP) and Self-Processes (SP).

Figure 3.2 Traumatic Stress Impacts to Structural Personality Dimensions in the Five-Factor Model

self-dimensions and their subsequent potential negative alterations and examples of trauma metaphors and how they, in turn, correspond to the FFM personality dimensions. Thus, Figure 3.2 offers a "lens" by which to understand and link trauma impacts to the self and personality processes and verbal expressions in trauma-specific metaphors (TSM).

Metaphoric Platforms and Continuums

Figure 3.3 moves our analysis to a different but critical illustration of how trauma metaphors change over time in psychotherapy and everyday life with significant others, family members, friends, and colleagues. Figure 3.3 has four levels or "*platforms of representation*." First, to examine the *continuum* from psychic distress and pathology to psychological health. Second, to view how states of PTSD and self-de-integration transform in time and space to states of trauma transcendence and self-integration. As such, this process reflects the *continuum or discontinuum of intrapsychic metabolic processes* and how the mind is coming to represent in metaphors the gradual resolution of traumatic life experiences.

At level three, there is metaphoric epigenesis (i.e., gradual unfolding of trauma disclosure) of metaphoric evolution, integration, and transformation. As such, this level of understanding reflects three basic stages: (1) unmetabolized traumatic experiences; (2) the reformulation of traumatic life events; and (3) the gradual but cognitively integrated understanding of the life experience and its impact to the personality, spirit, and soul of the person. Finally, level four illustrates *metaphoric vicissitudes* from states of fixation in primary metaphors to psychic synthesis and resolution of perspective.

As we continue the journey, Table 3.6 "rounds out" the major illustrations for Chapter 3. This table builds on Wilson's (2006) extensive and detailed analysis of how traumatic life events impact epigenetic development. In summary form, Table 3.6 illustrates that each of the eight epigenetic stages can be profoundly impacted by traumatic life events and produce trauma-specific changes in life-span development. These specific traumatic events not only potentially affect stage-specific ego-strength development but the genesis of trauma metaphors in simple but revealing nature as to inner identity processes (see Wilson, 2006).

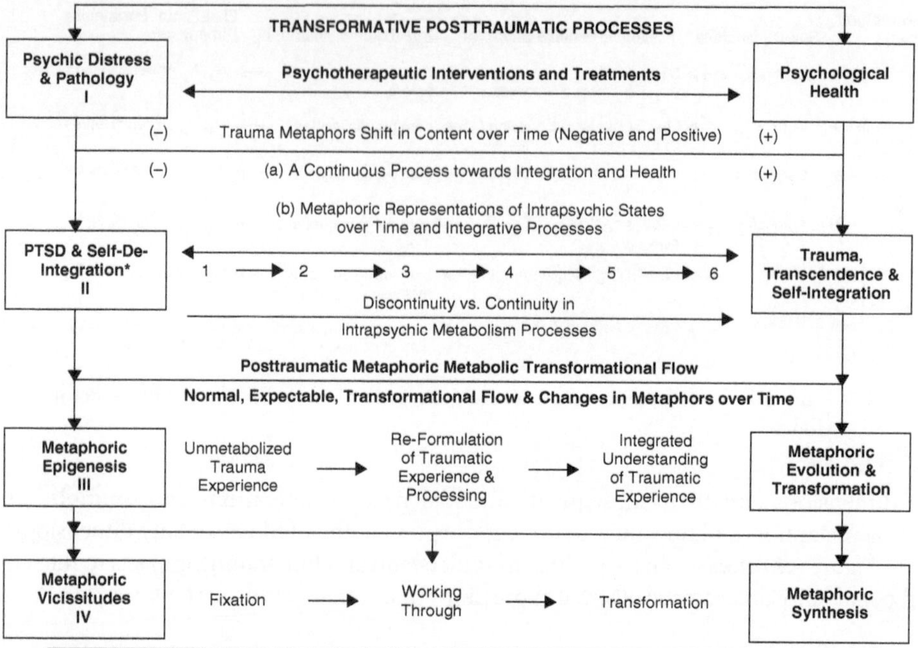

*Key:

1 – Unmetabolized Trauma
2 – Constructions of Trauma Images (Genesis)
3 – Constructions of Trauma Images as Metaphors in Language: The Origin of Transformative Process
4 – Metaphors as Organizers of Trauma Experience Over Time in the Life-Cycle: Epigenetic Transformation
5 – Metaphors as Reflections of Intrapsychic Changes and Integration: Towards Intrapsychic Integration
6 – Peace, Resolution and Acceptance of Fate: Final Integration and Synthesis, the Resting Point of Trauma's Legacy

Figure 3.3 Trauma Metaphors Change Over Time in Psychotherapy and Everyday Life*

Trauma and the Genesis of Trauma-Specific Metaphors (TSM) and Beyond

The genesis of trauma metaphors can be viewed by analysis of at least six major categories: (1) metaphors of the internal world of the PTSD patient; (2) transformative metaphors; (3) giving insightful identity to trauma metaphors; (4) linking metaphors to life-history; (5) the five dimensions of metaphors (e.g., symbols, somatic-sensory elements, etc.); and (6) re-enacting metaphors. These six major categories embrace over 20 sub-dimensions and are a rich source of clinical assessments and therapeutic insights as to patient dynamics.

Brief Summary

Our summary review of the major figures and tables of Chapter 3 has led to further departure points for consideration. We can, in the interest of limited publication space, summarize them as follows:

- There are profoundly significant posttraumatic psychic constellations at four complex inter-related dimensions as to how traumatic life experiences create intra-

Table 3.6 The Epigenesis of the Identity and Trauma Metaphors

Epigenesis and Psychosocial Development	*Potential Ego-Strength*	*Epigenetic Metaphors of Trauma*	*Stage-Specific Trauma Metaphors*
1) Trust vs. Mistrust	Hope vs. Hopelessness	Faith in Life	I cannot trust anyone
2) Autonomy vs. Shame/Doubt	Will vs. Engulfment	Degrees of Freedom of Choices	I feel shame / anxiety
3) Initiation vs. Guilt	Purpose vs. Futility	Vision of Self-Worth	I see no future
4) Industry vs. Inferiority	Competence vs. Inadequacy	Esteem & Mastery	I can't do it; I feel conflicted
5) Identity vs. Identity Confusion	Fidelity vs. Non-commitment	Authenticity of Self	I'm confused, not the same
6) Intimacy vs. Isolation	Love vs. Detachment	Human Connectedness	I am distant from the ones I want
7) Generalitivity vs. Stagnant	Intrinsic Care vs. Indifference	Non-Judgmental Care and Love	I am empty, lost, lonely, alone
8) Integrity vs. Despair	Wisdom vs. Surrender	Sense of End-Stage Wholeness	I am at the end, there is no more

Source: Erikson (1982).

psychic constellations and alterations in individual adaptative responses, both behaviorally and intrapsychically (Figure 3.1).

- All aspects of human personality processes, self-structure, identity, and traits may be altered by trauma and have long lasting emotional consequences (Figure 3.2, Tables 3.2–3.5).
- Trauma patients, no matter what the nature or precipitating event, will express traumatic life events in metaphorical expressions that are subtle, muted, discrete, disguised, or blatant and confrontational (Table 3.1).
- There are discrete categories of psychic symbolism which always demonstrate a connection/relationship between the traumatic life experience and specific psychic states, dreams, language syntax, and metaphor creation (Figure 3.2; Table 3.6).
- Traumatic life experiences are always reflected in internal life states and altered dimensions of the self and lead to metaphor genesis (see list below).
- It is a reality that trauma metaphors change and evolve over time as psychic metabolism occurs in due course. It is a gradual process, depending on the age and time of traumatic events for the survivor. However, there are at least four "platforms" of meaningful analysis. These platforms are dichotomous. First, psychic distress and psychopathology vs. the striving toward resilience, health, and integration. Second, PTSD and processes of self-de- or dis-integration vs. trauma transcendence and self-integration. Third, metaphoric epigenesis and metaphoric evolution and transformation amongst a three-pronged psychic journey of integration and understanding.

Trauma and the Genesis of Trauma Metaphors

1 **Metaphors of the internal world of the PTSD patient**
   a Body language as expressive of trauma metaphor
   b Somatic symptoms of experience of trauma and metaphoric expressions
2 **Transformative metaphors**
   a Evolve ways to metabolize and express the trauma metaphor
   b Serve as transitional mechanism to preserve integration of self and coherence of personality
3 **Nurturing and giving identity to the trauma metaphor by Nurturing Guides (NG)**
   a What changes in the patient's ego process?
   b Re-establishing nurturing experiences and healthy generations
   c Activate conscious awareness of trauma metaphors
   d Confirmation of the connection to the Nurturing Guide as one who will help as needed
4 **Metaphorical links to the past: When do the links become important?**
   a Connection to important previous life experiences and affective states to current trauma connection
   b Connection to previous trauma or psychopathology to current psychic representation in internal states of experience
   c Metaphors as clues to the unsaid repressed traumas of the past or recurrent ego-states of more recent trauma

5 **Traumatic metaphorical meanings: What are the dimensions?**
  a Metaphors
  b Symbols
  c Mythology
  d Symptoms
  e Somatic/bodily metaphors connected to trauma
6 **Re-enacting metaphors**
  a How is the treatment of the therapist provided to find these venues?
  b Unconscious expressions of trauma complexes and configurations
  c Universal trauma-specific metaphors (UTSM)
  d Influence the nature of (TST) trauma-specific transference
  e Unconscious influences (TST and CTRs) trauma-specific transference (TSTM) and countertransference modes of empathic strain
  f Influenced therapists capacity for empathy and empathic strain
  g Trauma-specific metaphorical transference (TSMT) and highly specialized traumatic reactions in PTSD patient to therapist

Personality, Self, and Identity Disturbances After Traumatic Life Experiences: Part II

Disturbances in Autonomy, Initiative, Independence, and Locus of Control

Trauma affects autonomous ego-functioning both consciously and unconsciously. The initiative that comes with autonomy arises in the context of the capacity to distinguish self from others and to regulate anatomical drives in an adaptive manner. Whereas before the trauma, the person may have felt the center of his own locus of control and initiative actions, spontaneous, independent, and self-determined loss of control of life. After trauma the same person might feel at the mercy of malevolent forces and humiliated, disgraced, and ashamed, with a loss of face and dignity. Whereas he or she initially felt the governor of his own internal processes, they now feel anxious, rigidly constricted, over-controlled, and fearful.

Metaphors give penetrating and useful insights as to the more precise ways that the competence and autonomy of the survivor has been damaged. They might feel as if they lost a sense of establishing a safe direction and therefore are about to crash or, worse, die, that a malevolent force (e.g., U.S. government) now controls life in a paranoid way.

Case Illustrations

The Tunnel Rat In Vietnam: The Small "Skinny Ass" American G.I. Upside Down In Cleveland, Ohio

A Vietnam veteran, some years after the war, found himself in a turbulent state with his friends, co-workers, ex-wife, and children. Micky, an Irish-American former U.S. Marine from the Irish-Catholic westside area of Cleveland, Ohio, used the phrase "upside-down" to describe his life predicament in personal identity and direction. Or, as he repeatedly said, "It's all fucked up Doc, everything is upside down after Vietnam." "Every day after the Nam (war) is always upside down to me."

He reported that as a stout but little "skinny assed" Irishman, he had been drinking heavily at night, as usual, at a party. While he had no memory of it, due to alcohol blackout intoxication, he had asked a friend to hold onto his legs while he (the friend) hanged Micky outside the fourth floor window in an "upside down" position.

In a general sense, the confluence of feeling upside down and asking to be held in that position led his doctor to ask if something dangerous had occurred in Vietnam while he was upside down. He responded that as a little guy (i.e., small in stature and weight) who was an athletic, high-school wrestler, he was the ideal person to be a "tunnel rat," i.e., the first to explore and to clear enemy Viet Cong underground tunnels that his unit came upon in Cu Chi in South Vietnam, Thy Ninh Province.

To begin that activity, a squad member would hold him upside down as he made his initial dangerous foray exploration into the enemy tunnel, and as such into the proverbial "lion's den," often after initially consuming a pint of Jack Daniels whiskey or more to steady his nerves and shakiness. The metaphoric term, "tunnel rat," evolved during the Vietnam war, although it also existed in World War II at Iwo Jima for U.S. Marines fighting embedded Japanese forces in tunnels and mountain retreats. The smallest unit members were trained to be the "tunnel rats," diminutive enough to go inside the Japanese tunnels to intercept and kill the enemy.

The tunnel rats were not only intelligent persons but leaders of assault, when necessary, under blind conditions as to what was in the tunnel. While they were combat instruments of interdiction, intelligence, and destruction, they were also constantly in the most perilous situations imaginable, especially since the tunnels were booby-trapped with deadly, poisonous snakes, punji sticks with infectious biological matter (buffalo dung, human waste, etc.), anti-personnel devices, mines, and toxic insects (spiders, etc.). Being upside-down, drunk, in his native home of Cleveland, Ohio, was a re-enactment of being upside-down as a tunnel rat in Vietnam. Micky's metaphor encapsulated these, then and there, war-related traumatic episodes in a few words.

It is a truism that much of the survivor's energy goes into maintaining his equilibrium with his emotions (i.e., affect modulation). Many of the usual psychosocial positive feedback loops that reward accomplishment and build self-esteem are often missing after trauma. Trauma often takes them away, i.e., to psychic (mental) and geographical isolation, to get away in different realities. The loss of these regulating functions is a hallmark of diturbances to ego-processes in posttrauma states and PTSD itself. They are complex, confusing, and disturbing. The survivor offers a helping hand to the clinician to access these damaged self- and ego-structures on a case by case method, as there is no other method.

Well, how so? We wish to underline that it may be through the unusual phrases, the trauma metaphors that offers the clinician the clearest window to trauma-related pathology. But, how does the sensitive, intelligent, intuitive professional read the cues that provide the portals of entry (POE) into the phenomenological space and world of PTSD and beyond (see Chapter 9)?

Disturbances in Emergency and Critical Defenses

When needed, metaphoric expressions capture emergency defenses, necessary in the trauma situation but maladaptive in the present. They give clues to such unconscious ego-processing activities as identification with the aggressor and the victim, turning aggression against the self, the externalization of blame, projective identification, isolation, and dissociating. These are common and important to understand in posttraumatic disorder processes and related conditions.

Stewart and the Instrument Panel: Iraq's Legacy

Stewart, an Iraq veteran, referred to his dissociative episode(s) metaphorically "as the time he spent watching the instrument panel." This phrase came out as he was trying to describe his subjective state during a period for which he was dissociatively amnestic. He described leaving his friends inside a bar and his sitting behind the steering wheel of a parked car. At that point the narrative broke off. There was a notable break in metonymy in his linguistic experiences. There was no memory for six hours while his buddies had gone into a bar which was in itself unusual as military command forbade drinking alcohol. Manifestly, he was remaining the safe driver for the group. But as others checked on him from time to time he was immobile and simply stared ahead. Watching the instrument panel, a trauma metaphor, he simply blurted out in an altered state of conscious awareness. It was an unconscious reference to his job during six-hour clearance missions in Iraq when his buddies cleared particular roads of IEDs while electronic reporting on the status of the roads was coming into his desk where he would relay information to see that they were safe.

Unconscious defenses, such as amnesia, dissociative episodes, repression, denial, as with Stewart above, are first manifest by discontinuities in the survivor's speech, points where the trauma narrative stops. The patient simply stares off as if in another world or seems to disappear in the therapy treatment office room. The damaged ego-functions protect the survivor, from first take of memory to the form of linguistic discontinuities rather than metaphors. Later, a trauma metaphor may intrude, giving survivor and clinician clues as to what has been blocked from memory. Metaphoric traumatic expressions are clues to the hidden channels of portals of entry into the world of trauma victims. The therapist needs to listen to posttraumatic metaphors (TSM) as they play out in trauma-specific transference (TST). These processes encapsulate capsules of information to enter the portals of entry to the inner-world of trauma survivors (Wilson, Friedman, & Lindy, 2001).

Somatic Distortions

As Freud and others discovered, composites or physical sensations, often in the form of bodily symptoms, are also psychological compromises that reference traumatic experiences. Decoding the symptoms into trauma-specific configurations constitutes much of the work of dynamic posttraumatic psychotherapy. How to decode the meaning of trauma-specific metaphors (TSM) and trauma-specific transference (TST) processes? Are they the same or dissociatively split in defensive ways, hiding secrets?

Saving Hearts After War: Josh and a Crushed Heart

Josh, a Vietnam veteran, experienced crushing chest pain and convinced he was moments away from death for which he was rushed to emergency rooms on numerous occasions only to be told that his heart was normal. He later recalled the image of a crushed child's chest as his truck ran over her on Highway 1 in Vietnam (1969). He feared that his crushing the hearts of those he should feel protective toward became an organizer for understanding all his relationships in the present and those anticipated in the future. Later he anxiously worried: "Because I crush the hearts of those I love or respect and honor, I deserve to die from crushing chest pain myself." His war-guilt permeated his present life and fears but without his conscious understanding of how the past was in the present.

Drowning: Kent and Electrocution

Kent was describing his state of being overwhelmed in the aftermath of the death of his friend. He felt questions of meaning and direction in his life were drowning him. He barely escaped being electrocuted when he jumped into a pool to save his friend, not knowing the pool was electrified. While stunned he escaped. The friend drowned. In the present, the traumatic past was associated with psychological stasis. He was psychically drowning and did not know how to move forward. He felt trapped in the traumatic experience.

Rev. Father Frank's Heel Pain: I Wish I Could Absorb Their Pain

Francis (Frank), a religious Franciscan monk who accompanied next of kin to identify loved ones at the temporary morgue following the disastrous Beverly Hills Supper Club fire in Kentucky (1977), developed unremitting pain beneath his Achilles tendon. Medical examination and x-ray showed no pathology. In psychotherapy, the brother remembered the pain that members of the family felt when it was he who identified the autopsy tag attached to an otherwise unidentifiable young man's heel. The somatic symptom, Achilles tendon, was a physiological metaphor for what was underneath both literally and figuratively. How to walk again with integrity and survivor guilt after identifying the heel of the dead?

Jason: Somatoform (Distorted) Autonomic Reactions

For Jason, an Iraqi war veteran, blushing at the neck line was a signal or possible posttraumatic clue that something was causing him to burn with rage, a feeling that he recognized but needed to inhibit as the result of an overreaction would be too dangerous in his civilian life. His therapist much later learned that Jason had carried out missions in which he strangled to death the enemy with piano wire (i.e., garrote). The erythema around his own neck was a point of connection with those whom he killed in Iraq. He somatically manifested his own projective processes of guilt, shame, and revulsion at his acts of murder. He never spoke the totality of the unsaid or unspeakable actions, the garrote of those he strangled to their deaths.

Traumatic Stress Impacts to Structural Personality Dimensions in the Five-Factor Personality Model (FFM): Case Examples

Our alternation of case examples with conceptual configurations in the figures and tables in Chapter 3 serves to further refine how traumatic experiences impact personality and self-processes and their subsequent correlation to the genesis of trauma metaphors.

The negative alterations to the self-structure and its constituent components can be individually (e.g., a personal sense of posttrauma discontinuity) or totally impacted (i.e., all self-dimensions altered) and disrupted. When these negative alterations occur in the core components of the self, corresponding trauma metaphors may be developed intrapsychically to reflect these important changes in posttraumatic functioning. To wit: "I am not the same as before; I am broken inside; I am disconnected and detached; I am not in control anymore as I was before; I have no energy; I am fragile and weak; I am totally gone; I exist in a twilight world between life and death."

These altered components of the self have a corresponding relationship to the Five-Factor Model of personality (FFM) (see Wilson, 2006, for a discussion). Each of the five major factors of personality corresponds with states of anxiety, vulnerability, depression, emotional lability, detachment, mental dullness, among other important possibilities. For the clinician, these aspects of personality and self-processes, as well as their relationship to traumatic metaphors, provides more portals of entry (POE) into the inner phenomenological world of PTSD and the survivor as a person struggling to sort out precisely how trauma changed their life as well as explorations into their personality dynamics.

Loss of Self-Continuity and Self-Sameness in Identity: Clinical Examples

Taking a closer look at the positive and negative polarities of the dimension of continuity of self, we note that subjective experience in the pre-traumatic condition tends to be continuous, sequential, stable, progressive, aligned, or cyclical. In its negative polarity, subjective experience (posttrauma) tends to be disconnected, disjunctional, episodic, fragmentary, and dissociated. Below are clinical examples of a self, rendered discontinuous by trauma, in clinical uses and more.

Splintered Inside: Angel Child or Dirty Whore? How to Differentiate

For example, Kristina, an incest survivor, persistently hyperalert that there was potential physical danger to herself or others, struggled with a sense of disorganization in her current life attachments. She felt splintered. Her sense of self and esteem was damaged in the capacity to maintain a continuous and steady idea of who she was (identity integration). This splintered state overtly referred to her as being: a good and/or bad teacher, empathic and abusive parent, kind or sadistically seductive partner. She struggled to inhibit impulses, especially sexual ones toward men, and when successful would say to herself "good job, good job." Alternatively she would say, "naughty whore." Gradually special words came out to capture which of her splintered (borderline) self-states was active, i.e., angel child or dirty whore.

These separate fragments were the derivative of actual splits in the continuity of self that originated out of her adaptations to childhood trauma. As a child when her stepfather's penis entered her, she imagined it was a huge rod that "splintered her into pieces like a piece of firewood."

Understanding some of the implications in the word "splintered" allowed the therapist to empathize with feeling cut-off from who she was only moments before to remind the patient of the other side of the splintered self and how a story of perceived danger led to the shift in the present.

Many veterans of combat feel that they became different persons during and after the war. Their preoccupation with the traumatic past often cuts-off war survivors from involvement in the present. The pre-war and war self is split-off from the post-war self and demands an unavoidable, inordinate amount of energy. In essence, there are multiple self-identities within one personality structure, all encapsulated into war-associated identity niches in the psyche, often, in an intrapsychic, metaphoric warfare with each other. The nuclear core of PTSD and self-transformations. The pre-war, war, and post-war configurations of the self and identity. How does the self reconfigure its internal psychic architecture?

The History and Importance of "Big John" and the "Marble" of His Eye: A War Veteran's Lost Eye: Big John and His Son

A Vietnam veteran, Big John, who lost his eye in combat, was startled when he learned that his child in kindergarten had been searching for a marble under a table with great urgency, explaining to his teacher that he had to find the eye his father lost in Vietnam.

The child, having understood his father's problem with his prosthesis in a concrete way, allowed the patient within a family treatment setting to see the same phrase metaphorically. Where, indeed, was his eye? For he failed to see his child as he should with his present self because he was preoccupied with a *discontinuous, damaged, non-integrated combat self.* The pun which the lost eye represented was clear. Empathizing with the veteran's state of feeling "cut-off" from non-combat was central to healing. Where is the eye (i.e., I or me or someone else) and what does it mean now? *Clearly, this is an internal identity conflict and existential dialectic and reality initiated by son and father in a common psychic search, to come home from the war and go on with living life to the fullest.* The son, being loving and sensitive, re-enacted his father's unconscious conflict and symbol of post-Vietnam conflict in soul.

Self-Structural Changes in Personal Identity Alterations in Coherence, Positive Self-Regard, and Identity

Looking carefully at the *polarities of coherence of the self*, the coherent integrated self is clear, comprehensible, direct, distinct in its detail and decipherable, while the view from the incoherent self is perplexing, amorphous, confusing, chaotic, and interrupted (Wilson, 2006). Survivors find remarkably apt phrases to describe the changes from a coherent self to a posttraumatically altered and damaged self that is unclear and finds the world dark and difficult to decipher. The self-coherence is altered, destroyed, fragmented, or no longer the same to the survivor and is typically associated with anxiety states, depression, emotional vulnerability, and amorphous fears.

Case Histories

Erica: In a Cloud after September 11, 2001 in New York City

In her spontaneous metaphor, Erica referred to her mental state as "*being in a cloud*." Erica had fled New York City after hours of walking away from the smoldering Twin Towers immersed in the ash that followed the terrorist attack. Weeks later she used the phrase to describe her confused state of mind as an inability to make decisions regarding where to live and what career and relationships to follow. Erica's therapist and she used the metaphor "cloud" to understand that the immediate aftermath of 9/11 was not the time to make permanent life decisions but rather, like a "toxic cloud," she would do well to return home to a safe place, waiting until the sky was clear to make major decisions for her life. From clouded sky to the safe home space.

Luke: Intrusive Swollen Brain Metaphor

Luke, an American Army medic in the Iraq war, describing his chaotic life after deployment, said he was trying to think with a "swollen brain." The unusual phrase covered the traumatic memory of being *unsuccessful as a medic in* providing treatment to an injured Iraqi girl whose brain extruded through her skull after a traumatic head injury in which the child had been used by insurgents as a shield.

Luke's case captured a self-state, overwhelmed by the suffering of others and the impotence of being unable to change the situation for the better. Luke's therapist empathized with the helplessness while valuing Luke's concern for damaged innocence and loss. Attending to the swollen head over time allowed Luke and his therapist to identify an interpersonal pattern seeking over-involvement and desperation with seemingly hopeless causes. How do you fix unfixable situations of personal responsibility when all goes wrong and out of control?

Broken Bodies and Spirits

Some clients or patients referred to damage to their posttraumatic sense of self-coherence in terms of how they felt their minds were working in the present. A rape victim, Karen, felt initially that her body and mind were broken, referring at once to a sense of hopelessness and the awareness of an inability to bring her life together but also of having the coherence of her body as a vessel having been broken by the rapist. It was crucial to Karen's recovery that both her fiancé and her therapist saw her as whole (see our discussion on coherence as a critical dimension of the self-structure).

The survivor sometimes describes spontaneously his or her posttraumatically damaged self in terms of images that arise from the trauma scene, i.e., indelible moments of images of the event. Unable to use metaphors from earlier in life as their source domain, the traumatized survivor falls back on the new all-powerful sensory-motor experiences of the trauma itself in order to describe the dilemma. They map onto current situations not the metaphors of past accomplishments but the frozen introjects metaphors of the trauma experience, i.e., what they would and could not do at that time, place, and space.

The Epigenesis of Identity in the Life-Cycle and Trauma-Related Metaphors: Life-Stage Specific Metaphors (LSSM)

The case histories and illustrations of disturbances in self-continuity and coherence represent only two of six central structural components of the self (Wilson, 2006). The issues of continuity and coherence in the self bring to light the necessity to know how trauma impacts the entire life-spectrum of the epigenesis of identity and personality. This fundamental question is essential to critical psychological analysis, scientific understanding, and diagnostic capability. How do traumatic events effect epigenesis, organismic life-span developmental processes within a ontogenetic framework? At present, there is little, if any, empirical, evidence-based data on this critical question (see Wilson, 2006, for a discussion).

Epigenesis and Critical Questions

In terms of epigenesis among the life-span necessary and most salient questions are these: (1) At what age and where, in the life-cycle epigenetic development, did the traumatic experience occur? (2) What was the specific impact to a specific stage of epigenetic life-cycle identity-foundation and self-processes? (3) How are the normative psychosocial crises and stages of the life-cycle potentially impacted by trauma? (4) What are the critical differential effects of trauma in infancy, childhood, adolescence, young or middle-adult and old age? (5) In a corresponding way, how do such age-specific traumatic experiences become incorporated in trauma-specific metaphors (TSM) at different phases and stages of life itself? Clearly, there are many more interesting and empirically testable ideas from these basic considerations which could potentially lead to both clinical evidence-based research and controlled empirical research investigations.

We presented, in a previous work, a complex analysis of trauma and epigenesis in the life-cycle based on Erik Erikson's (1968) and Lifton's (1976) seminal psychoformative framework (Wilson, 2006). Using this modified and expanded conceptual, theoretical, empirical paradigm it was possible to examine the normative (i.e., typical psychosocial) developmental crises and how traumatic experiences impacted them in developmentally specific ways for nascent or clearly emergent developmental processes. When trauma "hits" the child or adolescent or adult, it is not unlike a natural disaster (i.e., tornado, hurricane, tsunami, mudslide, flood disaster involving traumatic loss, etc.), it impacts existing structures of "self- and personality processes" (i.e., existing structural components). The disaster impact can "hit" some or all of the self-structural dimensions, ego-processes and personality traits, states, and ongoing adaptational processes. Like a tumultuous Hurricane Katrina, it can hit some or all of self and personality processes and structural dimensions. How, then, to assess properly the psychosocial and long-term developmental processes?

Alterations in Vitality, Resilience, and Self-Soothing Capacities

In a healthy self there is a positive valence in energy in the capacity to engage the world and to be self-soothing and resilient in the face of adversity. The pre-trauma person may experience himself as energetic, influential, competent, and capable. Under extreme stress he may not manifest hardiness, stamina, and courage by being overwhelmed by trauma. Trauma damages these self-states and internal psychic energies. Now the victim/survivor may feel weak, impotent, passive, vulnerable, defenseless, unresponsive, fragile, and depressed. Afterwards, when challenged, be withdrawn, demoralized, that they have lost nerve or breakdown, in terms of depleted resources of energy.

In this chapter, Luke said he is "wiped out"; Stewart said he "felt paralyzed." In terms of response to challenge, Jerome felt like a "flat *cardiogram, already nailed in his coffin.*" He might have described himself as an engine using 90% of its energy to prevent losing control and 10% to stay alive.

Paralyzed and in a State of Psychic Stasis

As discussed previously, Stewart, a depressed and anxious Vietnam veteran, complained to his doctor that in his current life he felt paralyzed. He was unable to make decisions, to get out of the house, and to take on tasks and challenges. He conveyed a sense of fear of doing harm if he were to take action and disparagement of his inactivity. The damaged sense of a vital self expressed as his paralyzed state was only growing worse as his treatment approached the actual content of his trauma in Vietnam.

There Stewart had felt paralyzed, separated, and silent on a hill and in heavy foliage but able to hear his buddy who had been captured by the Viet Cong who were torturing him and severing his limbs while alive. Choosing to stay alive had meant abandoning his buddy and remaining inert. This psychic inertia characterized his posttraumatic life. Paralysis captured Stewart's existential dilemma in war and his current life. His conscious and unconscious guilt for his friend's death made his inability to move on with his life in the present plausible but unconsciously unbearable. The self-preservative instinct to remain inert would have to find a new place in his self-image before he could move on. His therapist would need to be his receptive, open ally in this endeavor to manifest empathy and emotional honesty. In terms of his self-processes, all six dimensions were diminished: continuity, coherence, connection, autonomy, vitality, and energy. To regain a healthy, positive identity, he would need to transform himself and the difficult journey of the Hero (HS) that would exhibit a multitude of trauma metaphors along the way of his journey of self-understanding and transformation.

Jerome: The Nails Are Already in My Coffin

Jerome said he had seen too much death. When his therapist asked him if he was going to react in some way to seemingly unfair circumstances at work, he responded "The nails are already in my coffin." While capturing a self that has lost all capacity to respond to challenge, this survivor's phrase also harkened back to a mental image that had grown out of his role of bagging bodies in war. Here was the clinical challenge to empathize with someone who thought of himself as dead, identifying with the victims of combat. Here, he was using this state of mind to defend himself in the present from facing uncomfortable interpersonal pressures.

Alterations in Attachments and Personal, Intimate Relationships

Trauma metaphors give important clues to the clinician regarding the person's capacity for attachment and characteristic configuration of object relations. While some theorists categorize "connection" as within the structure of self, others see these capacities in terms of separate elements in psychic structure, namely object relations to others and attachment and societal engagement capabilities.

Psychic structure, following trauma, may be altered or damaged in all dimensions. Trauma metaphors are portals to understanding the nature of these potentially damaged structural and governing parts of personality and identity. The healthy pre-traumatic individual feels connected to others, experiences closeness as enhancing, and is positively tied to others in affirmative groupings. A basic sense of love and belongingness.

At its negative polarity the posttraumatically damaged person finds himself or herself separated from others, split off, and divided. All this leads to alienation, disconnection, disengagement, isolation, reclusive and secretive behaviors.

Dante: Haunted Memories and Hyperarousal Dispositions

Dante, a guarded, suspicious veteran, described his life as a constant worry about his family's safety. The intensity of the fear impacted his sense of efficacy and mastery as he had been a successful student, athlete, and young entrepreneur. He paused and emphasized the word "haunted" to describe his life. While he realized his fear was partially irrational, he also understood that the context in which he was assigned to kill the enemy was one of blood feuds among warring clans. The mental-health counselor, by taking the self-state "haunted" seriously, helped Dante describe the world in which he lived, a world where old blood feuds were likely to be avenged. For Dante the likelihood of retribution against him was credible. No one before had understood that. He left his understanding existentially alone and isolated and, indeed, "haunted."

Sarah: I Am on the Outside Looking In

Sarah, the mother of a 19-year-old, who had died suddenly in an accident (as described earlier), felt disconnected from her life course and from the world around her, particularly the young people who had previously been such a major part of her life. She painted an image of herself, her face peering into the light of an active world of young people, while her body was in total darkness. She described the image as outside looking in, as in the Motown hit by Smokey Robinson in 1963, the central lyric of which is: "I'm on the outside looking in, but I don't want to be on the outside looking in anymore." Her metaphor was found in the Motown music (get the CD recording).

Dominic: A Hole in My Heart

Dominic, the father of a 17-year-old who committed suicide, spoke of a "literal hole in his heart," one that he could not fill up with contacts with others or by reconnecting with previously fulfilling relationships including his wife. Both parents experienced intolerable traumatic loss and separation. Dominic's narrative of his son's death was filled with questions of blame. His clinician needed to understand and convey that the more central issue was feeling alone in the extraordinary degree of his loss.

Other survivors whose damage to psychological structures is in the area of altered object relations and attachment, warn their contacts in the present to be wary of the harm that will come by maintaining a connection to them. It is a posttraumatic, grief-stricken loss of a loved one in a hypervigilant/hyperaroused state and pushing others away to feel safe.

Mario: Look Out for the Hoodlums, Thugs, Con-Artists, and Sociopaths

Mario, a survivor of the Beverly Hills Supper Club fire that killed hundreds of patrons, withdrew from all contacts and isolated himself. He reported to his therapist that a recurrent image stayed in his mind. It was of hoodlums beating up innocents. The victim in the image would be left to die. But in the fire, in order to survive, this patron pushed his way ahead in the fracas at the partially blocked exit door leaving behind him those who would not escape. He had personal guilt placed on him in the role of enabling the death of others. The unusual phrase, "beware of hoodlums," was a warning and a self-punishment as he felt he had behaved like a hoodlum and had not taken action to prevent the fire and what happened. Later, he sought isolation, because staying in contact with him was a danger to others, or so he felt. To be alone was to be safe, secure, and free of reoccurrence. To be isolated was comfort, if not freedom, from others and unremitting survivor guilt. In this sense, a respite from recurring moral dilemmas and intrusive images of failed enactments.

Alterations in Identity: The Loss of Self-Sameness, Continuity, and Ego-Agentic Efficacy

Jake's Case History: Every Bone in My Body

What was striking in this quiet, mannerly Iraq veteran's expression was not so much the choice of words, but the shift in his pronouns. He was a former power-builder and weight-lifter; a very big man of 320 pounds. Describing his seemingly warranted frustrations, he burst out with: "I am so angry I could break every bone in *my* body" (a Freudian parapraxis).

This apparent misstatement of pronoun in the idiom was a clue to the discomfort he had with powerful avenging fantasies and sadistic impulses that burdened his everyday thinking. It was not a far step to explore the actual events in combat where he lost control of his anger at the captured enemy and now expected retaliations.

In his modified metaphor, one can see how the unconscious defense of identification with the victim turned the idiom on its head; indicating that the survivor struggles with the powerful forces of turning aggression against the self, inside out, inverted and other sublimated transformations. Unjustified killing became unjustified surviving and maybe a lot more in the future.

Altered Moral Judgment Processes, Tests of Intelligence and Coherence: Posttraumatic Guilt and Existential Dilemmas

With the turning against the self in "*every bone in my body*" we begin to see how central moral judgments exist in trauma metaphors. We have already seen such metaphors such as Dante's feeling haunted by others who would kill him in retaliation, Stewart's guilt over his paralysis while his friend was tortured and killed. Kent's surviving while his friend drowned; Francis's wish that it were his clipped heel at the morgue rather than the young man's.

Survivor guilt, the sense that the survivor could or should have done something to save others or themselves, is alive and well within many of the phrases and associations connected to them that we are calling trauma metaphors. There is damage to the structure of the mind, potentially long-standing, that assigns responsibility for one's actions. The long-term shadow of moral judgment metaphors that often presumptively blame the self for actions can be major blocks to the regaining of initiative and confidence necessary for the adaptation of returning home from the abyss of a myriad of natures, some unspeakable.

Throughout the discussion of ego-processes, self-functions, disrupted personality, internalized objects, and superego-normal functions, we have drawn corollaries between the metaphor and the subjective trauma experiences and the internal psychic processes they represent. One might infer that these connections are direct or facile.

Nothing could be further from the truth. The connection between the trauma-specific metaphor (TSM) and its meaning based solidly in or near the subjective memory itself, is often complex and requires trust, safety, a good working alliance, and clinical skill. We shall address this further in Chapter 6. We shall also examine in more detail the formal aspects of the baseline subjective experience, the Special Configuration of the Traumatic Event (SCTE).

Trauma Metaphors: Challenges for PTSD Trauma Therapists, Researchers, and Decision-Makers Over Funding the Critical Studies and Scientific Crucibles of the Omega Point

One of the critical and most urgent concerns of the clinician assessing the traumatized survivor is the question of suicidal risk, especially for Iraqi and Afghan war veterans (see Wilson, 2006, for a discussion of suicidality in trauma victims). This is particularly the case for traumatized war veterans. Are there clues from within the unusual phrases expressed, the trauma metaphors, that survivors spontaneously choose that increase our captured concern regarding suicide? Yes, a lot of them!

Approaching this question retrospectively, we know that of the 67 severe cases we reference in this book, three made serious attempts on their life to warrant hospitalization. Fortunately, none were completed suicides. All were cries for help and understanding, and their trauma metaphors (TSM) may have provided the therapist the portal of entry to their traumatic PTSD world.

It is interesting to examine these three cases in terms of their presenting trauma metaphors. Bill, an Iraq veteran whose case we shall explore in more detail in Chapter 5, wanted to bang or bash someone's head against the wall and in fact began doing so during the interview. Chris, a survivor of a civilian fire, awoke from a nightmare in which e was about to crash and burn. A Vietnam veteran, Chris, ended his session in a lissociative state, murmuring that he would have to "go back up the hill" (a suicidal nission with overwhelming enemy presence and dismembered bodies nearby).

In each of these trauma-specific metaphors (TSM) they referenced extreme violence (bashing, crashing, and a dismembered torso). Imagery in each metaphor referenced an impending loss of impulse control. Two involved violence proceeding to the point of the grotesque. All referenced traumas in which there was extensive loss of life, terror, potential death, or witnessed death. In context, each involved severe guilt. All three involved enactments in the clinical situation, where trauma was not remembered but was being re-lived in a dissociative state. All were men and each denied a specific plan for suicide out of unresolved PTSD and complicated intrapsychic pain.

In this small sample of suicidal trauma patients, we find that imagery of violence, self-destructiveness, loss of impulse control, guilt, and closeness to dissociation becomes a dangerous combination of factors. Depression and impulse are criteria clues to suicide attempts, especially with PTSD or major depressive diagnosis. It appears to us that careful assessment of the patient's spontaneous language may be of particular use in identifying those with the highest risks for self-injury and destruction. In short, PTSD + depression + impulsive existential despair = suicide risk. A formula for self-destruction to end posttraumatic pains.

Interestingly, almost all the patients referenced in this book from time to time considered the idea that life was no longer worth living. Their life journey, per Figures 1.2 and 3.1, was not a successful homecoming and re-entry. They were on the outside, sadly looking in, wondering, who gets understood which endured went through the foray of the journey. Will there be a Nurturing Guide (NG) to help them? Further research could test these hypotheses and would greatly help in this important assessment and treatment protocols.

This chapter has focused on trauma-specific metaphors (TSM) and traumatic injuries to internal psychic structures. How do traumatic experiences change the internal configurations of psychic states? Invariably they do to a greater or lesser extent to the core elements of personality, self- and ego-processes. This recognition is fundamental and essential for clinicians and researchers. Whether conducting a clinical examination, analysis for the purpose of diagnosis or interviewing a research participant for a study with approved IRB hypotheses, the greater the knowledge of trauma's impact to self-processes will open new portals of informed inquiry and significance.

In the way of summary, the relationship of ongoing and concurrent ego-states to the basis psychological journey of the Hero is essential to map out (see Chapter 1). As such, it is both simple and complex because it outlines aspects of the Hero-Survivor's journey that we have not yet explored but will in later chapters.

Summary

First, there are at least six agentic ego-states functions related to the posttraumatic self that represent the role of executive cognitive brain functions (see Figure 3.1). Second, we identify for clinical and research purposes ego-states functions: (1) agentic ego-strivings toward mastery of situations; (2) passive-agentic mastery-orientations, i.e., tendencies to depend on others for solutions; (3) dissociation and dissociative, disengagement and detachment processes; (4) the organismic drive toward integration versus disintegrative processes; (5) fragmentation in daily ego-mechanisms and information-processing abilities; and (6) synthetic functions; attempts to make things work and integrate in the service of good adaptations. These ego-processes are, of course, totally continuous with personality and self-processes, but more evident in day to day and hour to hour interpersonal relations. There are fluctuating states of ego- and self-processes following trauma. They vary hourly, daily, weekly, and monthly. As such, they reflect the Journey of the Hero (JTH), the Failed Hero (FH) and how all of this incredible journey gets experienced in trauma metaphors (see Chapter 1).

When lucky, the Hero-Survivor, as contrast to the Mythical Non-Hero (Campbell, 1949), finds a Nurturing Guide (NG) to assist the homecoming experience. The Non-Hero suffers enduring tribulations and disturbing memories. These troubling traumatic memories thus appear in trauma metaphors, often for a lifetime in complex, haunting, and creative forms (see Chapter 5).

We move our interest in the trauma metaphor in the next chapter, from the traditional clinical perspective where it is an adjunct to pertinent and accurate assessment of ongoing psychological functioning, to a non-traditional perspective where we see trauma metaphor as an expression of the Hero myth. In particular, capturing detailed way-stations along the perilous journey from the Abyss to home. The Mythical Hero of Joseph Campbell's work of five decades is also the source of wisdom gleaned from mythology and its extensions to other academic and clinical domains. It is universal in its knowledge and utility, especially to traumatic metaphor analysis and decoding of encapsulated mental states. The posttraumatic trauma journey is simply that of Campbell's Myth of the Hero, translated and interpreted for our times of abyss, war, trauma, and discovery pathways to healing that leads to transformed states of living with a sense of integrity and well-being in the here and now of everyday life.

4 Trauma Recovery

Perils in the Journey from the Abyss of Trauma to Self-Integration

We suggest that cultures share myths that serve as a metaphoric scaffolding on which to locate the life situation of a trauma survivor. Myths, rituals, and culturally-based ritual practices have evolved for a purpose and set of functions to assist survivors in their journey to personal peace and recovery (Wilson, 1989). Their design, structure, and evolution are inevitably culture-specific and yet universal and archetypal in nature, a common human pathway in psychological design. Scientifically understanding them leads to the discovery of portals of entrance (POE) to "unsaid posttraumatic constellations" across cultures throughout the world (i.e., posttraumatic secrecy, the non-disclosed and unsaid aspects of the Abyss Experience). How do we discover hidden posttraumatic places of its treasury of riddles?

As described in Chapter 1, Joseph Campbell's Myth of the Hero (1949) offers the classic mythological and essential phases of the journey to and from the Abyss Experience (AE). Onto this seminal literary structure we can affix the survivor's own trauma-related metaphors that best describe his or her place along the journey home to a desired posttraumatic place of safety, comfort, and respite. Understanding metaphors as way-stations along a mythical and unexpected life journey, psychic route, allows the survivor and the clinician or Nurturing Guide (NG) to see spontaneous language as a clue to the readiness to go further in recovery as well as the need to rest temporarily in protected spaces of protection and safety.

Our posttraumatic conceptual analysis builds the therapeutic alliance as a positive forward-looking journey for the survivor who will inevitably run into walls, blocks, detours, abysses, crevasses, further life-stresses, and encounter flooding states of emotional and overwhelming painful memories. Nurturing self-sustaining states require rest, safe way-stations, time outs, resources for resilience, and emergency psychic supplies of all sorts for psychic well-being. Posttraumatic recovery includes inventive strategies, bridge building and insights, to move beyond the traumatic-interference in the idiosyncratic life-journey road of recovery to eventually discover the often clouded or uncertain highway to home. The complex understanding of PTSD is the total discovery of the patient's profile of adaptation, from dawn to dusk, day in and day out, week to week. It is a very complex behavioral profile of adaptation.

As with emotional resistance to self-exploration and discovery of internal processes of any kind in counseling and psychotherapy, clinician and survivor must pause respectfully to absorb and understand the source of each obstacle or psychological block of resistance along the complicated pathway of recovery. In the best psychological sense, it is a mutually received reciprocal process of empathy and respect, often understood in "unsaid or unspoken ways" until the proper moment allows trauma disclosure. In short, the "unsaid" of trauma experiences in all of its ugly colors and realities. At that critical moment, the "unsaid" becomes the "said" and life, at that critical therapeutic or epochraphul moment, changes in new directions.

The imagery contained in these references to problems confronting the mythological trauma traveler on his or her journey home, captures the displaced shadow of a temporarily adaptive mental state within a portion of the trauma experience itself. As with other trauma metaphors, pausing to explore sometimes unexpectedly "opens" previously hidden areas of emotional-psychic distress that needs working through within the trauma history itself in order to clear the way so that the survivor may continue the journey home, if lucky, with a Nurturing Guide (NG) to assist. In a spiritual sense, what is trauma in its purpose for self-transformation? What are the lessons that traumatic experiences can teach about life living and day to day existence?

Trauma and PTSD are more than a single stress response syndromes. It is more than a self-limited pathogen. It is more than a faulty set of core beliefs about life, fairness, justice, wars, and political movements. Ultimately, it calls for more than neurophysiologic, psychopharmacologic, or educational models in its humanistic-educational recovery efforts to heal injuries to the self. To understand psychic trauma and its impact is to ultimately understand the complexity of life itself, as every therapist discovers. Every trauma therapist knows this as a transition in their own life-journey, a parallel to their patients, but often with avoidance to introspect into their own portals of entry of difficult life events. In this sense, therapists and patients are on a reciprocal, parallel endeavor but one that is not often connected reciprocally.

The Residue of Trauma in the Unconscious is Timeless

Since exposure to trauma bears on the existential core of the survivor, the task of absorbing its impact in the direction of recovery will take time and go through expectable stages of progression, regression, and self-reinvention. How else could it be in the troublesome tasks of sorting it all out? There is a lot of posttraumatic material to process in life's progression. As Freud noted, the unconscious is timeless. What is unconscious can emerge anytime, anywhere in the life-cycle at any age. So, what the trauma survivor thinks about the past may emerge at any stage or age in the life-cycle, with special transferred intrapsychic configurations and structures. Unprocessed, unmetabolized trauma memories may "rear" their "historical head" at any time in living, at any moment of being "triggered" by trauma-specific stimuli (TST).

Enduring such confrontations within the Abyss Experience (AE) strains the survivor to the utmost in terms of personal resources, physiological and psychological capacities. To help cope with such stresses, cultures worldwide have passed on for generations stories of their special Heroes/Survivors who have mastered such calamities, disaster, war, and catastrophe. These are the myths that Campbell elucidates in their complexity in mythology and are transgenerational educated resources of information.

The Myth of the Hero's Journey Redux

In the broadest overview, the tables in Chapter 4 condense and summarize the essential data and graphics of critical analysis for our understanding. To begin, the list below presents a capsule summary of the Hero's journey with respect to five major points of significance from the pre- and posttraumatic departure destinations: (1) the encounter with the call to duty; (2) the encounter with the "dark" forces of the mission and extreme stress; (3) entering foreign or unknown spaces of danger without proper guidelines, maps, or knowledge of what is to be expected or encountered; (4) actually traversing the travails of the foreign territory and difficult human decisions in that "forbidden" space; and (5) encountering the Abyss Experience (AE) and the near death realities of existential realities.

The Mythic Hero's Journey

- A call to duty, mission, or life-journey.
- In the journey the encounter with dark forces, trauma encounters, and life-threatening experiences of bodily or psychic nature.
- Entering zones of danger without prior preparation, knowledge, experience, or the dark encounter.
- Experiencing unknown territory, foreign domains of ecological and cultural existence, and the travails of the unknown and uncharted pathways of one's journey without certainty as to the future and life itself.
- Encountering the Abyss Experience and the specter of the life–death paradigm of imminent existential realities.

Enduring the Hero/Survivor's Task

- Emerging from the journey and new realities of life and oneself.
- De-illusionment or disillusionment upon return from the epic journey or legacy of trauma.
- Experiencing changes in identity, self, and personality and belief systems.
- Existential questioning of why the journey has to happen and what it now means.
- Seeking a Nurturing Guide (NG) for help and advice.
- Mastering the challenges of homecoming and re-entry from the trauma journey.
- The development of insight and wisdom as to the meaning of the journey: illumination.

This list further highlights the enduring tasks of the Mythical Hero following the Abyss Experience (AE). In brief form, there are seven separate dimensions connected to the re-entry or posttraumatic phase of life experience: (1) the initial emergence from the travails of the life journey of a taxing and arduous nature; (2) phases of de-illusionment and disillusionment upon returning to the home culture and environment; (3) the growing and increasing awareness of changes in oneself in terms of identity, self-processes, and beliefs and value systems; (4) the nascent need to seek out or find a Nurturing Guide

(NG) for advice, guidance, or wisdom as to the homecoming post-Abyss Experience environment; (5) to become resilient and masterful in the return from the Abyss Experience (AE), i.e., to be competent and posttraumatically efficacious in daily living; (6) to develop insight and wisdom, i.e., to transform the trauma experience into an illuminated view of the future; and (7) the graduation, ultimate synthesis, and framework of personal meaning of the trauma abyss.

Beyond the Successful and Failed Hero/Survivor: How Does the Posttraumatic Life-Journey Continue?

Trauma Impacts to Core Ego-Processes and the Self

Table 4.1 differentiates the ego-states and personality dimensions of the successful and non-successful (failed) Hero/Survivor and the common, significant metaphors expressed in language. On the left side of Table 4.1 are the six primary functions of ego-states ad then, correspondingly, are represented the various aspects of the trauma survivor's successful or failed journey and correlated metaphors. For example, "I feel trapped in the trauma; I am hopeless; I am split apart; I am broken; I am diffuse and unglued." These and other metaphorical expressions are representative of internal, disrupted physical processes by traumatic life-events. For the therapist, they are important clues to the portals of entry (POE) to the inner sanctum of traumatic memories and ongoing efforts of cognitive reconstruction.

Perils in Unsuccessful Heroic Journey

Table 4.2 illustrates the perils of the unsuccessful Heroic Journey: What can go wrong upon the return from the Abyss Experience (AE). Table 4.2 delineates at least three major categories of the significant and expectable perils of the trauma survivor. Respectively, they are as follows: (1) wounds of the unsuccessful hero, of which, ten are outlined as expected and typical after the posttraumatic journey in the realm of the Abyss Experience (AE); (2) the multiple ways to be non-resilient and maladaptive upon return from the traumatic life journey; and (3) multiple ways to be self-destructive after the traumatic life journey ranging from substance abuse to various forms of risk behaviors.

Tables 4.1 and 4.2 summarize a wealth of useful information regarding the nature of the Hero/Survivor's traumatic journey and changes in the self, personality, and day-to-day functions. As such, these tables are not only useful guides but pointers to future areas of empirical investigations of many scientific designs and clinical interventions (see Chapters 9 and 10). In this way, this chapter is a prelude to those that will follow with more detailed analyses.

The Hero's Journey and Survivor Modalities: Adaptive Posttraumatic Functioning

There are many perils of the Mythic Hero-Survivor (MHS) so that in the actual build-up to and confrontation with the survivors Abyss, the ultimate of life-existence. The

Table 4.1 Trauma and Posttraumatic Ego-States in the Journey of the Hero/Survivor

Ego-States Functions	*Hero / Survivor*	*Failed Hero / Survivor*	*Trauma Metaphor*
I. **Agentic (Active Mastery) Strivings**	Transitional, Process of Re-entry to Culture	Fragile / Static Disconnected Ego-States	I am trapped in the trauma
II. **Passive Agentic (Anaclitic Orientation)**	Reclusive, Dependent	Withdrawal, protective	I am hopeless
III. **Dissociation**	Striving towards integration	Sense of dissociation, detachment, denial	I am split
IV. **Integration vs. De-Integration**	Self-awareness of Hero Journey and impact to self	Feelings of disparate self, fractures and instability in self	I am torn apart
V. **Fragmentation**	Search for new modes for reconfiguration of self	Feelings of stasis and failure to reintegrate identity caps	I am broken
VI. **Synthetic**	Active, prosocial step towards self-reinvention	Diffusion of thoughts and disorganized behavioral style	I am diffuse

journey home for the Imperiled Hero-Survivor is therefore a complex and incomplete emotional task with pauses and important psychological work necessary at each point in the journey of recovery where disillusionment of trauma reality replaces mythic fantasy. In short, the journey is filled with bumps and challenges of unimagined sorts, sources of self-search and desperation. To use another metaphor, it is often "rough sledding in the worst winter snow and tough times." In this sense, the snow is piled so deep that the ability to go against it is impossible. Try to conquer, overcome or lose?

This chapter organizes the points of likely peril in the Hero's journey along chronological lines. For each point of traumatic disillusionment, the task of reflection and renewal is delayed. How and why did these "shortfalls" in recovery occur? To what extent is the Trauma Hero responsible? To what extent should he or she have foreseen these consequences? During the situation of trauma, what else could or might have been done? What adaptations of resources did they have to use? If effective, do they find necessary coping strategies [unconsciously] repeating themselves along the journey home?

Our concerns are the phrases, behaviors, language, and communications that help the treating physician or trauma therapist understand the specific ways in which the journey has gone awry, the metaphors that tell the story and implicate much more about posttraumatic functions and adaptive behaviors as solutions to different encounters.

Table 4.2 The Perils of the Unsuccessful Heroic Journey: Beyond Trauma and PTSD

I. **Wounds of the Unsuccessful Hero**
   1. Inability to continue the journey dictated by Historical Fate.
   2. Sense of being stuck in the life-altering experience (i.e., trapped in the trauma).
   3. Sense of being in between the worlds of trauma and the world of re-entry.
   4. Sense of disillusionment to overcome the power of the Hero's immersion into dark, sinister and powerful forces.
   5. Feelings of ego-alien character change, personality alteration and identity confusion—stuck in the abyss.
      a. Redefine self in negative ways with emphasis on Shadow Archetype (Wilson, 2006).
      b. Addiction to hyperarousal and numbing cycles (i.e., prolonged stress response patterns).
      c. Profound difficulty in committing to a purpose greater than oneself.
      d. Choices available in society do not permit purposeful commitments of higher order.
      e. Hope at a critical stage for a future dissolves and results in hopeless bewilderment, similar to that experience in the trauma encounter.
   6. Rejection at homecoming after emerging from the Hero's journey due to alienation from a significant other.
   7. The genuine absence of a nurturing guide (i.e., necessary social, personal and emotional rebirth) makes successful adaptation and coping more complex and complicated.
   8. Feeling alienated from family and others who lack understanding of the Hero's journey.
   9. The emergent trend toward maladaptive patterns after failed initial attempts or successful reintegration.
   10. Spiritual disillusionment as to the meaning of life and beliefs in a Higher Power.

II. **Multiple Ways to be Unsuccessful Upon Re-Entry from Trauma Journey**
   1. Stagnate in the journey, inability to commit to a higher purpose.
   2. Extreme avoidance behaviors of all types (e.g., social) of commitment.
   3. Failure to confront the impact of trauma to oneself.
   4. Premature foreclosure on experience and self-reinvention possibility.
   5. Other creative vicissitudes of self-denial, hiding, and staying away from the world.

III. **Multiple Ways to Self-Destruct**
   1. Substance abuse.
   2. Pathological interpersonal relations of a destructive nature.
   3. High-risk behaviors that recapitulate fears experienced during trauma.
   4. Avoidance of reinventing a new sense of personal identity.
   5. Other creative ways to destroy the posttraumatic self.

Blindness to the Traumatic Encounters Incurred in Preparation for the Hero's Journey

For the Hero, difficulties, at least at the beginning, arise in the preparation and commitment to the task. He or she may be poorly prepared for his or her journey's task, may fail to have made a commitment to the cause or duty or may feel ostracized and disconnected from others; may be in the midst of negative morale, or find the leadership and logistical support wanting; his or her protection absent or defective; his or her supplies impaired or absent, or judgments about his actions or inactions may be harsh, misconstrued, or correct.

The beginning of the Mythical Hero's journey (MHJ) may come about as a surprise as it did to Jonah in the Old Testament story where an ordinary person is simply confronted with God's assignment. Or it may arise through volition as in a grown man's volunteering for combat as in Odysseus or the youthful volunteer of the Vietnam war. In either case, the Hero-Survivor, perhaps after periods of protest, embraces the challenge by committing him or herself to something ideologically transcendent (e.g., an ideal or ideological cause, mission, or special task of special or secret governmental importance).

Clearly, one form of the Hero's task is when disillusionment in the righteousness of the cause sets in, fermenting psychological doubt, anger, and uncertainty. While certainly this is not true of all difficult historical situations, it was the case for many Americans during the Vietnam war. Anger and uncertainty prevailed after the war experiences.

During this era, for veterans of World War II and Vietnam war draft age, there was such disaffection with the goals of the war that draftees chose to retreat to Canada or elsewhere, rather than fight a war that they believed was wrong. For others, it was after prolonged engagement in the Hero's task when disillusionment in its cause settled in even more profound ways. In the metaphors they brought to their postwar therapies, war-related metaphors became apparent and painful. Simply said, their disaffected voices were "What was it all about?"

Case Histories

Pete's Story: Twisted Steel Metaphors

Pete, in Vietnam, learned that the village he had advised had become a target of American aggression. While initially enthusiastic about America's goals, he later expressed his disillusionment to his therapist by bringing him a recording of Jimi Hendrix's "National Anthem," a musically distorted version of patriotism, expressing in tonal discord the view that he and his country had lost its way.

Pete volunteered to disable explosive ordnance in Vietnam in order to save lives. His skills ultimately led to the maiming of the enemy. He and his therapist believed that the recurrent dream in which a single image of "twisted steel" dominated a scene of devastation also conveyed "twists" in his ideals and behaviors away from idealistic ones he had first brought to Vietnam. His past was in the present. Where does it go from here? The dream symbolism and metaphors are his portals to the unconscious of the Vietnam war legacy.

The Nurturing Guide (NG): Wise Presence of Advice, Guidance, and Wisdom

Having received the initial outlines of his or her special mission, the Hero, as in *Star Wars*, meets a mentor, for example, Obi-Wan Kenobi, gains access to his light saber and practices with his new weapon until he has reached technical proficiency. In our Hero-Survivor's journey, the mentorship as a Nurturing Guide (NG), discipline and skill mastery that go with this preparation for his task leads to a state of readiness. It is hyperarousal readiness. Luke Skywalker is prepared to meet Darth Vader (i.e., his evil father) as is Achilles to attack Troy in ancient Greece. The mythic cycle completes in modern times (e.g., a state of readiness equals PTSD-related hypervigilance and states of excessive hyperarousal). Luke Skywalker was hypervigilant and prepared. Darth Vader believed he had the "Force" with him. In the end, he almost had it but lost it to his beloved son.

In the Imperiled Hero-Survivor's journey, the mentor may be absent and the uniform he wears may become a tattered, torn, tainted, or a disgraced blood-soaked old one. For example, Butch, trained as a U.S. Army infantryman, was suddenly placed in charge of a large number of Afghani prisoners without training as a prison guard. Fears of the new role frightened and embarrassed him lest his Farsi (Arabic) speaking prisoners would get out of control. In order to maintain control, Butch would suddenly break into life-threatening sadistic nonsense speech. He was consciously imitating a murderous character as in the Hollywood movie *Pulp Fiction*, played by actor Samuel Jackson. He brandished his weapon and threatened to kill or maim the prisoners for speaking a language he did not understand, frightening some to the point of losing control of their bowels. Upon return from the war, threatened by situations that might get out of control, he unconsciously re-enacted his traumatic dilemma when he would shout a string of threatening expletives and non-words at his wife or son. These "pulp fiction" outbursts became his unique metaphor for non-heroic functioning in a role for which he was not prepared. His therapist and he could name the identity of a "trauma shadow" from Iraq, this time affecting his new roles as husband and father of a toddler. Butch came to understand his war-related re-enactments. His life improved dramatically in due time. His trauma-related metaphors became a road of discovery and recovery.

Confrontation with the Abyss Experience (AE) and the Aftermath to Self-Structural Reconfigurations of the Self: Reinvention

Exposure to Death, Dying, Chaos, and Destruction

A profound sense of being stuck in the life-altering experience (i.e., belief in sense of the self dying, feeling trapped in the trauma) is always overwhelming and life-threatening. What is the horrible, phenomenologic feeling the survivor experienced with no exit or way to freedom?

In confronting the Abyss, the Imperiled Hero-Survivor may have been startled and shocked by the experience of death at close range, killing and seeing others killed, injured or maimed, bodily penetration (e.g., rape), catastrophic destruction, being exposed to the grotesque, or simply absorbing the overwhelming content of the trauma exposure.

The experience may have been one of total powerlessness or the opposite; someone holding power of life and death of others. Hence, the paradox of omnipotence versus helplessness and freedom to decide one's course of action. He or she may find fault with actions or inactions particularly as it relates to others with potentially worse outcomes. The Abyss Experience (AE) opens the Hero-Survivor to experiences beyond the expectable, a world in which the basic benevolence of the universe has gone awry and then raises questions about his own innate characteristics and the measuring of human life itself.

The Star Wars Trilogy: Myths of Characters and Personalities

In the rich worlds of mythology, after many confrontations and trials, Luke Skywalker must fight Darth Vader, David must do combat with Goliath, Odysseus must outwit the One-Eyed Giant. The result may be death to the protagonist or the maiming or killing of monsters. And the intensity of the experience will be forever life-changing. The Hero then emerges in self-defined character and striving.

In mythology and reality, history will now take a different turn. The protagonist Hero will come to appreciate the powers that rallied to his cause and celebrate. The Hero's journey has become imperiled.

The Traumatic Journey and Beyond: Case Illustrations

In illustrating the former situation, Stewart hid in the "bush" in Vietnam while the medic in his unit was ensnared, entrapped, and helpless. Stewart saved his own life by staying "frozen and paralyzed." The phrase "paralyzed" returned during his homecoming as a metaphor for procrastination in terms of taking action for his own adjustment to civilian life. His therapist also understood that "paralyzed" referenced his own accusation of cowardice in combat while the enemy tortured his friend and platoon member. In his psychic paralysis, in the present, Stewart was unconsciously maintaining the safe steady hidden state that kept him alive in war but now infused his life with survivor and moral guilt and prevented him from re-engaging life tasks. The metaphor (TSM) permitted the clinician to empathize with Stewart rather than argue against his resistance of feeling paralyzed. His psychic paralysis hid his guilt, grief, and profound sadness.

In another situation, a waiter at the Beverly Hills Supper Club bravely marched through the main dining area announcing the outbreak of the fire early on and instructing the patrons as to safe methods to exit. Later, his effort was thought to have saved many lives, honored at the U.S. White House. He afterwards continued to repeat outrageous brave and dangerous announcements until he collapsed in a hypomanic over-stimulated physical state. His repetitious brave announcements functioned as a metaphor casting a shadow on his ability to resume his less dramatic ongoing life tasks. Thus, being a "Hero" in the club fire became a new identity; one he could not readily accept or acknowledge.

Indeed, sometimes success at the summit breeds maladaptive repetitions in behavioral patterns. For example, a boy soldier in the Congo was taught to overcome fear and previous inhibitions to murder the "enemy." He felt ecstatic excitement in his new power to kill the identified enemy. Upon return to normal civilian life, he did not want to return to the ordinary experience of the adolescent in an adult world. He did not wish to trade his murderous power for civilized impotence, and remained stuck. The child warrior had become a precocious killer of God-like life and death power. Afterwards, he was an impotent person without his weapons of power and destruction. The boy morphed into a man of killing and destruction.

Managing Temptations: Values of the (Safe) "Middle Way" and Beyond

Faced with posttraumatic situations including total helplessness or total power over the life of others, the Hero/Survivor must manage the paradoxical twin temptation of falling victim to total passivity as a result of being fixated at the peak of life's power. The Imperiled Hero may be unable to hold his ground and maintain a middle way. The "middle way" is a ground for negotiation, resolution, and transition. Ultimately, the birth of a new posttraumatic future and self although initially amorphics in shape.

The Hero-Survivor's victory, when it occurs, comes about because he manages to survive amidst raging, emotional extremes within himself. As Odysseus sails between Scylla and Charybdis, he must avoid the seductive and the turbulent, the attraction to unnecessary danger and to the erotic components of violent tasks and foreign lovers. The existential dialectic of choices in extreme situations. To sustain focus or succumb. Dialectics of mind and body dominate consciousness.

The Imperiled Hero-Survivor gets caught up in the moment of power and finds pleasure in using his powers excessively and is self-serving. The result may be the death of innocence and persisting guilt or shame. For example, Jeb, a reconnaissance scout in Vietnam, precipitated a My Lai (1968) type massacre and atrocity. He referred to himself afterwards not as a elite American warriors but rather as a member of the vilified World War II Nazi Gestapo or S.S. The negative self-identification with the Nazi S.S. captured his ongoing guilt and self-recrimination. It represented a position of self-loathing, an affect and belief that his therapist could ultimately clarify and helped him to understand, although with great difficulty and effort.

The Imperiled Hero-Survivor may succumb to these potential realities and experience an ego-alien character change, a personality alteration and a sense of identity confusion (see Chapters 1 and 3). For example, Bill, an American Iraq war veteran, found himself in such a situation. He captured his dilemma metaphorically in a photograph he took of himself in battle gear, in which his innocent youthful face is contained in the aggressive uniform of full battle gear.

Bill succumbed to the sadistic desire to beat to death a captured Iraqi and became caught in the web of its adrenalized excitement and power so that it became addictive and obsessive to him. The photograph captures the contradiction produced when the innocent self abuts the simultaneous presence of the cruel and sadistic all-powerful distorted warrior self. The shadow side of personality shows itself. This personifies what Jung described as the Shadow Archetype. In short, the "dark side" to human personality and the self, or stated simply: The evil, ugly, demonic, disavowed, or hidden characteristics of personality.

Positive Changes in Character Structure and Personality

Within the confrontation with the Abyss Experience (AE), the Hero-Survivor may learn important human qualities that he or she possesses (Wilson, 2006). On the one hand they may be of a humbling humanly fallible nature, or on the other, they may reveal powerful strength of character previously hidden in the self that they did not know or recognize.

In the midst of the confrontation with the Abyss Experience (AE), features of characters evoked sometimes become fixed and as such impair the Hero-Survivor's journey home. Wounded Heroes like Bill, as presented above, have a sense of disillusionment in their own capacities to overcome the power of immersion into "dark, sinister and powerful forces or places." He and others redefine self in terms of their negative Shadow archetype. They feel as if they have been inhabited by the Lucifer effect (devil), and remain stuck in the Abyss Experience (AE) of negativity or personal entrapment for their actions.

Paradoxically, other wounded warriors and survivors of psychic trauma deny positive unconscious character states present at the height of the trauma that would help them in the continuing journey, if only they could access them via memory and integration to the self-structure. Furthermore, memory of these states can sometimes arise during the reflection that is part of the treatment experience or during re-enactments of the trauma with the therapist. For these Heroes-Survivors, who are unable to make progress on the journey home driven by shame and guilt, it turns out that the traumatic situation actually evoked highly positive character traits, forgotten behaviors which memory had consigned to the sidelines. These survivors edit their experience to conform with coincident negative character change while suppressing additional parts of the picture that underscore altruistic, life-saving, and positive character traits. How do they do it?

For example, Pete, whom we discussed previously, could not remove the picture in his mind of the excruciating experience of shooting a child who had been booby-trapped and the self-blame that went with his picture. But in his clinical session, while recounting the tragic, overwhelmingly traumatic situation, Pete made a protective gesture with his shoulder and elbow as though to keep his therapist clear of the "explosion" he was describing. Through this spontaneous, protective, and symbolic gesture, Pete and his therapist reconstructed the trauma story in more detail: To wit, that as the bomb (strapped to a Vietnamese child) was heading toward his comrades, Pete had shoved them aside before he fired his automatic rifle and the shell exploded. The gesture, with his shoulder in the therapist's office, carried the motoric symbol of his actual experience which was to push away his friend so as to save him from the scene of the killing and the explosion. This clinical case example is a good example of somatic, metaphoric, and symbolic expression of unresolved PTSD. Pete's characteristics of protecting those he loved had survived even in the midst of the inevitable contradictions of war, where he protected his friends while having to explode a bomb strapped on to a child, the killing that condensed his confrontation with the Abyss Experience (AE). With his memory frozen at the death of the child, Pete could only see abandonment of his life-long value of looking after the less fortunate in life. Reframed by his gesture both therapist and Pete could place in perspective the ongoing wish to protect them even in its seeming ironic traumatic complex situations and their aftermath.

In another case example, Nick, remembering his slipping on an industrial cleaner just before it caught fire, causing 70% burns to his body and complete transformation of his face, had a forgotten that one of the reasons he fell was that he was simultaneously pushing aside the superior who had announced the fatal chemical mixture was safe to use. The shove saved his boss from the fire. Later, as framed in the initial memory, Nick was at fault for clumsiness. He reframed using his gesture in the office, showed how his deep character of altruism had been evoked at the very moment that threatened and altered his life. Thus, the creation of an existential dilemma: Fire burns vs. survival, who wins?

Others find that admired qualities of trauma victims became hypertrophied or grandiose righteousness and guilt to the extent that in the face of the Abyss Experience (AE), they become consuming without achieving the desired end. For example, Luke, as a teenager, was highly religious. Growing up in a world in which the helpless and downtrodden were taken advantage of, he wanted to change the world, to be a witness in a community of believers. In Iraq, Luke's biblical devotion to saving others as a medic became an addiction characterized by prolonged stress with accompanying hyperarousal and prolonged numbing at the conclusion of these episodes. There were no limits to his willingness to risk himself to help others; to be a devoted medic.

Once back home, Luke reported the trauma metaphor of being consumed and wiped out. He sought needy women to rescue. Inevitably his offer to help was overruled or rejected. For example, he tried to console a girlfriend with leukemia in the hospital but she refused to let him see her. In response to the rejected help, he felt wiped out and consumed, as with most attempts with securing the affection of women.

Luke's particular way of describing his exhaustion in the present had its metaphoric origin in a traumatic situations in the geographical Sunni triangle of Iraq. In addition to American injured warriors, there were Iraqi children who needed medical help. Because of limited resources, these children were triaged elsewhere. One child, whom he tried to help but was overruled by superiors, had her skull crushed when she was used as a human shield in front of a rocket grenade (RPG) launcher. His thought was, "In this war where children become sacrificed as weapon shields, my wish to help the downtrodden has no effect." Rather, his being prohibited from helping the child left him with the conviction that, along with the victims, he had failed in his values. They and he had been wiped out by forces of politics, malfeasance, and the U.S. military.

The hope of changing the world was being replaced by the conviction of being unable to help and consumed with his powerlessness. Hope that reappeared during his recovery, retreat and at critical stages, dissolve temporarily, regressing to the state of being consumed and wiped out that characterized his war experience. But here, knowing that the setback along the journey home was temporary, helped both Luke and his therapist retain a positive attitude during the working through phase of the recovery process (see Figure 1.1 and Chapter 5 in totality).

Then and Now: Killing Monsters and Illumination of Universal Mythic Polarities

While the Hero of Myths kills "monsters," the Hero of trauma takes aim at the monsters of the contemporary world: war, rape, incest, disaster. His or her task is to carry out his mission and to survive with physical wholeness and integrity. In confronting the unimaginable he or she also gains insight as to the nature of humankind, the universe and their role in it and subsequently readjusts goals for the future.

In the *Star Wars* movies by George Lucas, Luke Skywalker must fly his spaceship to deliver a fatal knock-out shot to the heart of the Darth Vader. He must use his laser-sword to defend himself and to unmask his father, Darth Vader (i.e., mythological representation of evil) in his abode. Armed with commitment to a virtuous mission, careful discipline from a mentor and the right equipment, Luke, the cherished positioned war veteran, warrior, Hero-Survivor, immobilizes the monsters in his world and gains illumination regarding insights concerning evil, power, love, and consumption. He, having confronted the Abyss, then prepared the journey home, to re-enter the world left behind. But the Nurturing Guide (NG), Yoda, is now gone. Who is to be the next Nurturing Guide (NG)?

The Imperiled Hero-Survivor often feels stuck in the life-altering experience (i.e., trapped in the trauma). For some, the "intoxication" of the power of life and death over others may become exciting and addicting. Alternatively, the conviction that failure in the moment of confrontation with the Abyss leaves the survivor full of guilt and shame, without the energy to continue, a depletion of soul energy. These two psychoformative realities co-exist in consciousness and unconsciousness and are not easily resolved and may persist for an entire lifetime. For example, in Chapter 1, we describe posttraumatic emotions and symptoms in Pearl Harbor survivors, 45 years after the Japanese attack.

In yet another example, Bill abhorred the idea of readjusting to civilian life; he longed now for what he called "metaphorically" the "sadistic experience" of his life. Similarly, Vince, whom we met earlier because his language lacked organizing syntax and clarity, had signed up for three tours in Vietnam, longing for the adrenaline high in combat, the hormonal rush and living on the edge of life itself.

The Inability of the Hero-Survivor to Come Home as Wished and Hoped for as Before the Trauma Abyss

Case Illustrations of Failed Heroes

Sometimes what remains from the confrontation with the Abyss Experience is the knowledge that the Trauma Hero's efforts were not vindicated nor validated. The Imperiled Hero (IH) feels compelled to stay in the trauma-reality, refusing to comply with the outcome dictated by historical fate or the authorities.

A veteran client, Bennett, can still see the Afghanistan village from which the RPG was fired that killed everyone in his military vehicle but him. His wish to avenge the deaths of his buddies represents for him an unfulfilled mission. Nothing at home can substitute for the drive to return to the scene of battle in efforts to change the outcome of historical fate. Yet, he is hyperaroused and desires to kill the enemy all the time.

Wayne was an acknowledged Hero in Afghanistan, decorated for saving the life of a comrade hit by enemy fire. Yet, his own nightmares and recurrent images were of the many individuals he accompanied who were fatally wounded. It seemed to him that he should have been the one to die, yet fate had singled him out to survive. Why me, he asks?

A Native American veteran spoke of dreams of birds of prey losing their kill because a larger predator was threatening. He sought help from the shaman and the sweat lodge of his tribe for release from the impact of traumatic images. His dream image referred to an incomplete mission; an order to retreat before he could avenge the death of his best friend, fate interfering with completing the mission.

War combat means confronting death, especially death of one's enemies and comrades. Caring for their bodily remains and honoring funerary rights including grief and mourning is a special task. There are psychic retaliatory demands to avenge wrongful deaths.

Re-Entry Difficulties: Rejection by the Home-Based Culture of Origin

The perils of the unsuccessful Heroic Journey are legendary and tragic in nature as they existed long before PTSD as a diagnosis in the self. Table 4.2 highlights and summarizes the three major dimensions of the Failed-Hero's journey: (1) the ten wounds of the unsuccessful Hero; (2) the specific ways the Hero is unsuccessful upon re-entry from the trauma journey; and finally (3) the multiple roads to self-destruct in the post-recovery environment.

Alienation and Rejection From Close Friendship Networks and Affectional Relationship Bonds

Although it seems counterintuitive, the returning Hero-Survivor is often rejected by the larger community of which he or she was a part and left on their journey. The roots of this rejection are complex, and involve the wish on the part of the unaffected community to deny and disavow the full impact of what they have been spared, the corpus body of the non-involved.

The returning trauma survivors may feel rejected by those who need to keep their distance from their trials and adjustment tribulations. Once again, metaphor plays a role. This time in its negative form. To be alone, to be rejected, to be isolated, to be without a Nurturing Guide (NG), is a harbinger of bad faith and the future.

Americans greeted returning Vietnam veterans by literally spitting on them as "baby-killers, drug addicts and killers." In this most pernicious form of public vitriolic protest against the war in Vietnam, American protesters, non-survivors themselves, could blame the warriors for the unpopular war they had served in at the summons of the whole body politic (i.e., everyone who voted for their elected representatives), for the war to be accepted.

After the Buffalo Creek dam disaster (1972) and flood placed pressure on the coal companies for their responsibility (i.e., the Buffalo Mining Company), in the catastrophe, the governor of West Virginia said in a speech that the event was an Act of God, thereby refusing culpability for a political and economic gain. A subsequent precedent lawsuit found differently for the trauma survivors: PTSD, anxiety, depression, and other psychological problems were recognized and awarded compensation. They were awarded a precedent 13 million dollars in damages.

In another case, after a crush killed youngsters waiting to enter the Cincinnati Coliseum for a "Who" concert, journalists implicitly blamed the victims when they described the event as a mob scene with the villains being new barbarians. Similarly, "don't touch them, they glow in the dark" was the metaphoric phrase used by neighbors not exposed to the radiation spill that endangered others. The metaphor stigmatizes and ostracizes the victims, as occurred in Hiroshima and Nagasaki as well (Lifton, 1967).

In the film-video *Eighty-first Blow*, a Holocaust survivor speaks of the impact of trying to explain her experience of being struck 80-plus times by a Nazi guard. Nevertheless, none of the blows was so great as the "unwillingness of her former neighbor" to listen to the story upon return home. The larger society's wish to "wash their hands" at the homecoming of the survivors' plight is often captured in negative terms as in the above illustration. In this way the larger society can avoid culpability, blame the victim, and ostracize and alienate them which they do after extreme stress.

These powerful societal ways of organizing trauma for those not directly affected enable bystanders to keep their distance from the existential despair of their fellow family, friends, and citizens. They can villainize those who return from the Abyss Experience (AE) offering demonizing metaphors that further drive the wounded survivors away. They stand as hindrances to developing constructive metaphors in the aftermath of trauma and in the recovery process of their disrupted lives.

PTSD Syndromes and Self-Destructive Behavior: Adaptational Patterns of a Maladaptive Nature

The Imperiled Hero-Survivor, once home, surprised by a world of potential comforters who sometimes make matters worse, then finds characteristic ways to self-destruct out of unmetabolized trauma. There are levels and degrees of these self-destructive behavior, actions, impulses, and processes. While some of these behaviors have their origin in the homecoming reception itself (i.e., from Vietnam, Korea, Iraq, Afghanistan, etc.) more likely than not the behaviors are also remnants of the trauma circumstances themselves. The tension between the trauma experience(s) and the self become so paramount that engaging in self-destructive, "action-junkie" extreme activities is paradoxically enlivening, and on the surface, sensical while being paradoxically self-destructive in nature. Living on the edge in feeling shame, guilt, and despair (Wilson, 1989).

Rejection by close family relationships and society pale in comparison to the damage the returning Hero-Survivor unconsciously brings on himself or herself. An arrangement of self-destructive behaviors arise in response to reminders of the trauma. They come about as the survivor fends off the fear that the original trauma, based on similar precipitating sensations or configurations, will repeat in full force at almost any time. So, what is left? Hypervigilance, hyperarousal, and being alert on the edge, to go on with life as known at the moment. For these Iraqi and Afghani war veterans, it is, for many of them, just another fucking war.

Case Examples

Helen: Pathological Intimate and Personal Relationships

For many trauma survivors, trusting relations become suspicious ones. Loved figures become objects of attack and mistrust. Annoying but innocent provocations result in extreme behaviors that drive a wedge between the loved ones and friends.

Helen, having reported her rape to the police, could not return to work for over one year, fearing that in her absence, harm would come to her children as promised by the perpetrator. The phrase "it's not safe to go out" captured her specific fear, said everything.

A survivor of rape, Helen had recurrent dreams repeating the threat her rapist left her with, untold fear and trepidation. He threatened that he would come to her house and kill her children. In fact, she could not return from the Abyss Experience (AE) because her current life was heavily weighted with the fear of the threat that he made to her. She felt trapped. A generalized agoraphobia had set in post-rape, altering all of her key relationships. She felt unbalanced and always afraid, wondering about the next moment in life. What is tomorrow's angst?

For many war veterans, especially those in combat areas of operations, maintaining a marriage after return from combat was difficult. Many combat veterans drive their spouses away by frightening them with combat-based hyperarousal states especially in their sleep, or when intoxicated with alcohol. The friends of war do not abate.

Vince's wife left him because of his non-stop confrontations with violence and alcohol. Understanding these assaults posttraumatically offers empathic opportunity that other approaches do not. Unconscious re-enactment is just one of many forms of re-enactment or re-experiencing of traumatic psychic states and PTSD symptom phenomenology.

Chris: High-Risk Behaviors and PTSD Actions

Chris, a survivor of the Beverly Hills Supper Club fire (1977) could not stabilize his life after trauma. Rather, as such, it was an ongoing series of catastrophes. He complained that his life was "too hot to handle." He lost two jobs because of impulsive action, rode his motorcycle recklessly despite the death of his brother in such an accident, and impulsively considered divorce. The metaphor that life was too hot to handle aptly described his hazardous journey home from his near-death in the fire. Over a hundred persons died in the supper club fire from which he escaped. Some survivors continue high-risk behaviors and activities as unconscious re-enactments of the hyperarousal and adrenaline-infused action during the traumatic event.

Harold: Substance Abuse

Efforts to numb the recurrent intrusive images of the trauma lead to alcohol and drug dependence and abuse. This in turn adds new layers of separation from previously positive relationships and, with impaired judgment, may contribute to the high-risk behaviors as well.

Harold, an Iraq war veteran, described his current situation as one in which he felt blank and black at times. This referred to periods where he could not remember his behavior and was often precipitated by excessive alcohol consumption. If the road home from the war was a journey, when Harold preferred to blank out and black out his vision and his steps rather than to see them clearly. Harold was adopted as three-year-old after severe child abuse and abandonment. He found relief in discharging aggression as an effective gunner in Iraq, but then was knocked unconscious by a roadside IED. Harold lost his career and fears the long-term impact of his traumatic brain injury (TBI). The blank and black sensation repeats both his experience of the explosion in Iraq and the sensation he seeks and enjoys with alcohol.

Suicidal Behaviors and Self-Destructive Tendencies

The extreme version of self-destructive behaviors is suicide (Wilson, 2006). Extremity of existential stress, guilt and recrimination, distress at failure to readjust, broken relationships and loss of hope make suicidal thinking an intrusive-medicated response phenomenon. Keeping one's eye on the traumatized survivor who is apt to carry such thoughts into action is a primary consideration of the clinician. Depression, PTSD, impulsivity, and a lack of a viable future are red flags for potential suicide, as without a vision of support and a future existence there is nothing to prevent suicide. Suicide is obliteration of self. It is the end of personal identity and the survival of life processes itself. In dividing, identity is destroyed forever.

We have previously examined three cases where self-destructive actions were so severe as to require hospitalization: Cliff, Chris, and Bill. In each of these, there was a combination of violence, loss of impulse control, severe guilt, and a tendency toward dissociation. Their trauma metaphors, "back to the hill," "I'm going to crash," and "I feel like bashing a head against the wall" gave important clues to dissociated trauma events and to violent despair in the present moment.

Avoidant Behaviors

The fear of confronting the memories of trauma (i.e., the Abyss Experience) and pain remembering, the survivor would rather that his problem simply go away. He turns to medication or alcohol to numb him. He engages in a variety of avoidant behaviors to provide some safety from the threat of the trauma's repetition, and the fear of further psychological working through.

There are multiple ways for the imperiled survivor to lose his or her way along the journey home (see Figure 1.1). He might stagnate in the journey, find himself unable to commit again to a higher purpose, engage in extreme avoidance behaviors, fail to confront the impact of trauma, or prematurely foreclose the risk of engaging new phases appropriate challenges. Finally he or she may be reluctant to engage the task of posttraumatic self-reinvention. In short, they surrender emotionally and psychologically in posttraumatic states until transformed.

We identify many metaphors that "war veterans and other survivors" use as referencing ways in which their journey home has run into obstacles, while they remain un-engaged with the next steps in the life-cycle process. Metaphors of immobility along the path to recovery in the present often allude to something comparable within the trauma itself.

Helen, Scott, and Others: Hidden "Unsaid" Metaphors

Helen, the rape victim mentioned above, afraid that her rapist would return to kill her children, was not only immobilized in her interpersonal relationships, she was also unable to take action in her life posttrauma as she felt paralyzed. She hid from her colleagues and from work. Paralysis, it turned out, was one of the ways that she coped with the rape itself. During the extensive trauma, in which a gun was held against her, she felt she survived by imagining herself to be paralyzed in a psychoanalytic sense of hysteria. The metaphor that describes her delay in recovery, also captures an ego-state of paralysis as part of coping with the trauma itself.

A returning Iraq veteran, Scott, was in his third year of supportive psychotherapy for his PTSD and had returned to college to move on with his life. He had confronted many of the unconscious demons plaguing him from his roles there during two tours as combat medic with dead and dying men. Nonetheless he felt stalled and on hold in his current life. While going through the motions this Imperiled Trauma Hero had a profound difficulty in finding a new commitment to a purpose greater than himself. Being stalled, he was thinking of a vehicle whose motor was capable of generating power but had lost its spark and temporarily died. Scott had made considerable progress, but he could not engage his own psychic gears. His metaphor expressed a particular point in the journey home where he could make the motions of readjustment (going to school) but could not yet find the energy to set direction in his life.

Lost My Footing and My Soul

Two years after the Buffalo Creek dam collapse in 1972, Otis was feeling that his life was slipping away and that he had lost his footing. He was estranged from his wife and distant from his children. He was facing his retirement years alone and this was frightening to him. The phrase "lost my footing" overtly referred to his inability to work through the effects of the trauma flood disaster and to complete his journey home. But the phrase also captured a segment of the trauma itself. During the flood, Otis was confronted with the impossible choice of floating downstream in a torrent of black, debris-contaminated water with his obese wife when he could not swim, or scrambling up the mountain side on his own, as she, weighing over 300 pounds, had decided there was no chance for her to make it on the ground against the rising waters. Without as much as saying goodbye, he chose the latter, losing his footing as he climbed, but ultimately scrambling to safety while leaving her to die. Miraculously she survived the powerful water by grabbing on to the detached roof of a passing house. But neither she nor he would forgive his abandoning her. Otis had lost his footing both during the flood and on the road to recovery.

Helen, Stewart, Scott, and Otis were using avoidant behaviors that were slowing their journeys home from the abyss. Their trauma metaphors conveyed the halt in their progress. It also represented an emergency coping strategy useful at the time to endure the trauma itself but that was now serving as further avoidance of confronting the impact of the trauma.

The Shivers: The Shock of Disbelief in the Horror of the Iraqi War

Bennett, an Iraq veteran, interrupted a current task by physically shuddering. In daily life, as he tried to readjust to being home, the symptomatic metaphor occurred when a given task had an unexpected challenge. As he felt himself shivering, he lost contact with the present, feeling detached, cut-off and without feeling, as if near some dangerous situation that he was watching, like a movie. Shivering along the route home was a repetition of the same phenomenon within the context of trauma. He was gunner on a combat vehicle, standing on an armored base as he looked, finding the enemy in the distance. Then, the vehicle exploded. He saw his buddy's blood-covered lifeless body being evacuated directly below him. He shivered in shocked disbelief. He was alive, unharmed because of the metal platform under him, while all around was death. In combat, the shivering state preserved a state of limbo, prolonging disbelief. Now, along the journey toward recovery the same metaphor was preventing grief, prolonging survivor guilt, and delaying the successful journey home. To be able to shiver in therapy would be to mourn with a Nurturing Guide.

Resting Spaces Between Trauma and Recovery: A Normal Process in Psychotherapy

In the context of necessary retreat from being overwhelmed, the survivor seeks resting spaces in the present. Often these represent actual places of relative safety from within the trauma context. Their occurrence in the treatment represents a necessary pause in the work, not a willful running away from the treatment contract and understanding.

A way-station on the journey to recovery is a relatively safe place where one is free to move in between the worlds of trauma and the world of re-entry. Sarah tried to interact with the friends of her recently traumatically killed son, but sensed that she was in a separate space, as though there were a physical barrier between the teenaged kids and herself. She said, "I'm outside, looking in."

Temporary retreats to safe places from which one might be close enough not to escape the traumatic memories, yet not endangered by them, are conveyed in trauma metaphors. Kristina, as memories of incest threatened to flood her, fled with her mind to a safe place, as dissociated in the past to safe psychic spaces. She said she wanted to be outside the consultation room so she could stand with the overcoats in the closet. Specifically she imagined herself hiding in the darkness of the closet and soothing her face by gently rubbing it against a fur cuff. As a child, when she sensed her father to be drunk, she sought safety from his molesting her by hiding inside the closet. The metaphor returns in the present of the psychotherapy as an indicator to patient and doctor that current traumatic memories require a safe place from which to remove oneself before further self-disclosure of intimate information.

Lawrence: In My Cave

Lawrence, an American veteran of the war in Afghanistan, explained to his therapist that he could not "connect" to his current life. He had gone back to his cave, conveying overtly a withdrawal from a female relationship that had gone badly, his refusing work opportunities, isolation from the therapist, and not following through with a referral to the pain clinic. His disconnection expressed frustrations with the ordeals of the present. But it was also important to understand, that, in Afghanistan, he found refuge in a cave during an exchange of fire that killed several of his buddies. Thus, by extension of his past experience with caves, it more closely represented a necessary resting point than a total disconnection from the struggle to return home. The difference in perspective, temporary safe resting place verses a permanent hiding spot, allowed a sense of forward movement in the therapy despite the respite and blockage. He wanted to come home safe and sound in a place he knows and treasures.

Reinventing the Self in a Pancake House

Commonplace metaphors, projected from the outside onto the survivor, are full of negative value judgments regarding a pace of recovery that is slower than expected. "She is stuck in the loss." "He has dug his heels in and won't move." "You know, at some point you just have to move on." Clearly, no one is more sensitive to these phrases than the survivor, who feels he or she is too slow, or can't get beyond it (i.e., the trauma).

While we have been examining many of the variables that may be leading to understandable difficulties along the path to recovery, it is sometimes the final step, the reinventing of a posttraumatic self, that is the most difficult. Here survivors may choose the very words of these clichés to describe their predicament yet the metaphor may have vivid meanings in a particular context.

For example, Angela, a child survivor of the Buffalo Creek flood, had moved out of the valley to pursue her career as a medical technician in a city in a neighboring state. Her world was full of energy, challenge, and opportunity. She remembered the escape from the rising black waters as a great adventure. She remembered, in the aftermath of the flood, meeting a public health nurse who lived in a far-off place and she vowed she would one day find such a life for herself. She concluded her interview with the researcher by saying simply that she had decided to move on.

Her sister, Anna, still lived in the valley. She insisted on being seated with her eyes looking out the window in the direction of the creek, while she hovered over her children as they stretched the perimeter of their play. When she drew a picture of the flood, it was from the vantage that she first saw it, rising rapidly soon to be over her head. This phrase, "things are over my head," continued to resonate with her current life. The day of the trauma was still alive 20 years later. For Anna, the disaster was part of her identity. She could not move on. Things were simply too difficult to manage; they were over her head.

Pete, a Vietnam veteran whose knowledge of explosives and inventiveness with light materials led to black ops missions in which he set traps to maim the enemy, was able over many years to convert his energies postwar into the building of light-weight heat exchangers which his company exported to Asia. He spoke of his meticulous work at repairing the damage he had done as getting it right.

Spike, on the other hand, experienced the illusion that a basketball rolling on a school gym floor he was trying to repair was too much like the rolling of a severed head in Vietnam for him to continue in his work. The intrusive image came out in the morbid phrase "get that head out of here." The phrase sealed any opportunity of continuing his profession after the war. In essence, Spike confronted the heads he did not see any more.

The Mythic Journey Home: The Work of Jonathon Shay

In *Odysseus in America*, Jonathon Shay examines Homer's epic, and finds stories of soldiers' behavior after war that aptly describe the generation of American combat veterans as they tried to come home from the war in Vietnam. Homer's warriors, like the Americans, banded together in military gangs (cf. motorcycle gangs) and resorted to wanton violence. They were haunted by lost comrades. They sought isolation, retreated to their caves for years. They resorted to mind-numbing drugs; they discharged feelings sexually. They struggled on the edge of suicidal thoughts and succumbed to the lure to return to the past. They failed to take advantage of opportunities to readjust when they were offered and were suspicious of the world which had changed as they had changed during their absence. It is as if each of Homer's chapters were a metaphor for actual maladaptive coping strategies of Imperiled Heroes millennia later. In terms of the relative weight of the strain of enduring trauma versus the strain of challenges upon homecoming, Shay points out that for Odysseus there were ten years of war and an equal number of years required to come home.

Shay makes another point relevant to the use of language in Homer's classic. Shay notes certain words that Homer uses in the world of the homecoming of Odysseus are the identical words he chooses from the world of combat of Achilles. Poignant words describing coping in the homecoming repeat words and phrases that go to the heart of problems in war situations. For Achilles, metis or deception is an ego-dystonic but necessary tactical maneuver in warfare at Troy. It becomes a hardened and fortified character trait in the returning Odysseus. Pothos, or yearning of deathly proportions, refers both to his intensity of feelings at the death of Achilles' comrade-in-arms and to the later emotional state of Odysseus' mother. Here Homer is using metis and pothos as if they were metaphors taken from the scene of trauma whose shadows become central to understanding the psychological organization of posttrauma scenes in Odysseus' life.

For Campbell (1949), using a cross-cultural pen, the same epic story illustrates the perils of the mythic quest, the confrontation and survival of exposure to absolute evil, return from the Abyss, as an organizing story for each of us in our venture into life. He points out the necessary role of a Nurturing Guide (NG), be it in the form of a god, Athena, or an old loyal servant who recognizes Odysseus and advises him as to the nature of the intervening changes he must understand in order to proceed into the future.

Culturally, our bards tend to describe mythic Heroes as idealized and idealizable figures. After all, they have traveled to the edge of the abyss, confronted the depth of chaos and evil, and won victory over the monsters and returned home, like King Arthur or Luke Skywalker or John Wayne characters in World War II movies. Late adolescents, the traditional source of combat troops, hold to these idealizations as part of their personal growth. When compared to these ideal figures, the quest component of trauma survivor falls hopelessly short of the fantasy but impels desires to be just like him.

But there is an equal tendency for the literary bards through the ages to describe Heroes in an all-too-human and flawed light. So, Odysseus is not only clever and scheming, he is also forgetful, impulsive, selfish, and dismissive of the needs of the troops he leads. Moses is irritable and a poor speaker. Jacob is clever but deceitful if need be, to gain his ends, and Jonah on his own has no heroic qualities; he simply runs away from God's command. What characterizes some of these Heroes is their happenstance closeness to events that have aroused the interest of the gods. Great wars, natural calamities, historic events that mark the life and death of nations and institutions, private hells: all these methodologically draw the flawed to take on heroic roles. It is this link that binds the ordinary and all-too-human trauma survivor to the extraordinary Hero's story. However, this being said, our trauma survivors have no access to supernatural guidance, no guardian angel to ensure survival, often no words that can match their trauma experiences, and certainly no bard to truthfully tell their story. In the view from the Abyss they saw all the imperfection of human beings and experienced their own failings as well. Their trauma world, from the beginning, turned out to be a world of danger, loss, disillusionment, and de-idealization, overwhelming in scope, but perhaps developmentally less devastating to those who have successfully negotiated Erikson's epigenetic stage of maturity rather than to children or adolescents caught up in its terror (see Wilson, 2006, for a discussion).

The Beneficient Hero's Future: Finding a Nurturing Guide (NG)

We suggest that for many the presence of a Nurturing Guide, a mentor, friend, and significant other confidant with whom to review the dilemmas of his or her trauma is a central ingredient to recovery. In the following chapter we shall explore some of the characteristics of this mythical figure cross-culturally. Here, we simply wish to make the point that the absence of such a figure adds to the difficulties of the already complex way home, as we have attempted to illustrate.

When the wounded Hero is ready to turn home to someone for help, there are many reasons why the Nurturing Guides (NG) are not present. For example, shortly after the Vietnam war, many mental health professionals, heavily influenced by the anti-war movement, had taken positions in opposition to the war, and were not ready to hear what happened to their brothers and sisters, who had actually served in the warzone. Families, often frightened and anxious about the experiences of their sons and daughters, covertly communicated to the warriors that they would rather the subject of what happened in the war should never come up. Friends and well-meaning helpers assume the problem should already be gone and not discussed. Holocaust survivors and resistance fighters were confronted with those whose guilt as bystanders made it impossible for them to bear witness to the experiences of their fellow citizens and younger children who went to war.

Functions of the Nurturing Guide for the Hero and Failed Hero's Journey

1. The Nurturing Guide (NG) understands the woundedness and helplessness of the Hero's special journey.
2. The Nurturing Guide (NG) finds appropriate opportunities to provide missing opportunities for nurturance, guidance, advice, and useful counseling – e.g., experiences that bolster self-esteem and well-being.
3. The Nurturing Guide (NG) acts in consistent, empathic, non-judgmental ways toward the fearful, disenfranchised, alienated, alone, abandoned survivor in ways that restore faith in a tangible justice of hope and self-realignment.
4. The Nurturing Guide (NG) provides, through the process of countertransference and personal being-of-character, what was missing in the past, i.e., critical relationships in the development of life-experiences as to provide a sum of ongoing care, trust, safe-holding space, and to provide a safe haven for a sense of new life in the future.
5. The Nurturing Guide (NG) establishes a non-judgmental and critically accepting attitude toward the Hero or Failed Hero who after re-entry has tendencies toward many forms of self-destructive behaviors.
6. The Nurturing Guide (NG) restores faith (i.e., hope and attainability) of a tangible and good future.
7. The Nurturing Guide (NG) helps the Unsuccessful Hero see the value of his or her trauma, struggles, travails, and horrific set of hurdles after the journey's end. The Nurturing Guide sets the foreground and background of possibilities which gives historical examples to the struggling Hero and assists in finding the new pathways for self-reinvention.

8 The Nurturing Guide (NG) facilitates personal and emotional empowerment of the Failed Hero. The Nurturing Guide helps the Failed Hero to once again see the bright side of dark personal-historical circumstances. Life-as-a-journey metaphor becomes strongly salient at this point in time. How does the Failed Hero not self-destruct?
9 The Nurturing Guide (NG) assists in providing information about the intrapsychic difficulties of living psychobiological with study of hyperarousal or psychic/emotional numbing, and how they alternate to set up complex states of PTSD, personality alteration, and character warping.
10 The Nurturing Guide (NG) can provide a sense of hope for a tangible future with goodness and grace. The Nurturing Guide can be a facilitator for self-integration, self-reinvention and inner harmony.

The list above presents a summary of the major functions of the Nurturing Guide (NG). The ten functions apply equally to both the successful and failed Hero's journey from the Abyss Experience (AE) to the homecoming reception and posttraumatic adaptive efforts. In Chapter 5, we explore the critical importance of the ways that the Nurturing Guide (NG) facilitates recovery and healthy societal re-integration.

For as long as we have written myths, like the comforters in Job in the Bible, there is the tendency to blame the Wounded Hero for his moral imperfection. Developments within the Western mental health community since Vietnam have added their own dimension to the problem. Today's Western therapists, committed to manualized treatment protocols (e.g., CBT) risk hiding from the existential dilemmas of their trauma patients. By knowing the right interventions perhaps they risk denying the survivor access to indispensable assets in recovery, the function of the Nurturing Guide.

In light of the hardships of the Hero-Survivor's journey home after confrontation with the Abyss of Trauma (AE), it is understandable that the path has numerous way-stations, cul-de-sacs, pitfalls, and obstacles. The specificity of these challenges to recovery, as conveyed in metaphoric expressions, often repeat actual dilemmas within the trauma experience itself. Thus, understanding and utilizing trauma metaphors is one of many "royal roads" to discovery of the psychic embodiment of extreme stress experiences in the life-cycle itself. It is often a useful therapeutic way to facilitate processes of self-re-integration and transformation.

5 The Nurturing Guide (NG)

In this chapter we focus on the complementary part of the Hero-Survivor mythology, their life journeys and their needs for a post-re-entry Nurturing Guide (NG). Nurturing Guides (NG) are posttraumatic mentors to recovery, who wear many cloaks, robes, uniforms, and garbs of all possibilities within cultures. Joseph Campbell's lifetime work in mythology suggests that each culture seeks to make available informed and gifted members of their community who, especially, assist the wounded Hero-Survivors on their journey home from the Abyss Experience (AE). We represent, as described in Chapter 4, this person as the Nurturing Guide (NG) (see Figure 5.1). He or she possesses certain qualities of character that will assist the survivor in fundamental and functional ways essential for recovery and re-integration from trauma. For example, bearing witness, providing a moral compass and honoring the Hero's experiences and travails in the journey simply as validation and affirmation of what has happened in their lives.

The Nurturing Guide (NG) brings with him or her some intuitive or personal knowledge of the perils of mythical metaphors: e.g., "dark woods, inhuman monsters," "the most evil place in the world," "the dark side of the Force" as per the *Star Wars* trilogy, as well as the transpositions from one mythic space to the next level that characterize the world of disaster and human capacity for self-transformation. In short, themes of life versus death; forces of energy and transformation from victim/hero to posttrauma survivor and many more thematic representations in a modern life.

The Nurturing Guide (NG) intuitively knows that the road home is lined with danger and perils to self- and well-being. Returning from the Abyss Experience (AE) brings with it a residue that frightens those who have never "seen" the Abyss and those professionals who treat its mythic, realistic posttraumatic spaces with disbelief (i.e., fear) and trepidation. The horror of traumatic experiences can be much worse than fiction or the most powerful Stephen King novel. The Nurturing Guide (NG) understands that the pre-traumatic significant others "back home" have changed and their various roles have evolved and altered during the survivors' absence. *Thus, experienced discontinuity post-traumatically in the self becomes, for the survivor, potentially preconsciously salient and anxiety-provoking upon return from the life-journey from their Abyss Experience (AE) in exposure to extreme stress life-experiences.* It is, in fact, a profound transition stage of recovery on a life journey. It is a transition of mind, soul, body, and spiritual essence.

The Nurturing Guide (NG) may be imbued by society with knowledge of the supra-natural and spiritual powers in many different ways within a culture (Wilson, 1989, 2007). He or she has learned, by life experience and ritual, some of the mysteries necessary to perform rites of passage, healing rituals, those that demarcate the transitions of the life-cycle, from the womb to life; from childhood to adulthood; from bachelorhood to marriage; from life to death and from death to the afterlife. He or she may be endowed by cultural rituals and healing practices to expiate guilt, revive vitality, and offer the emotional ways to peace. For many survivors, however, these helpful Nurturing Guides (NG) may not be available and, when they are absent or non-existent, lead to pathological consequences. What happens to the distressed survivor upon re-entry to their hopeful place of re-integration when there are no guides to provide comfort and wisdom as to what can be materialized next in life?

Where, indeed, do these Nurturing Guides (NG) come from? What is, in fact, the epigenetic-ontogenetic life-journey of the trauma victim? And how does the Nurturing Guide (NG) "walk" the posttraumatic journey with them in a healing and helpful way?

Recognition of the Trauma Survivor's Journey: Asking the Nurturing Guide (NG) for Help

Across cultures there are many formally sanctioned professional roles that have evolved and whom the survivor might seek out as he or she tries to adjust coming home from the Abyss Experience (AE) of trauma exposure (Wilson, 2004). Where do they find the Nurturing Guides (NG)? Amongst different cultures, the returning Hero-Survivor will eventually seek out and turn to these individuals in one of these sanctioned or non-traditional roles and ask that person to take on the task of being his or her Nurturing Guide (NG), albeit without conscious, lucid awareness of doing so, but out of psychic necessity, inner tension, and anxiety and fear of the future.

Cross-culturally, the Nurturing Guide (NG) shares many qualities and attitudes toward and with the survivor similar to and with the Western psychotherapist while engaging in other areas that would stretch the responsive range of the traditional Western clinician to uncomfortable limits and proper professional structures and proper role-boundary limits (see Chapter 1, Figure 1.1). These culturally-rooted qualities and attitudes, in turn, create identifiable characteristics of the psychic-socio-emotional space of the encounter with the survivor. We spell out some of these qualities and attitudes and a few of the characteristics of their shared communal space. We illustrate how the returning Hero-Survivor confirms these elements via trauma metaphors (see Chapter 1, Figures 1.1 and 1.2).

The Nurturing Guide (NG), in an oversimplified analysis, refers to an ideal or archetypal set of interrelated skill sets, abilities, or special sensitivities. Linguistic groupings that may feel foreign to the Western or non-Western clinical therapists are enumerated and explored in Chapter 2 and later in Chapters 7–10. Nevertheless, the Nurturing Guide (NG) has the ability to connect psychoformatively to the victim/survivor in ways of sustainability of emotional health.

Like a kaleidoscope picture, the very listening to and trying to respond to these pertinent and at times imponderable questions stretches the perimeter and boundaries of what the Western therapist defines as the "usual range of action."

In wrestling with these boundaries the therapist both widens his or her perspective and opens the door for collaboration with other professionals and their writings in the interests of the progress of the Hero-Survivor's return. We believe that when proper empathic attunement exists, both survivor and therapist grow in character and wisdom (Wilson & Thomas, 2004). Through this effort, we begin to appreciate how broad and deep are the concerns and needs of the traumatized survivor(s) and how narrow may be some of the fixed, conventional ideas about healing from the Western medical, scientific mindset. While these concerns cannot be ignored, they must be explored and studied, and we do so in Chapters 8, 9, and 10. At the core set of issues is: What cannot be ignored any longer to progress science and knowledge?

Cultural Considerations: The Complexity and Relation of the Nurturing Guide (NG) to Trauma and the Journey of the Hero-Survivor

Table 5.1 presents an overview of the Nurturing Guide (NG) in its complexity and functional integration within the life journey of the Hero-Survivor perspective. In the most inclusive sense, a Nurturing Guide (NG) is one whom, by personal life experience and empathy, has *implicit knowledge* of the trauma survivors' posttraumatic travails, struggles, conflicts, frustrations, and potential for anxiety reactions, depressions, PTSD, substance abuse, and self-destructive behaviors. They are "down to earth people" with a tempered wisdom about the profound disappointments, "hard knocks," and "rough sledding in life." The survivor, progressing through spiritual and emotional challenges to the self, personal integrity, evolution, and wholeness, struggles to be whole again in identity and self. In greater or lesser degrees, the Nurturing Guides (NG) possess knowledge of the "big picture" of the Hero-Survivor's posttraumatic journey and are able to be empathically attuned to the "wounded soul" of those they encounter in different ways at different times in space and time in a specific, given cultural context. *The Nurturing Guide (NG) connects in limitless time and psychological space to the inner psychic reality of the person, as if, on a coetaneous virtual reality trip in history together.*

In artistic film productions, such as the *Star Wars* trilogy, for example, the role of the Nurturing Guide (NG) for the Hero, Luke Skywalker, was woven into the character of Yoda and Obi-Wan Kenobi, who guided and advised Luke, protagonist Hero, as how to deal with Darth Vader (his father). The characters portrayed the archetypal images of universal life forces; positive and negative; light versus dark; good versus bad; black versus white; love versus hate; good versus evil. The Nurturing Guide (NG) was as a mythological figure representative and existentially-based person with unique, and special insight concerning the Hero-Survivor's posttraumatic journey, can, and often occupies a pivotal and transitional role relationship that potentially facilitates healing, recovery and the wholeness of personality. The critical importance of recognizing, referring, and educating Nurturing Guides (NG) for trauma survivors. They are often unrecognized "tour guides" to recovery from the abyss. In Chapter 9, we outline the pedagogy of posttraumatic educational needs and processes.

Graphic Representation of the Nurturing Guide (NG)

Inspection and analysis of Figure 5.1 enables a detailed, cross-sectional complex understanding of the roles and functions of the Nurturing Guide (NG). At first impression, this figure appears somewhat daunting in its architecture and computer-assisted design (CAD). *The graphic images are intricately interrelated in a holistic way which reflects the*

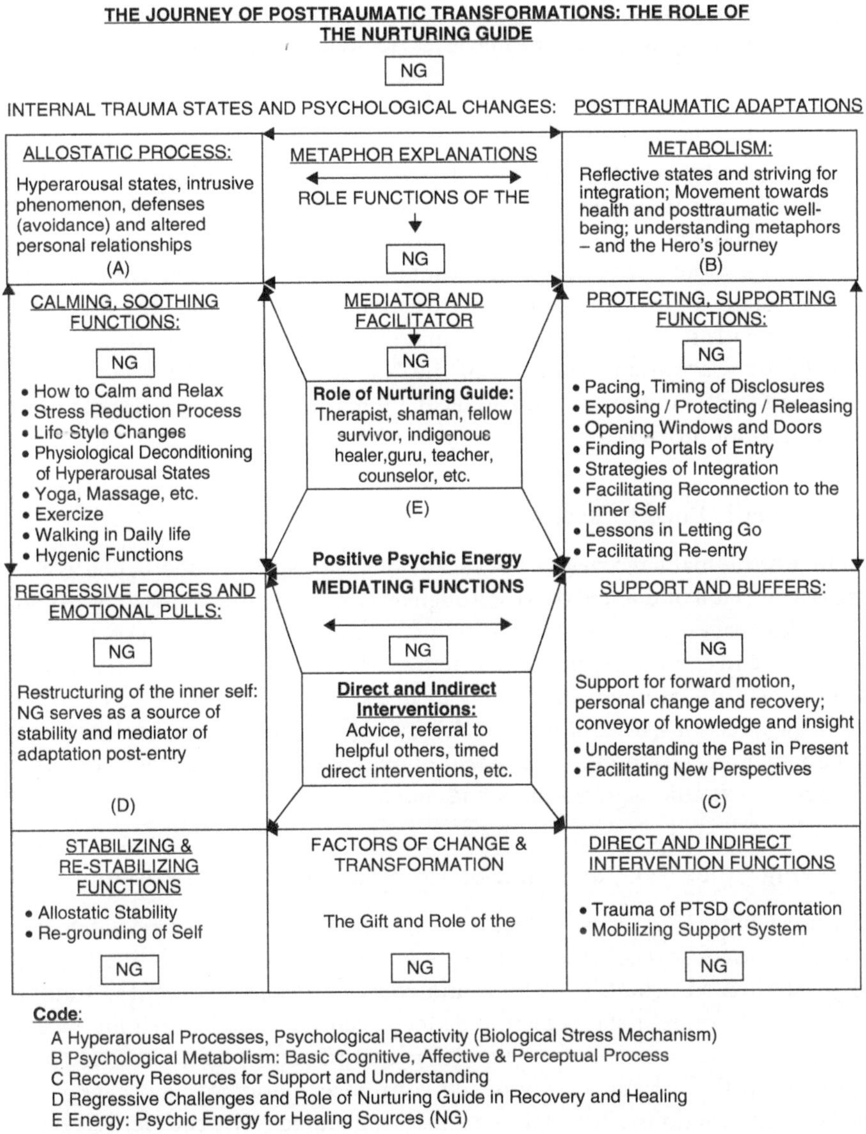

Figure 5.1 The Nurturing Guide

synergistic processes of the organism at all levels of biological and mental functions. Holistically, it is a representation of the roles of the Nurturing Guide (NG).

To begin, analysis of Figure 5.1 can be broken down into examination of internal traumatic states (i.e., physiological and psychological allostatic processes connected to hyperarousal nervous system reactive processes) and posttraumatic adaptational mechanisms that are governing attempts at the psychic metabolism of trauma and, eventually, integration in the self-structure and personality (see Chapter 3). There is an interplay, or isomorphic relation, between simultaneously occurring physiological and psychological processes. In short, the epiphenomenological events of a psychobiological nature in PTSD at the systemic organismic level (see Wilson, Friedman, & Lindy, 2001, for a review).

Figure 5.1 can be further dissected by evaluating the codes for the capital letters A–E, which represent the following: (A) hyperarousal processes and psychophysiological stress reactions of the body; (B) the processes of psychological metabolism of trauma at cognitive, emotional, and perceptual levels that reflect the striving for self-integration, wholeness, and well-being. For PTSD patients, it is often here that awareness of one's own metaphors emerge more clearly into consciousness. In terms of the interaction between posttraumatic states of hyperarousal and psychological expressions, the Nurturing Guides (NG) provide support and buffers to mobilize recovery and trauma integration (C). As such, the wisdom and guidance of the Nurturing Guide (NG) can assist in understanding the past in the present and facilitate new perspectives of trauma in the Hero-Survivor's journey (D).

The Posttraumatic Road to Recovery

The road to posttraumatic recovery is not usually or customarily a smooth, linear, non-conflicted one. It is full of ups and downs, "rough terrain," and difficult life journeys and further stressful challenges to self and the existential meaning of life. Indeed, there are regressive forces and emotional pulls to return to maladaptive patterns of posttraumatic adjustment which can be manifest in many forms: severe hyperarousal states, hyper-vigilance, drug addictions, alcoholism, impulsivity, high-risk behaviors, adolescent-like or childlike demands, and emotional outbursts of irritability and requests for dependent care and support, extreme aggressiveness, and more.

The Nurturing Guide (NG) as Source of Strength and Spiritual Wiseom

The Nurturing Guide (NG) serves as a source of strength, stability, and a mediator when unhealthy regressive forces come into existence in the trauma survivor's life. Through nurturing, calming, and soothing actions and conversations, they help the trauma-affected person recapture a state of groundedness, centrality, and proximity in psy-choformative processes to be "here and now." The trauma survivor gets their "feet back on the ground" with a greater feeling of self-coherence, autonomy, and energy (see Chapter 3 on self-functions). Through the Nurturing Guide (NG) the Hero-Survivor (HS) experiences further recovery and integration of the trauma experience in the context, and opportunities confines of their culture and healing rituals. When this happens, their psychic energy is bolstered.

In the center of Figure 5.1, (E) is a box labeled *Mediator and Facilitator*. This computer-assisted graphic design (CAD) is purposeful in several respects. First, to illustrate the critical and central role that Nurturing Guides (NG) play in life journeys, personal dilemmas, and crises of an unexpectable or unpredictable nature. Second, for many PTSD affected victims with overwhelming posttraumatic life-stresses, the absence of connection to a Nurturing Guide (NG) can be psychically injurious for a positive, successful and healthy recovery.

Nurturing Guides (NG) and Mobilizing Positive Psychic Energy for Posttraumatic Recovery

Nurturing Guides (NG), in all their forms (invocations, medical roles, traditional cultural masks, cultural rituals, societal roles, psychological role-sanctions, counseling, medicine man or woman, manifestations, and characteristics) have similar properties of their social status. Whether a shaman, priest, counselor, recovering addict, psychiatrist, psychologist, social worker, guru, indigenous healer, African witch doctor, etc., they not only understand that the Hero-Survivor is pursuing a posttraumatic journey but needs *psychic infusions of a positive energy* (see Chapter 3). *In this sense, the Nurturing Guide's (NG) positive psychic energy is a requirement to mobilize the internal resources for recovery, healing, self-transformation, and self-reinvention.* The absence of good positive psychic energy is passivity and depressive withdrawal and an inability to move forward beyond emotional, bodily, and psychic injuries to the posttraumatic "hole" in the self. It becomes a state of stasis and lack of forward movement. Psychological trauma can be profound injury to the self and soul, but psychic infusions of positive energy can reverse these negative processes in profound and immediate ways.

The Need for Psychic Infusions

In medicine, patients that are dehydrated, sick, or suffering from various illnesses need "infusions" of water, antibiotics, or other medications to assist in recovery. Similarly, patients suffering from the effects of psychic trauma and the potential deletion of their mental energy during recovery often need psychic infusions of positive energy and hope.

When not treated, the "self and soul" freeze, avoid, and stop active living (i.e., stasis) on an everyday basis. To fully recover, the Hero-Survivor needs to mobilize and effectively employ positive, self-directed psychic energy to make important and significant personal changes. When all goes well, the Nurturing Guide (NG) provides the necessary psychic infusions of positive energy and hope to change the direction of their lives. Whether or not the survivor accepts it is another consideration. If no depressive states prevail with negative consequences, co-morbidities and further risks for self-destructive behaviors.

The Spectrum of Roles and Responsibilities of Nurturing Guides (NG)

Cultures demand of their Nurturing Guides (NG) prolonged and arduous periods of study, knowledge of the central stories of their culture, passing difficult tests and practicing for many years under the guidance of seasoned, professional practitioners of their specialization. The Nurturing Guide (NG) might be empowered to prescribe and dispense pharmaceuticals, herbal medicines, traditional potions or lotions, or substances. He or she may prescribe bodily activities such as deep breathing exercises, yoga, Qi Gong, imaging a safe, secure, protected space, meditations, mantras, participating in a sweat lodge ceremony, or literal hands-on touching rituals; order changes in diet, the eating and drinking of special fruit juices or herbal teas, etc. He or she might have medicines or acupuncture to reduce anxiety and pain. They might use powerful words to reduce the fear of nightmares or prescribe rites and ceremonies to achieve the same results. They might guide by prayer to God or induce communication with supra-natural forces such as ancestors and spirits. They might educate regarding PTSD or instruct about the world of the gods, the ancient stories of trauma in a particular culture or ancient tribal secrets of the underworld. These are unique and fascinating cultural rituals and traditions which always involve the Nurturing Guide (NG). How can we ignore them when they produce salutary outcomes in culture-specific archetypal forms? The pressing scientific question is what we can learn from the diversity of worldwide cultural healing rituals? How and why did they evolve? Why do they "work" or possess efficacy in outcome? How to assess and further deepen understanding of them? Why does modern science not employ methodologically sound studies of these long evolved cultural healing rituals?

Cross-Cultural Examples of Nurturing Guides (NG)

In many cultures, the Nurturing Guide (NG) is a symbolic figure whose role joins two poles; approaching the imponderable and managing in the world of the practical and real. Such considerations apply to [in English] the Native American shaman, the African witch doctor, the Shinto and Buddhist monk, the Asian wise elder, the Zen teacher or guru, Navajo elders, and so many others. In American society, indeed, it takes many professions to encompass the "masks" that might be considered part of Nurturing Guide's (NG) functions amongst other cultures throughout the world. In fact, what do the ancient Greek cultures teach us about the roles and masks of the potential healers?

Qualities of the Nurturing Guide (NG) Across Cultures

The Nurturing Guide (NG) brings to bear a set of attitudes, training, and skills that uniquely prepare him or her for the task. It is not necessarily formal training or education. The role is typically acknowledged by the larger society and their worldview is a broader one capable of dealing with contradiction and paradox. Trauma is more than individual experience. The understanding and knowledge of traumatic experience falls within a broad and mythic historical context. Some of the perspectives he or she carries are philosophical, medicinal, anthropological, religious, ethical, theological, historical, psychological, and mythological. We highlight characteristics of the Nurturing Guide (NG) that cross cultural boundaries in Figure 5.1.

The Nurturing Guide (NG) is concerned with the emotional stability and well-being of the survivor, with ways to sooth periodic, emotionally painful posttraumatic storms, to manage sleep, to reduce pain, to tend to physical and emotional wounds. He or she is concerned with basic needs for shelter, food, nurturance, and opportunities to work and have positive social relations. He or she is interested in educating and counseling those associated with the returning Victim/Hero. They are interested in helping the returning survivor to understand the mission and life journey he or she has been through and will continue to pursue and embark on in ways never expected for their future. Taken together these socially defined roles represent the important psychical dimensions of the Nurturing Guide (NG) in a very condensed manner or representation.

Many of the specific qualities of the Nurturing Guide (NG) are ones held in common with the Western psychotherapist such as concern for physical well-being, the capacity for empathizing with loss, grief, and alienation, retaining non-judgmental attitudes, monitoring self-awareness, intervening so as to alter self-destructive cycles and remaining a beacon of hope in the midst of obstacles, challenges, and setbacks of the journey home from the Abyss Experience (AE).

The Functions of the Nurturing Guide (NG) in Terms of Trauma Metaphors, PTSD, and Mythical Dimensions

Table 5.1 summarizes the ten major functions of the Nurturing Guide (NG) that we have identified from various sources including the seminal work of Joseph Campbell (1949) and our work with many sub-populations of trauma and survivors.

The ten dimensions include, respectively: (1–5) the functions of the Nurturing Guide (NG); providing assistance and insight as to the pre- and posttraumatic changes in existence and how to manage them; (6) to assist the process of bearing witness to history, humanity, trauma, evil, and their psychohistorical realities; (7) the therapeutic functions of bearing witness in the role of Nurturing Guide (NG); (8) to assist in illuminating the nature of the trauma and spiritual journey; (9) to execute the major responsible functions of the Nurturing Guide (NG) posttrauma; and (10) the persons, occupations, etc. who serve within different cultures as Nurturing Guides (NG).

In the most panoramic, encompassing perspective, Nurturing Guides are persons of an archetypal nature and roles that reflect Jung's archetypal description of the Wise Old Man (WOM). In our modern 21st century, the Nurturing Guide (NG) is the WOM or Wise Old Woman (WOW) of Jung's archetype, who helps PTSD trauma patients and others. Gender is an equal opportunity (NG) provider on a worldwide basis

When clinically analyzing the dimensions of trauma metaphors and mythical aspects, the functions of the Nurturing Guide (NG) become more central and clearer in focus. Table 5.1 provides a "capsule snapshot" overview of these important role functions that often facilitate posttraumatic healing and recovery.

The Nurturing Guide (NG) and the Navigation of the Homecoming and Recovery From Trauma and the Abyss Experience

The first of the functions highlighted in Table 5.1 has five specifications. Once the trauma survivor finds and connects to or with the Nurturing Guide (NG), they hopefully find a spiritual, empathic, compassionate person who helps transition from the Zone of Danger (ZD) to re-entry into their community and culture. Metaphorically and mythologically, this is movement from the "dark side of the force," to a new and beneficial, salutary environment of creative self-reinvention. *This then is the initial transitional phase of a nurturing relationship. In many cases, this phase allows the survivor to trust the Nurturing Guide (NG) to help illuminate what their journey will be all about and why it happened the way it did.* While the Nurturing Guide (NG) non-judgmentally and compassionately provides insight and necessary protection and caring, they serve as a psychic and spiritual bridge to the inevitable processes of change in recovery, self-transformations, and eventual metabolism of traumatic memories. The Nurturing Guide (NG) has "intuitive, useful, caring knowledge" of the survivor's journey and then, when possible, provides the guidance and wisdom for adaptive ways to *navigate re-entry* and reintegration to culture

Table 5.1 Traumatic Metaphors, PTSD, and Mythical Dimensions to Therpeutic Orientation: Functions of the Nurturing Guide (NG)

The Functions of the Nurturing Guide (NG) in the Journey of the Hero (after Campbell & Wilson, 2007; Wilson & Lindy, 2011)

1 The NG facilitates transition from the world of trauma (i.e., out of darkness; zone of danger; the woods or confrontation with sinister forces (dark side of the "force") to the new entry point/place upon return from perils and trauma.

2 To provide assistance to facilitate understanding of the Hero-Survivors' journey. This includes protection, caring, nurturing, guidance, advice and providing useful advice as to sources of recovery, stability, autonomy, security and basic need gratification. To help re-ground the Hero upon re-entry.

3 To provide insight and necessary protection from forces, situations or people that would cause further damage, harm or problems in re-adjusting after the Heroic journey.

4 To provide advice, guidance, and wisdom as to the tasks of re-entry, transformation and considerations for protected recovery, healing and survivorship.

5 **To provide Insight between the pre- and post-trauma changes in existence and how to manage them.** For Example:
- a) The ballgame has changed, There are rules.
- b) Rules and realities may not seem the same as before. The need for new ways to adapt.
- c) The experience of fluctuations in continuity vs. discontinuity as normal but discordant in consciousness and everyday life experiences. Internal self and identity functions.
- d) Self-reinvention is a meaningful task, but a difficult one with no or very few road maps.

6 **To assist bearing witness to history, humanity, trauma, evil and realities:**
- a) Provide validation as to what happened in the journey itself.
- b) Confirm authority of survivors' legacy and its personal significance.
- c) Articulate the need for self-reinvention.
- d) Help place the hero's journey within a cultural and contemporary historical perspective.

7 **The therapeutic functions of bearing witness in a role of nurturing guide:**
- a) *Preservation of historical realities*: Embracing through empathic-orientation the patients' accounts of their traumatic experiences, struggles, and difficulties.
- b) *Honoring*: Confirming the authority of experience, security, hardship at ungodly and horrific encounters, some never evident before.
- c) *Transgenerational legacies*: Continued recognition of the horrific, burdensome, and over-taxing nature of the survivors' journey.

Critical Issues:
- d) Morality, ethics, values, and the sanctity of Human Existence: The recognition of the need to preserve and protect the bases of values, morals, laws, and ethics that affect the Goodness of Human existence.
- e) Re-establishing and recognizing higher human values so that sound judgments can be made about extraordinary historical life events.
- f) Recognize that the therapist can experience existential despair and distance it from the treatment process, a personalized internalization of the patients' experiences.
- g) The role of the Nurturing Guide facilitates preserving parts of ego and personal identity challenged by the traumatic experience.
- h) The Nurturing Guide helps the survivor bear witness to the unbearable, the unsaid, the secrets and hidden pockets of psychic shame and guilt.

8 **The illumination of the trauma and spiritual journey:**
   a) The Nurturing Guide helps the hero/survivor to understand the posttraumatic journey (PTJ) and its vicissitudes in the life-journey.
   b) The guide helps to normalize that the posttraumatic journey has starts and stops along the way and will be, at times, emotionally overwhelming, confusing and uncertain as to direction and meaning.

9 **The execution of the major functions of the nurturing guide after trauma and why they are important:**
   a) *Soothing, calming, re-assuring*: After emerging from the encounter with dark, sinister or destructive forces, the nurturing guide provides soothing, calmness, an anchor of security and trust, and a place where clear-headed understanding is possible and necessary to provide effective thinking as to the future.
   b) *Protection and wisdom*: The Nurturing Guide provides education, personal wisdom, and knowledge about the reality of the task of recovery, adaptation, self-transformation and immunity against negative forces that cause secondary stressors and potential traumatization. This also involves helping to identity faulty expectations about re-entry into the post-trauma environment.

10 **The role of the Nurturing Guide: Advisor, shaman, medicine man or woman, confidant, mentor, wise counselor, spiritual figure, guru, priest, mental health professional or next-door neighbor:**
   a) Assist in preparedness for hero's journey, if possible, with realistic information about physical, mental and moral challenges.
   b) Use their wise counselor judiciously and with practiced discipline.
   c) Bear witness to existential challenges.
   d) Facilitate integrity of changes upon completing the heroic journey.
   e) Facilitate re-entry upon completion of the journey and the next phase of motivation.

---

and a home in the posttraumatic return. Mythologically, this is the journey of the Hero-Survivor in its psychic essence, from the Abyss Experience to a new home for recovery. An eventual homecoming of expected and unexpected encounters, obstacles, and difficulties.

The Nurturing Guide (NG) is more than a mediator, facilitator, and special God-given spiritual connection. He or she is fundamentally a compassionate teacher. A teacher of life itself, among other critical Nurturing Guide (NG) roles, they have the unique ability to provide insight as to pre- and posttraumatic changes in adaptive functioning, complex and deeper personality processes. As a guide and a practical, wise, day-to-day, informative teacher, they can explain how the "rules of living" and "existing" have changed after the trauma and that there may not be very many road maps or emotional manuals on how to reach desired destinations for a sought-after tangible future. The road of recovery and destiny may be confused, vague, blocked, blurred by sandstorms and hurricanes. The natural disasters of life have direct parallels to human ones.

The Major Functions of the Nurturing Guide (NG), Clinical Therapist, or Mental Health Professional

Table 5.2 presents the major functions of the Nurturing Guides (NG) working with trauma survivors and trauma-specific metaphors. Each of the six functions has

Table 5.2 Roles of the Therapist in Working With Trauma Metaphors Divided Into Six Major Functions

A	**To Assist Wounded Hero-Survivor in Reconstructing Trauma Configurations and Events**	
	1	Metaphors as windows into the trauma experience. Portals of entry (POE).
	2	Decoding: How do psychotherapists learn how to decode trauma metaphors that are presented during treatment?
	3	Understand the relationship between (TST) and (TSM), i.e., trauma specific transference and trauma specific metaphors (TSM). How do they inform each other?
	4	The therapists' own metaphors as countertransference to the patients (TST & TSM).
	5	What are the therapists' TST and TSMs? What role do they play in treatment?
B	**To Assist Wounded Hero-Survivor in Clarifying Damage to Self and Ego-Processing**	
	1	Psychotherapists need to respect posttraumatic behavioral adaptation in all of their normal vicissitudes and pathological variations. Reinforce resilience.
	2	The client with PTSD has obstacles to re-engaging epigenetic tasks of self-confrontation.
	3	Unmetabolized traumatic experiences reflect damage to the inner dimensions of the self-structure and ego-processes.
	4	Trauma metaphors are conscious or unconscious expressions of internal self-schemas.
C	**To Assist the Wounded Hero-Survivor in Identifying Complex Post-Traumatic Affect States and Mental Processes**	
	1	The Lucifer effect: The clients' awareness of the dark side of self, life and the propensity to engage in morally devalued actions. The devil or demons exist, to some extent, in everyone.
	2	Traumatic experiences produce ego-syntonic and ego-dystonic experience.
D	**To Contribute to Building Alliance Between Wounded Hero and Therapist**	
	1	Clinicians need to recognize the therapy metaphor of recovery and treatment as a journey out of the Abyss to self-reinvention.
	2	At what point of education, professional training, etc. do psychotherapists realize that they occupied the role of the mythic Nurturing Guide?
	3	This refines the metaphors in terms of timing, pacing and respect for resistance.
E	**To Assist Wounded Hero in Working Through Trauma and Healing the Process When Possible**	
	1	Clinician bears witness to the trauma history and narratives.
	2	Therapist becomes co-participant in the recovery journey of the patient.
	3	The construction of trauma metaphors is a step in moving forward in psychic metabolism and cognitive processing of the traumatic experience.
	4	The therapist jointly constructs the process to understand trauma metaphor and its meanings.
	5	Provide empathy in the metaphoric expression of the trauma.
	6	Understand condensation of paradox and ambivalence within the trauma metaphor.
F	**To Respect the Wounded Hero's Most Regressive Positions**	
	1	The absence of trauma metaphors reflects an absence of active metabolization of experiences that have been entombed, walled-off or repressed.
	2	There are states of raw posttraumatic psychic function that exit before the creation of trauma metaphors.

sub-functions making a total of 22 distinct role functions. Each of these six categories reflects different methods or ways to assist the wounded Hero/Survivor.

The Nurturing Guide (NG) as Witness to Humanity and History

In the broadest moral dilemma or perspective of going right or wrong in the ethical sense of humanity, the Nurturing Guide (NG) has an important role in bearing witness to history and trauma in all of its sordid variations and ugliness.

The authentic inner character strength, integrity, and honesty of the Nurturing Guide (NG) empowers them to confront the stark and often unimaginable realities of Holocaust, genocides, wars, atrocities, calamities, torture, natural disasters, and much more. *Historically, this collective grouping of the world's worst traumas shares a common need for survivors that the Nurturing Guide (NG) often fulfills and brings unparalleled empathy for understanding the Hero-Survivor's journey. It is a rare gift.*

The Nurturing Guide's (NG) role in exposing, recognizing, and honoring the victims of historical events and atrocities of all types then leads typically to two critical issues for the Nurturing Guide (NG) which they feel impelled or necessary to share and discuss with the survivor. First, the historical presentation of events that unfolded at a given moment in history: What actually happened? Second, and equally important, is the need for the Nurturing Guide (NG) to discover knowledge, information, and details of atrocities, abuse, torture, killing, rapes, mutilations of the body and spirit, and much more in the way of specific and disturbing details.

In this sense, the Nurturing Guide (NG), where possible, can convey, teach and counsel or guide understanding of transgenerational legacies of how powerful historic events effect survivors and generations. The critical moral issues, central to these basic dilemmas, are delineated in Table 5.2 (a–h).

The last parts of Table 5.2 address the question of the primary functions of the Nurturing Guide (NG). Table 5.2 illustrates these in clear graphic forms. To focus and abbreviate: There are two major functions of the Nurturing Guide (NG) as illustrated in Table 5.2 (6): (1) soothing, calming; and (2) reassessing, protection, wisdom, and a common-sense guide to living life on a daily basis.

To summarize in a brief way, the Nurturing Guide (NG) occupies many roles, positions, titles, professional responsibilities and more, such as being a friend, neighbor, fellow addict, or war veteran. Thus, the Nurturing Guide (NG), per se, is a metaphor of the soul spirit.

A Nurturing Guide: Hearing Existential Despair: As Witness to Individual Life Suffering

The Nurturing Guide (NG) hears despair and the woundedness and helplessness to both the trauma itself and the Hero's journey home afterwards. It is painful to listen to the stories and narrations, and sometimes it is unbearable, if not overwhelming, for the treatment provider. In response, where possible, the Nurturing Guide (NG) offers opportunity for nurturance, guidance, advice, useful counseling, and shared wisdom. A psychological place of shared quietude.

Case History: Gretchen

When Gretchen, for example, repeated the lament that she had lost too much blood to go on, her therapist heard in that phrase, more than the reference to her actual injury, her radial artery being severed as she fell through a glass door. It was indeed factual that she had lost so much blood she lost consciousness and nearly her life. But a year after her accident, the phrase "too much blood" was also referring to difficulty in the route to recovery, her profound state of woundedness; she was afraid that there was no blood left in her veins, no energy left (self-structural reference) to resume her struggle back into the energetic life (self-structural reference) that preceded the trauma. It was important for her Nurturing Guide (NG) to understand the metaphor in a particular sensitive, soft way. As a Jehovah's Witness, transfusion of blood from another was a sin. New blood metaphorically speaking would come from Gretchen's own growing capacity to generate her own life-sustaining energy from her own healing marrow.

The Nurturing Guide (NG) attempts to be sensitive to all facets of traumatic experience. He or she listens to the grieving, alienated, alone, abandoned survivor and acts in ways that honor the loss, promote connection, and restore faith in a tangible justice of hope and self-realignment. More essential, he or she, on a regular basis as a Nurturing Guide (NG), helps the person to feel whole again.

Case History: Dominic

When his second therapist heard Dominic, a prominent civic leader, refer to the wound of the death of his son by suicide as a "hole in my heart" he heard more than the initial psychiatrist provider who had incorrectly focused exclusively on guilt. The Nurturing Guide (NG) noted how the "trope," "hole in my heart," had transposed the actual bullet hole in his son's chest where he shot himself. He understood the hole as representing the existential loss Dominic felt at his son's successful suicide. In fact Dominic had literally brought his son back from the brink of death on numerous occasions during preceding months while professionals, medical, psychiatric, psychological, incorrectly minimized the son's suicidal danger. Dominic's "hole" captured his profound despair in feeling abandoned by helping professionals, even by God, in spiritual intervention. The empty space in Dominic's chest was in grave need of filling not simply via the relief from interpretations about neurotic guilt. The Nurturing Guide (NG) understood how Dominic's words unwittingly recapitulated the etymology of the word trauma itself (see Chapter 2). What was at the time of suicide became his unconscious reality and only to be consciously realized later as to the total sadness and pathology of the situation.

Self-Awareness

The Nurturing Guide (NG) monitors his or her own reactions to the survivor's narrative and, by way of using self-awareness, enables the work to continue in the face of horrendous obstacles. He or she provides something otherwise missing so as to provide ongoing care, trust, safe-holding space, and a haven for a sense of new life in the future.

Case History: Jeb

Such was the situation when Jeb, a scout leader in Vietnam, walked his Nurturing Guide (NG) through a "My Lai" type massacre (1968 Vietnam) for which he was responsible. The therapist became uncomfortably aware of wishes for retribution, specifically a counter-transference wish to kill his own patient for his war-related crime. Jeb's choice of words was revealing. He called himself an "S.S. agent" as though his task had been to exterminate Jews and his Jewish doctor. In turn, the treating doctor felt like a survivor of the Holocaust, and fantasized retaliatory justice. In ways such as this, the Nurturing Guide (NG), "tasting his own wish to kill and have justice," was able to hear a profound self-loathing present in Jeb. The doctor, through this internal work, was able to become the other capable of understanding an impenetrable sense of self-loathing without disrupting totally what had been until then a safe place for recovery.

The Nurturing Guide's (NG) Capacity to Hear the Unsaid, Tragic, Sad, Unspeakable, Untold Story

The Nurturing Guide (NG) recognizes that the healer, therapist, or helper can experience existential despair. The Guide normally gets beyond a personalized internalization of the patient's experiences by being able to place it in a larger mythic or personological worldview context (Wilson & Lindy, 1994). Psychoanalysts who participated in the "Vietnam: Casebook" project (Lindy, 1988), came to feel the existential despair of their patients deeply. The therapists came to match the veteran's dilemma with shared myths and personal feelings. One veteran who was marginally adjusted as a teenager before Vietnam became so angry at the enemy that he radioed instructions to shell suspected enemy hospital sites because, he argued, they (the VC) were all guilty. His Nurturing Guide (NG) came to think of him as the Jonah of the Old Testament, so angry at God for being placed in the role of Hero, and so angry at the people of Nineva for their sins that he would instruct God to destroy them all, the injured as well as the hardy.

Non-Judgmental Moral Attitudes and Ethical Dispositions

The Nurturing Guide (NG) establishes a non-judgmental and critically accepting attitude toward the wounded Hero who, after re-entry from the Abyss Experience (AE) journey, has tendencies toward many forms of self-destructive behaviors. The voracity, clarity, and forceful impact of the trauma story is engulfing. The Nurturing Guide (NG), in whatever societal role function, becomes a witness to history through empathic understanding and compassionate regard.

Case History: Chris: The Fire Victim

Chris fled from a deadly fire without warning or tending to the needs of his nearby wife who might have died. In treatment, he unconsciously re-enacted the traumatic exit scene with his doctor, mistakenly thinking the medical building (with his doctor in it) had warm walls and was about to be destroyed by fire. He, once again, fled, this time not warning his doctor. Understanding the re-enactment as metaphor, the doctor was kind and understanding, despite Chris' conviction that the doctor would judge him harshly for trying to save himself without even thinking of saving the doctor first. In response, Chris dreamed of a holy figure who had forgiven him the sin of self-preservative impulsivity, someone half-way between the doctor and Jesus. Metaphors, in this case the doctor as Jesus, confirm the presence of a non-judgmental and critically accepting attitude toward the survivor, especially in the presence of repeated self-destructive behaviors. Thus, trauma metaphors connect to both personal (traumatic) experiences and cosmological life-experience metaphors.

Illuminating the Multiple and Diverse Pathways to Recovery

The Nurturing Guide (NG) tries to place the traumatized survivor along the recovery path, empathizing with "tough spots" and "detours" along the way while expecting, in the long run, positive movement to occur and manifest itself in healing transformation. When Scott reported feeling stalled while at the same time his engine was working overtime, his Nurturing Guide (NG) heard not only the frustration at not moving along on his journey, but more particularly she inferred that his energies had not found a meaningful place for their expression. She suggested and then arranged a temporary volunteer position at a hospital as a specific form of support.

The Nurturing Guide (NG) Facilitates Self-Reinvention Posttrauma

The Nurturing Guide (NG) occupies a state of expectancy regarding long-term improvement and emotional empowerment of the Imperiled Hero. The Nurturing Guide (NG) helps the Imperiled Hero to once again see the bright side of "dark" and difficult personal-historical circumstances. The NG acts as a facilitator of self-reinvention. In the best sense, the Nurturing Guide (NG) is an iconic figure of hope and a light beacon for the future.

Case Histories: Mario, Fred, and Others

The life-as-a-journey metaphor becomes strongly salient at this point in time. For example, Mario, survivor of a Kentucky supper club fire, quoted his dead violinist friend's phrase, "You have to love your instrument." While initially Mario used this phrase as a negative judgment on his behavior during the club fire (his friend had died trying to save his violin), his guide understood that he, too, had great love for his violin and would in time see the phrase as a metaphor for a tangible and attainable future (i.e., to play music again with joy).

In another case, Fred's Guide was supportive, a chemical engineer, who came to see his major role after exposure to Agent Orange in Vietnam as an advocate for the safety of workers and consumers. While it cost him his job, he was proud of his stance with a chemical company when he decided that in his new identity he could not shrink from telling the truth and being a whistle-blower.

The Nurturing Guide (NG) can provide a sense of hope for a tangible future with goodness and grace. The Nurturing Guide (NG) can, sometimes, be a facilitator for self-integration, self-reinvention, and inner harmony. Metaphors affirm when the Nurturing Guide's (NG) consistent, loving ways have helped the survivor move from the fearful, disenfranchised, alienated, alone, abandoned old self to ways that, at least minimally, restore faith in a tangible justice, one of hope and self-realignment. For example, Micky had left Vietnam feeling that if he did not see that justice was meted out, it would never come. As he was concluding his treatment, he was surprised by an impulse to physically maim a dangerous driver on the expressway, to take justice into his own hands. Then he thought he heard a siren, an indication that the traffic police would stop the offender, that others in society had this job and would carry it out. He noted his relaxing, regaining a sense of safety that he had not experienced since the war. In fact, the sound was not a siren. His Nurturing Guide (NG) pointed out that Micky now felt more of a sense of restoration of justice in the larger world so he might not have to carry that burden himself.

Josh and his guide understood that he had regained a sense of hope and self-realignment when he used the phrase "heart" to no longer refer to his (heartless) misdeeds in war, but with reference to his own commitment to courage and love in the present. We elaborate in greater detail the dovetailing of metaphor and recovery in Chapter 7.

In Table 5.2 we attempt to move beyond the attitudes that overlap with conservative roles of the Western psychodynamic psychotherapist. Here we examine some of the general characteristics of the structure of the encounter, cross-culturally, with the wise person or Nurturing Guide (NG) that stretch traditional realms. Sanctioned by each society the Nurturing Guide (NG) seeks to assist the Hero in his journey home from the abyss. It places the Western trauma therapist in a wider multicultural perspective and facilitates our efforts to understand globally how survivors and their healers approach the problems of PTSD.

Universal Myths and Education: Establishing Mythic Space for Recovery

At a cross-cultural level, part of the healing process involves the survivor and the healer establishing a setting that resonates with a world of universal myths. The survivor, or Imperiled Hero, is one of many who has been close to or seen the Abyss of Trauma, lived beyond it and tried to return home as "before" in wholeness of identity and personality. The Nurturing Guide (NG) together with a healing society helps the survivor place this unique journey into its larger cultural and social context. By conventions or rites, they form a temporary mythic cocoon with certain sustaining properties that facilitate the transition back to the world of return. Within it, the Wise Elder or authentic friend offers advice, both practical regarding managing in the world of return and mythic regarding re-establishing meaning, encouraging integration growth and reinvention. The Nurturing Guide (NG) provides the space and trust, so that the survivor can give testimony to his or her extraordinary and overwhelming, extreme experiences. The guide bears witness by honoring it, embracing it, and placing it in a larger ethical moral and cultural framework. In so doing the Nurturing Guide (NG) illuminates the trauma journey, per se, and provides psychological support and offers specific forms of help.

Across cultures, the Nurturing Guide (NG) encourages and identifies movement in mythic space, facilitating the return from the world of trauma to the re-entry point upon return from peril (see Chapter 1, Figure 1.1). Metaphor helps to mark movement in this co-constructed mythic space. Indeed, the special place where the survivor and Nurturing Guide (NG) come together has transcendent properties. It is a place where transition is to take place. The survivor moves from the world of trauma (i.e., out of darkness; zone of danger; the dark and dangerous woods or confrontation with sinister forces (dark side of the "force")) to a new entry point or place back to home from a land of peril, trauma, and unexpected encounters.

Safe Spaces and a Haven of Quietude and Serenity

The survivor may refer to this "safe haven" metaphorically as his hideout, perch, hooch, cabin in the woods, closet by the stairs, country resort, nook in the attic or elsewhere. The Nurturing Guide (NG) and returning Hero need a space of physical and psychological protection, a space of security, safety and to be self-contained. While one of its purposes is regained insight, this safe haven must offer protection from forces, situations, or people that would cause further damage, harm, or further-imagined problems in readjusting after the Heroic journey.

The co-constructed space is one where the Nurturing Guide (NG) takes a practical interest in the survivor's basic human needs: stabilizing dysregulation, helping sleep, providing shelter and food, accessing support networks. In short, "just looking out" for the vulnerable, afflicted, and injured "soul" survivors and their personally neglected needs.

Finally, a *posttraumatic safe space* defines itself from which the recovered Hero and his or her Nurturing Guide (NG) can look back on the ordeal of trauma in an almost dispassionate manner, observing the self who was victimized by the perpetrator, taking in the bystanders and their guilt, as well as the disinhibitions and illness of the perpetrators, as if from afar or in real-virtual time. For example, Ariel remarked to her Nurturing Guide (NG) that it was "as if" the two of them were safe, as adults, on a hill overlooking the house where she had been molested by her grandfather as a child. From that safe space on the mountain (one actually was near the house), they could piece together and bear witness to her trauma. The mythic space took a place of metonymy, next (i.e., near to far) to but at a safe distance from the trauma memories. For years Ariel felt smothered by her traumatic memory. For example, she covered her head with her pillow when her grandfather approached at night. She now breathed easily, as there was plenty of air in her new safe mythic place.

Where possible, the survivor and Nurturing Guide (NG) work to create a safe haven. In this way the Nurturing Guide (NG) provides assistance to facilitate understanding of the Hero survivors' journey. This includes caring, nurturing, guidance, advice, reassuring, soothing, and making useful comments as to sources of recovery, stability, autonomy, security, and basic need gratification, all of which require a sense of security and safety. These ingredients, of course, are not present all of the time yet the survivor feels that for the most part the Nurturing Guide (NG) has offered a safe haven from which he can reflect on the past, the present, and the future. For those working with CBT, breathing exercises and imaging exercises that produce an internal safety complement these goals.

The Practical World of the Survivor: Useful Clinical-Counseling Interventions

The Nurturing Guide (NG), across cultures, assists in opposing destructive forces, internal and external situations, relationships, or opportunities that harm adjustment, protective functions providing advice, guidance, and wisdom. The Nurturing Guide

(NG), as a special form of *psychological emissary or ambassador*, possesses cross-national immunity because of natural compassionate empathy and connection to persons who suffer.

Metaphor marks the common space as one where the survivor will obtain practical help, where the Hero-Survivor receives guidance and wisdom that assists in the tasks of re-entry and transformation, help that is practical, concrete, and adaptively related. In moments of frankness and openness, the survivor refers to his practical helper as "Doc" or "teach" or the wise "old man" tell me what I need to know.

The Nurturing Guide (NG), within the safety of their common space together, helps the survivor assess the changes, positive and negative, that have occurred as a result of exposure to the Abyss Experience (AE). In their general form these involve expectable losses similar to those in other conditions of life stress. There are losses of friends, changes in physical, bodily capacities, and the ability to regulate affective states. The returning survivor, like the returning traveler, or migrant worker, may experience culture shock on return home. Rules and norms may have changed and there are needs for new ways to adapt. But it is in the details of the exposure to the abyss (AE) that we note real differences from other psychological returns. There are profound changes in attitudes toward the self and the world.

The survivor and Nurturing Guide (NG) note that change is a fluctuating matter and volatile affective concerns. At one moment, feeling continuous with the past and at another quite discordant and discontinuous with his or her idea of themselves. The Nurturing Guide (NG) understands the psychic balance, impatience, frustration, anger, and despair in adapting to these changes. The survivor knows, in most instances, that they fluctuate on a balance beam of emotional dysregulation. He or she knows there may be few useful and adaptive roadmaps along the way that will enhance their quality of life and well-being.

Proper education as to how to manage these changes is another element in the activities of the Nurturing Guide (NG). Rules and realities are not as they were before in the world of trauma. Metaphors capture insights regarding the changes that have occurred from the pre- to posttrauma condition and also illuminates important self-discoveries of self-reinventions.

The survivor may refer to these changes with a phrase such as "I'm in a new ballgame and all the rules have changed"; the guide explains the new rules and why they have come to be, however inaccessible. Metaphors capture the Hero's experience of fluctuations in continuity vs. discontinuity, as feeling normal one moment but discordant and disconnected in consciousness in the next. The survivor may feel he is switching on and off, or moving suddenly from a state of being tuned out to being ready to explode. The guide empathizes and suggests helping measures for these internal states of ego- and self-processes that are most distressing (see Chapter 3).

Bearing Witness and Giving Testimony to the Historical Truth

Characteristics of the Nurturing Guide (NG) and of the encounter space that he creates with the returning Hero seem to stretch the bounds of ordinary psychotherapy. How so, and in what ways? To confront the unconfrontable!

Testimony: To History, Disaster, Evil, Humanity, Trauma, and More

The Nurturing Guide (NG) provides the space so that the survivor can give testimony to the details of his or her experiences. History: An honest, complete history! In bearing witness to this testimony he or she provides validation as to what happened in the journey, confirms the authority of the survivor's legacy, confirming their personal significance. In so doing, the Nurturing Guide (NG) places the narrative back into cultural and contemporary history. The space that the Nurturing Guide (NG) and the survivor create together allows testimony and portals of entry to enter history at a given time and space. This entry is a journey through "portals of entry" to a historical virtual reality in "time and space" for the therapist and patient (Wilson & Thomas, 2004).

The language of trauma testimony is stark and unusually, if not overwhelmingly, tense. The narrative of how the world behaved against the stars is filled with horrendous concrete detail told within the sensory experience of the survivor who can barely find words to convey the events. Metaphor takes form here from within the experience of testimony itself: a journey into and out of the black sun inside oneself, a journey toward erasure, a rolling train, or enclosed death van.

The survivor giving testimony seeks validation as to what happened in their Hero's journey. In making the narrative of testimony real, the Nurturing Guide (NG) seeks their own metaphors that organize chaotic detail into more manageable conceptualizations. Tom's guide captured the death game by which prisoners of war were chosen to be executed as a sadistic version of the childhood game of musical chairs in that the winner survives only by seeing his comrade lose. Judd's guide understood the missed hand-off for which he felt responsibility for dozens of lives in a plane crash only when the metaphor was re-enacted in the doctor's office. How does one hand-off in the specter of death and dying? It is not spiritually possible to do so despite all moral protestations under non-negotiable human life challenging circumstances.

Bearing Witness: The Role of Nurturing Guide (NG)

Psychological bearing witness is the reciprocal experience of giving testimony. The two cannot happen without each other. Testimony of trauma alone is trauma repetition; accounting and testimony before the significant tribunal or Nurturing Guide (NG) who hears and decides the road to healing is another story in itself. Whenever possible, the Nurturing Guide (NG) helps the Hero preserve historical realities and truths. He or she embraces through empathic-orientation the patients' accounts of their traumatic experiences, struggles, difficulties and horrific realities—all of them! In the case of Lee, both he and his Nurturing Guide (NG) understood how a simple piece of military paper money worth ten cents came to represent a complex story of betrayal and assassination that became understandable only in light of rigorous knowledge of Vietnamese and American tactics of terror and counter-terror. Metaphors such as the ones we present below emerge out of the trauma narratives themselves to reveal the unsaid, hidden, and non-illuminated realities of trauma experiences.

Michael: Honoring the Hero From Stalinistic Terror

The Nurturing Guide (NG) honors the Hero, confirming the authority of his or her experience, insecurity, hardship at ungodly and horrific encounters, some never evident before disclosure and revelation. For example, Michael, repeated to his Nurturing Guide (NG) the phrase of his torturer in a Communist Romanian prison 40 years earlier, "you must yield." Yielding meant giving up his fundamental integrated self and denying that his life, memories, and attachments were other than he knew to be true. His Nurturing Guide (NG) helped him understand the torturous historical and personal context in which Michael yielded to save his life as a 20-year-old student while honoring his lifelong yearning never to yield, never to give up his sense of integrity, autonomy, coherence and self-vitality, spirituality and future. In the long historical retrospect, Michael survived and flourished, Stalin died.

Moral Compass: Ethics, Values, and the Sanctity of Human Existence Itself

Because the narrative of the survivor stretches the limits of human understanding, it challenges the most fundamental assumptions about humankind and the universe. It taxes the survivors' moral compass and understanding of life and the nature of humanity. Because the narrative is filled with evil events it often challenges notions of God, his presence or absence, or his benevolence. Because the narrative includes all manner of depraved, bestial behavior among people and toward people and within the survivor's world, it challenges the nature of ethics at the basis of human existence itself.

The Nurturing Guide (NG) recognizes the need to preserve and protect the bases of values, morals, laws, and ethics that affect the goodness of human existence even in the presence of horrendous trauma. In working with therapists who conducted therapy with torture survivors while Pinochet's reign of terror was still in effect in Chile, Inner Agger noted that the therapists invoked the charter of the United Nations as a protector of human rights in order to remind the participants that the traumas to be discussed occur in a greater world that seeks to re-establish the value of human existence.

Re-establishing a moral compass permits recognizing higher human values than the laws governing behavior within the trauma, so that sound judgments can be made about extraordinary historical life events and future judgments can bear a moral stamp. Spike (see the previous history), a Vietnam veteran, saw himself at the beginning of his journey with his Nurturing Guide (NG) as a crazed veteran-killer capable of and at times wishing to stand on a tower like a mass killer (i.e., like the Texas killer Charles Whitman). Agreeing to act as point-man (first in a military platoon) to rid his unit of dangerous officers, had made him, in his moral eyes, a contemptible murderer. With his Nurturing Guide (NG), Spike came to value his role as spokesman for his patriotic union, representing others who have been wronged with passion and effectiveness but without violence or malevolence in a warzone. Yet, those TSM and TST would change in time to a difficult level.

The role of the Nurturing Guide (NG) facilitates preserving parts of ego and personal identity challenged by the traumatic experience. For example, Jonah, another Vietnam veteran, began his journey as dissociated fragments of a personality. He ended his work wearing his headband, military boots, and pony-tail in a jaunty way as an integrated and proud Vietnam veteran.

The Nurturing Guide (NG) helps the survivor bear witness to the unbearable, the unsaid, unspeakable secrets and hidden pockets of psychic shame and guilt (see Chapter 1). Pete's internal image, one of being immersed in foul-smelling blood-filled creeks, alternated with episodes of standing waist high being cleansed through clear mountain streams. This contrast represents evil versus good, bad versus good, conventional versus pure, and, ultimately, death versus life.

Nurturing Guide (NG) as Ceremonial Leader for Prayer and Rites of Passage: Advisor, Confidant, Counselor, Spiritual Figure, Guru or Wise Old Man (WOM) or Woman (WOW), Sweat Lodge Medicine Person

The Nurturing Guide (NG) in its more secular form as advisor, confidant, and counselor, and in its more spiritual form as priest, spiritual leader, medicine man or woman, or guru shares many functions: assisting in preparedness for the Hero's journey, if possible, with realistic information about physical, mental, and moral challenges, using their wise counselor role judiciously and with practiced discipline, bearing witness to existential challenges, facilitating integrity of changes upon completing the Heroic journey and facilitating re-entry upon completion of the journey and the next phase of motivation (see Chapter 1, Figure 1.1).

Sharp distinctions between the two exist as well. The priests, Native American medicine persons, spiritual advisors, or gurus participate with the survivor in religious and community rites including prayer, meditation, and ceremonies. They call upon higher powers, interpret personal metaphor in keeping with spiritual belief systems and cultural myths. The informed, educated, PTSD competent and knowledgeable clinician blends his therapeutic relationship with scientifically founded activities, treatment protocols, and psychopharmacology. Yet, activities in the gray area between the two are not so rare, non-specifically defined.

Nurturing Guides (NG) and Journeys to Memorials: Metaphors Can Become Rituals and Life-Changing Moments

Lee invited his therapist on a pilgrimage with him to the sacred space of the Vietnam Memorial Wall in Washington. Kent's therapist empathized with the frightening image that haunted him, the recurrent image of his friend's hand movements under water as indicating "save me" prior to his friend's death by electrocution, while Kent burst from the water only mildly shocked. But Kent's priest gave a different interpretation. The priest explained the gesture meant, "go in peace, save yourself from this electrocuting water a communication from his friend to go and live, do not die here with me."

One African-American pastor after the Buffalo Creek Dam flood, brought peace to his congregants by explaining that the reason there were no deaths of American blacks during the dam collapse and flood, was that it was God's act of a modern-day Passover. In another useful religious interpretation of trauma, African-American survivors of Katrina turned their agony of walking in fetid, smelly, putrid water without knowing if they would be rescued, into the Spiritual Song, "I'm walkin' on water." Oh, yeah!

All of the above indicate how central spiritual interpretations are to the meanings given to disaster situations by Western survivors. Awareness of their impact expands the

Western therapist's vision not necessarily of his own role and expertise but of the need for collaboration with others in the Hero's environment of return.

We employ our earlier definition of metaphor as expressing through seemingly ordinary language, an extraordinary use of words and phrases, this time linking concrete images rooted in trauma to extraordinary posttraumatic, metaphorical themes (TSM). We suggest that listening carefully to such verbal creativity (TSM) offers entry points to areas of psychological therapies and work that might otherwise go unnoticed. A given everyday expression often has referents in the present and in the traumatic past. In this case, it must be seen also as an allusion to potential work with the Nurturing Guide (NG). It is an invitation for interaction often stretching the limits of the science-bound practitioner.

The Seven Masks From Mythology: Implications for Trauma Metaphors in the 21st Century

I The Mask of Asclepius: Iconic Greek Medical Doctor Who Addresses Bodily Dysregulation and Illness

Asclepius was a Greek icon of a medical healer, the ancient precursor to modern medical practice. We have observed earlier how survivors express their feeling states in terms of *bodily dysfunction*. They say their nerves are mixed up, jumbled, unsettled, overwhelmed, and can't quiet down. Proprioceptively they can't find where they are or are upside down, sometimes disoriented to time and space (the Inversion Experience, Wilson, 2006). Referring to sleep, they are afraid to sleep and up all night, referring to muscle tone they are uptight and unable to unwind (i.e., hyperarousal). Referring to respiration they feel smothered, unable to take a deep breath, in Burundi-Rwandan, their condition is "ihahamuka," literally the inability to inspire (i.e., suffocated by trauma exposure). When this family of bodily metaphors is dominant, the survivor is proposing posttraumatically that the survivor experiences a failure of self-regulatory and restorative bodily mechanisms, a loss of self-control and self-soothing capacities. As the survivor finds words to express his concern with bodily malfunction, he is calling for that aspect of the Nurturing Guide (NG) who, like Asclepius, knows how to soothe pain and discomfort, an authority who gives primacy to the bodily needs of the survivor and possesses prescriptive knowledge. Wearing the mask of Asclepius, the Nurturing Guide (NG) prescribes medication for anxiety and sleeplessness, herbs or acupuncture. The Nurturing Guide (NG) offers instruction in deep-breathing exercises, mindfulness and meditation, rest, relaxation, and calming exercises and more. The Nurturing Guide (NG) gives instruction regarding restoring physiological balance. Asclepius understood synergistic organismic functioning and now has ancient masks throughout the world.

II Mask of Mythic Space: One Who Comprehends Transitional States Between the Present and the Abyss

Survivors, depending on the circumstances of their trauma, speak of pausing at certain transitional geographical spaces that represent mythic entry-ways or transitional spaces en route to ultimate danger or abyss experiences as in the deep forest of primary Hero myths: Vietnam veterans speak of entering the bush, being surrounded by elephant grass, unable to see, getting lost. At these way-stations they switch on a hypervigilant readiness for danger and action. They also refer to mythic safe zones like the magical meeting place where the Hero comes upon his guide during his journey. They seek isolated spots away from civilization, a cave, or a hooch, or a canopy of trees, points of respite from battle places to recover, refuel, and once more face monsters. Each trauma zone has its own special vocabulary. Veterans of the Korean war may refer to the coldest day or a dangerous mountain pass. African boy soldiers may refer to a dangerous marsh or a safe rocky mountain hideaway or muddy diamond-digging field. The survivor's metaphors suggest that mythic spaces of impending danger and magical safety inhabit the current world as well as the world of trauma. He expects the Nurturing Guide (NG) to understand these references in his daily life and in his trauma experience and respect them.

The trauma survivor may allude to transitional states in terms of weather rather than geography. For example he might refer to his state of mind as misty, cloudy, foggy, or confused, or he may speak of transitions in terms of time of day such as dusk or twilight or first light. Often these descriptors capture not only figurative transitional zones of great importance but also actual spaces that were present on the way to or away from trauma. To the Nurturing Guide (NG) they are descriptors of feeling the pull back forces to the land that presaged trauma or the movement away from that land.

Trauma and Regressive Polarities

Veterans, especially soon after returning from the abyss, seek transitional collective groupings as well, groups with characteristics reminiscent of their period of exposure to trauma, such as veteran organizations (e.g., Disabled American Veterans, DAV), motorcycle gangs with ranks, uniforms, blood oaths, loyalty, being prone to violence but only in the right cause. The Nurturing Guide (NG) is led to consider the power of regressive pulls back to the scene of trauma, and to read metaphors of transition as measured in terms of the subjective sense of relative safety or danger in the present. In short, the generation of Vietnam veterans sought out not only comrades but the critically needed Nurturing Guide (NG).

Later on, the survivor must commemorate loss of life in the form of ritual and memorial. The Nurturing Guide (NG) hears his patient's search for sacred space. Lee sought sacred places in remote rock formations reported to be where an earlier more primitive people performed animal, even human, sacrifice. He and others are intrigued by blood oaths that bond, like those that bikers sometimes make. They are enormously anxious lest this intrusion of the irrational mean they have lost all sense of rationality. Others in more conventional terms are drawn to the societally sanctioned sacred places of commemorative monuments. Following the enormity of the number of deaths being commemorated they make pilgrimages to such memorials as the Vietnam wall, the Shoah monument, Omaha Beach, Normandy, France and the Gettysburg battlefield where the memory of comrades and relatives who perished comes alive.

III Mask of Hades: One Who Lives at the Interface Between Life, Death (Hell), and the Afterlife

Confronting the abyss experience of trauma contains survival in the midst of the very extinction of life. The survivor's continuing existence is colored by images of those left unburied, be they comrades or enemy, bystanders, bartenders, or monsters. The move toward and back away from those without funeral rites, those who shared the trauma experience but died in its midst, opens an ordinary life to one exposed to an uncanny world of spirits, that is of the wandering souls of those who died in trauma but who are yet denied access to the afterlife, in short of a spiritual world on the edge of the natural one.

Survivors uses phrases and words such as "ghosts, the angel of death, guardian angel, elders, grandmothers, grandfathers, old spirits," etc., the sense of being haunted, to describe an active supra-natural presence in their worlds born from their exposure to trauma. Unlike other families of metaphors, these remain somewhat hidden, expressed with caution or undue emphasis and only after considerable trust has been assured in a counseling relationship. If not picked up and explored they may disappear or never be spoken of again. The survivor is leery lest the Nurturing Guide (NG) interpret these phrases as evidence of a break with reality, of psychosis or mental decompensation. Their posttraumatic language supports the supposition that there must be some order to the way the spirit world, in its effort to move to the afterlife, intervenes in the world of the living. They seek from the Nurturing Guide (NG) a listener who can hear how such extraordinary events intrude in an otherwise ordinary life and conscious reflections (see Wilson, 2006, 1989).

As a case example, Dante, an American who served in the Iraq war, after many visits to his therapist, reported that in the morning when he looked at the mirror as he was about to shave, he saw two faces next to his one on either side. The images were clear and terrifying, although he was aware that they were in all likelihood illusions, not in fact occupying physical space. Noting the faces, he felt anxious about the safety of his kids at school that coming day, and about his wife who was staying home. He was also aware of a sense that his own life had only a short span in front of him. As he related the phenomenon to his doctor, his eyes grew very wide. There was no history of or other evidence of paranoia or psychosis. He was asking the Nurturing Guide (NG) to wear the mask of those who understand the nature of the connection between life, death, and the afterlife. The doctor said, tell me about the ghosts.

Dante explained that the two figures were Iraqis whom he killed with his hands. At the time of their death he thought he heard them swear something in Arabic that he interpreted as a blood oath, that their spirits would kill him and members of his family before they left earth. The ghosts would avenge the deaths. Dante's language of ghostly illusion was crossing into the world of spirits; he was asking the Nurturing Guide (NG) what organizes such phenomena, how might he protect himself and his family, or should he give in by suicide.

Gretchen, described earlier, wanted to give her guide the painting she drew after her accident. It captured the moment of her crashing through the glass looking into the face of death. On one side of the painting is a female figure, with facial figures that reference her sister and her own suffering yet also with the subtle suggestion of wings. While her therapist initially misidentified the figure as Gretchen herself, the artist clarified, "No, it is what I saw as I went through the window, my guardian angel who was standing beside me (not only then but in the apparitional journey home afterward)." The figure in the painting was ethereal, life-saving, yet grim, a reference to her religion as a Jehovah's Witness, and perhaps her Nurturing Guide (NG) as well.

In some Central American cultures we see the influence of spirits around disaster even more clearly. In an interview following the deaths of scores of Dominican American youth at the Happyland Fire in the Bronx, NY, two English-speaking psychiatrists were interacting with the mother of one of the deceased young men and two other adult siblings of the deceased who acted as translator. The mother had recently emigrated from a rural village where ancient customs were still very much alive. During the interview she was mostly silent, but non-verbally expressive of her deep grief. It was as if she were in another world while the surviving son and daughter spoke for her as was the custom. The overt task was directed toward gaining standard PTSD type information about the mother in the weeks since the funeral, her sleeping habits, concentration, irritability, decision-making, etc. The daughter and son were cooperating with the interview while she sat still or rocked. It was general knowledge that the fire killing her son had been set by a scorned male lover of a particular young woman in the club at the time. When the interviewers asked about the feelings about how the fire had started and about the perpetrator of the fire, the mother looked up startled and the son and daughter informed the psychiatrists that the interview would need to stop immediately. Later the psychiatrists learned that the mother felt the spirit of the deceased girl (former lover of the perpetrator) to be present in the room. She did not want to say anything that would disturb the spirit of this young woman as there was unfinished business between the families going back several generations. The mother explained to her children that she was uncomfortable that something might be said to anger the spirit who was uncomfortable with the Western guests, so the mother ordered the psychiatrists to go away.

In the case of Abram, the appearance of a ghost-like presence emerged only gradually. This time it was the head of a 12-year-old Vietnamese boy whom Abram had killed in the war. There were orders to shoot at the sign of any movement close-by. It was dusk, in a free fire zone in Vietnam. The boy fell toward Abraham after he was shot and had lain close to Abraham's shoulder throughout the night, with Abraham ironically comforting him as life oozed out of him and he died. Now, showing only the bent shoulders of a burdened man, Abram revealed to his Nurturing Guide (NG) the ongoing presence of this boy's head sitting literally on his left shoulder. The boy was now demanding that Abram refuse to hug his own son who was now the same age as the Vietnamese boy had been at his death, 12 years old. Abram turned to his Western therapist for advice as to what to do. Again there was no history or evidence of psychosis save for this isolated phenomenon.

As a family of metaphors, these references to the spirits of those who perished in this and similar disasters, challenge conventional beliefs about the relationship between life, death, and the afterlife, requesting to understand an order to the supra-natural. The presence of this vocabulary of the spirit state between life, death, and the hereafter alerts the Nurturing Guide (NG) to cultural, religious, and idiosyncratic organization of thought about the ongoing presence of the dead in the life of the survivor including the regressive pull to join comrades by suicide. The survivor addresses that ancient mask of Hades, the Nurturing Guide (NG) who is expert in the hereafter and its role in present life, a mask cherished by shamans but eschewed by most mental health workers today, even at times by their theological colleagues.

IV The Mask of Chronos: Time Keeper Who Knows How to Be There at the Right Time and Space in Chronology

Survivors' words sometimes remain fixated in the moment of trauma, even years later, while consciously unaware of their predicament. From the perspective of their dreams what is past is, in fact, present: it's happening now, not then. It's like yesterday, the images are so clear they won't go away; the same dream comes back over and over. "I'll have this forever." As the wounded Hero dissociates, unconsciously merging into the details of the trauma itself, time elongates to occupy the same temporal period as the original trauma. Beneath the simultaneous re-living and disavowal of trauma is a yearning, that under the right circumstances with the right companion, the survivor would like to revisit his trauma, so as to better understand his *actions and reactions and to appreciate its impact on his life and to see if alternate methods of coping with it might release him from remaining a prisoner in time.* Gradually, and with the building of trust he turns to the Nurturing Guide (NG) with the wish to revisit the scene of trauma with a wise companion who will not abandon him there. In this way the Nurturing Guide (NG) allows himself to be taken along to experience the details of the trauma, it is as though the past were present with the slight change of the presence of the Nurturing Guide (NG). These enactments, phrases, and temporal quality or grammatical tense of the sentences form another family of metaphors, this time referencing the "fold in time."

"Chronos and Tristan": Metaphors and Recovery

Some describe the trauma survivor as being caught in a fold in time formed by the trauma itself, as though the past could be activated at any moment, and as though nothing of significance has happened ever since. These metaphors seem collectively to make the statement that the central unmetabolized core of trauma "remains the center of life as it has ever since its occurrence and until I can find someone who will re-visit the trauma with me, it stands in the way of my continuing on with my life." This unique use of expression seeks to evoke the mask of Chronos, the Nurturing Guide (NG), as fellow traveler into the time plane of the trauma. In the case of one patient, Tristan, who described himself as a "groggy boxer," ultimately invited his therapist to share his experience of letting go of his sister's hand as she ran across a busy street, watching her being hit (boxed) by a vehicle and thrown like a rag-doll to her death. In the therapy it was as though the therapist too were on the very street corner as a participant observer in the tragedy (i.e., empathically-based virtual reality) (Wilson & Thomas, 2004). Responding to such a request to enter the trauma experience extends and significantly challenges the range of most therapists. While Western therapists are taught to expect a variety of transferences and countertransferences, they are usually not prepared to travel in time with their traumatized patients. It is the rare clinician who accepts the invitation to enter this door. But when we do, psychotherapy moves to a new and more profound level (see Wilson & Thomas, 2004, for a discussion).

V The Mask of Themis: Equity in Life Who Knows What Is Just and Fair

Survivors use phrases such as "no one will ever believe what happened." The world doesn't want to know. We couldn't have been doing that. It was a system of degredation and humiliation beyond comprehension. Or, on the other side, what I did can never be forgiven; I deserve to be executed; I am an evil son-of-a-bitch or guilty for being aloof.

For every culture there are figures that represent final judgments on these questions, be it Themis in ancient Greece, Jesus, Yahweh, or an ideal court of law.

This family of collective-reflective thoughts often utilizing concrete details of trauma without overt metaphors deals with survivor's need to place the unspeakable nature of trauma under a magnified moral lens. Together, they form the thought, trauma, so horrendous that it is unspeakable, that must be judged in the court of universal justice.

From Judgment to Witness and Testimony

The task of finding the words and the intimate other with whom one can give testimony and bear witness has many obstacles. Yet when that opportunity to give testimony, to tell the details of their story, finally emerges in the environment in which the listener becomes that other (NG) with whom trauma can be shared, when survivors experience being listened to carefully, when the other bears moral witness to their experience, the subjective state changes as for example in the cases of Lee, Judd, and Helen. Now the thoughts are along the lines of "I hope my story will help others understand." I feel some relief, as if a burden is lifted.

In its finally articulated form, complete with testimony and witness, this family of thoughts challenges the survivor's previously held position that ordinary people who simply live their lives do not intersect with history. In the end, quite the opposite is the case. They do give testimony and as the Nurturing Guide (NG) becomes that other who listens, these ordinary people do enter history, one that is theirs, both individually, culturally, and transgenerationally, a history that is now part of a collective culture's memory. While the Western therapist too often avoids the roles above, the Nurturing Guide (NG) does not. Instead, they engage like warriors in battle.

VI The Mask of Apollo: To the Universe and Beyond

Survivors say God looked the other way as they refer to their experiences as hell, depraved, bestial, and evil. They say that no one should have to endure or participate in it: the sadism and destruction of the innocent. They say there was no reasonable order to the universe. Earlier more naïve belief systems are not broad enough to encompass the tragedy. Survivors may feel estranged in the church, synagogue, or mosque of their childhood. They speak of existential despair, they say there was no God in Auschwitz, Vietnam, or the Twin Towers, yet on the other hand their own life was randomly spared. For others it seems that providence spared them for a reason, that a greater power was at work when, for example, the latch on their firearm locked and did not fire when a veteran could have killed innocent children. Incongruous thoughts pass through their minds, on the one hand the wish for benevolence and peace, on the other an intrusive image of wishing to hack off the head of someone who has only irritated them in a minor way.

This family of visual images, questions, and ideas challenges conventional wisdom about the order in the universe threatening to fracture beliefs in the goodness or the very existence of God. It underlines a challenge to an all-knowing, benevolent deity, while it also searches for theological answers to the question, "Why did I survive?" Each culture identifies a deity or totem animal who sets in motion the order of the universe. It is from that deity that the survivor demands to know why.

Indeed, within the past two decades in the West the new fields of traumatology and trauma theology have taken root, with a large literature on spiritual connotations to trauma experience, trauma narrative, and traumatic loss (Wilson & Moran, 2004). It is crucial that the Nurturing Guide (NG) listen to the protests aimed at Apollo that he or she not shrink from encountering the meaning of these questions, fears, and altered fundamental beliefs. But to listen to the questions is not identical to having answers. Indeed, particularly for the Western therapist, it may be important to spread the functions of the Nurturing Guide (NG), calling for the involvement of clerical colleagues.

VII The Mask of Hermes, the Trickster and One of Sick Seduction: One Who Understands Contradiction and Is a Jungian Archetype of Seduction and Temptation

The trauma survivor speaks of the apparent randomness of his survival. He says it was an accident that the explosion killed my friend but spared me, he points out the irony and paradox of catastrophe. He speaks as if the dead were an ongoing part of his life and as if he would confront the gods with their injustice if only given the opportunity. It is as if through his metaphorical language the trauma survivor were protesting a world of absolute causation: his proposition is that in the world of trauma it is accident and chance that rule.

Lewis Hyde (1998), reviewing mythological trickster stories and others from ancient and contemporary societies, concludes that through stories of the trickster, many cultures other than our own place great weight on the roles of contradiction, ambiguity, chance, the simultaneity of accidental loss and gain in our lives. The trickster, Hermes, is master of cunning, quick to meet the needs of appetite and human desires. Coyote loves to perform contradictory behaviors leaving the uninitiated stunned. Eshu brings out hidden conflict by being two things at once. The trickster is always on the move, crossroads being his home, movement a phenomenon of opposite directions. He transcends earthly bounds, traveling into the netherworld to bring back his partner from the dead and into the heavenly world of the immortals to rankle their authority. The trickster exhibits irreverence for the powers that be, a willingness to question and challenge the gods, with cunning and contingency as his technique. It appears the trickster is the god of chance but he is willing to suffer grave consequences in the name of redefining moral boundaries.

We might think of the very experience of trauma, as for example in the field of military combat, as a world in which there is a sudden over-concentration of events from trickster-land. In the flick of an eye, the survivor is confronted with the contradictory experience of death of friends, and survival of self, a surfeit of chance, where a turn in one direction is life and another is death.

The accidental intersection of a personal need, for example to relieve oneself with the ballistics of enemy tactics might mean life or death. The survivor has faced acutely dangerous circumstances and acted or hid based on contingency, intuition, and reflex. For years after, he puzzles over how and why did he react the way he did, why did his friend die, why did he survive? He tries to fit these happenings into previous categories of religious clarity, feeling blessed or cursed, and moral rectitude, feeling guilt or shame, but comes out of his investigations convinced that it was chance that ruled the day.

It is as if the trauma survivor's internal world has changed from one where rational choices led to natural consequences to one where accidents determine irony, paradox, and coincidence.

Trauma survivors, especially war combat veterans, understand the world of the trickster so well that it appears they have taken on trickster behavior in their everyday world. For example, Merritt, like many Vietnam veterans, found his life filled with contradiction. On homecoming, having risked life and lost his friends in combat, fellow Americans spit on him while he is wearing his uniform. He pondered why the best men in his unit were killed in the artillery explosion while the careless ones were spared; why so many argue that the country he believed in and fought for may have been on the wrong side of the war; why his superiors risked danger to the life of his buddies without cause. He thinks, even today, of giving in to sadistic impulses as though in the heat of battle, while wanting at that very moment to hug his grandchildren whose love for him is palpable. He thinks of a life-long character trait of optimism sitting next to the contrary thought of wishing he were dead. At one moment he finds himself in the land of the dead where his fallen brethren and enemy lay; and in the next, in the heavens where he confronts the gods with the injustices they have permitted and he has witnessed first-hand. Homeless for long periods, Merritt traveled what seemed to be endless roads moving in opposite directions, firing warning shots to any who will listen, stopping only to relieve his body of aggression and bathing in mind-altering substances, all of these traits being characteristic of the mythic trickster.

For those familiar with the totality of the trickster story, his paradoxical actions are only random on the surface of things. Rather he is part of a larger schema that affects the larger history of society in addressing inequities in how boundaries are currently drawn. For example, Hermes both pleased Apollo by offering him the lyre, and displeased him by carving and eating the forbidden cows of the gods. But in this process he taught humans how to sacrifice to (and therefore feed) the gods, ultimately changing the social customs of the land, altering the boundaries between gods and mortals.

This leads us to ask if the very contradictions inherent in behavior of the Vietnam Veteran that didn't force the larger American society to change. The trickster Vietnam veteran insisted we re-draw social boundaries regarding responsibility for warfare: no longer would the general society blame the warrior for the war; no longer would the mental effects of combat be divided from the physical ones; no longer would a protesting public displace its frustrations on the wounded soldier. Such changes widened the concept of ownership for war, and altered society's share in responsibility for its aftermath.

Yet another effect on society of the trickster/trauma survivor's stories of contradiction and opposites, is the role of acting as prophet in his own times, as whistle-blower for his society. Like Fred, earlier in this chapter. He warns of the unraveling of simple-minded plans that in their complex execution in the real world will likely lead to tragedy and death. The trickster/survivor is potentially a leader in society's efforts to modify itself.

For Hyde, while the devilish trickster is largely banned from positive aspects of Western religion, it is in the world of art that we find his influence alive and well in the contemporary world. Like the trickster of old, it is the artist who prepares and shoots arrows to strike at the articulations of our societal structure. We see this in clinical illustrations. It was through art (in this case music) that Lee found an expression of his disillusionment. Lee wanted his therapist to listen to Bruce Springsteen's or Jimi Hendrix's "National Anthem," to hear anguished betrayal of patriotism through harmonic discord reflecting how he felt his country's policies betrayed him.

The trickster's story is unlike the mythic stories of those who strive for perfection as warrior, whose ideals are in pure form, such as courage or strength. The trickster's strengths are cunning and effectiveness in contingency situations. His or hers is not the story of destiny but of accident and purposeful manipulator.

Confronting trickster elements in the language of memories and metaphors, the trauma survivor acknowledges that finding an integrative concept to pull together his trauma experiences cannot work unless it is broad enough to encompass irony, paradox, contradiction, and chance.

The trauma survivor today seeks a listener who will hear and understand his trickster stories. When our empirically based protocols no longer tolerate chance, ambiguity, accident, and contradiction, we deny the world as it actually is. And we deprive the trauma survivor of myths which might help him find his rightful place in it. Hyde argues that it would be better to play with him (the trickster), better especially to adopt styles (cultural, spiritual, artistic) that allow some commerce with accident and acceptance of the changes contingency will always engender.

The Nurturing Guide (NG) possesses the uncanny ability to listen without judgment and compassion, to follow the survivor's unlikely trickster story, without prematurely fitting it into a pre-existing diagnostic niche such as psychosis, paranoia or grandiosity or PTSD. The Nurturing Guide (NG) compensates for a fault in the larger society by tolerating and valuing the unusual and the accidental. He or she finds a way of listening so that the survivor is given his due.

Taken together, the seven masks of the Nurturing Guide (NG) stretch the Western therapist in ways that classical psychotherapy does not or has not explored. In the following chapter we shall keep some of these dimensions in mind as we return to the technical matters of how the clinician might more comprehensively understand and respond to his trauma patient's words and metaphors.

We see how the various functions of the Nurturing Guide (NG) work, together over time, as the returning injured Hero or survivor faces different clinical and existential challenges. Here, we break down the functions into their major groupings: assessing, soothing, explaining, protecting, and advising (i.e., primary functions of the Nurturing Guide). The survivor presents in a chronically unstable allostatic state, in which areas of his mind and body have been overcompensating in order to adapt to the ongoing pressures of reminders of trauma with their psychological and physiological consequences.

On the one hand, the Nurturing Guide (NG) is sensitive to assessing and responding to the survivor's needs for some physiological stabilizing or soothing activities directed to such needs as nourishment and sleep. On the other hand, the Nurturing Guide (NG) through careful listening is able to help the survivor explain what it is that has happened to him during his confrontation with the abyss that is contributing to his current state of disequilibrium. Each step forward in understanding is accompanied by risks of intolerable re-experiencing of the abyss or withdrawal from its confrontation. Each understanding creates new and more profound questions about existential issues arising from what one saw, what happened to others, what one did, and did not do, and what one now expects as a consequence. Thus, accompanying the understandings, explanations, and insights that evolve from the effort to give testimony, and to bear witness, comes new disequilibrium and fear. Sensitive to this, the Nurturing Guide (NG) insists that the space of the encounter remains a protected and safe one. At this point, there is need for ongoing support, and containment within the journey home paradigm. While the primary activities of the Nurturing Guide (NG) go on in the top half of the figure, important secondary functions go on in the bottom half. For, soothing and protecting functions after new insights are only a part of the recovery road. There are practical needs for supportive action that come from others in the community that need to be accessed at different moments in the process. With regard to these needs, the Nurturing Guide (NG) takes on mediating roles with others.

There are periods of more or less disequilibrium and symptomatology, periods of more or less need for soothing, periods of readiness for insight and progress followed by periods requiring protection from regression and fear; there is a progressive consolidation of bonds with the Nurturing Guide (NG) but also need for cooperation with fellow helpers. Finally, there is growing attachment, but only in the service of ultimate autonomy. Guiding to and from the Nurturing Guide's (NG) work is the language of the survivor, who in phrases prosaic and profound, routine and surprising, concrete and poetic, conveys where his primary current dilemma rests. It is the survivor's language that in turn defines the mask the guide must temporarily wear, the one from which he can understand and out of which he can speak in the current moment, often moments of critical usefulness at the right time and right place, that creatively facilitates transformational and integrative states of being and psychic consciousness.

6 Trauma-Specific Metaphors (TSM) and Mapping Clinical Pathways

In this chapter, having expanded our understanding of the linguistic features of trauma, and, in light of cross-cultural insights, we return to central matters of clinical technique for the Western therapist or others worldwide in working with trauma survivors. How to understand posttraumatic transformation. Our attention focuses on listening to the survivor as he or she tries to convey and we try to co-construct the nexus of their trauma experience. It is only from within this frame of reference that we build a safe place, a constructive working alliance and the potential for change in psychoformative processes. But, what does this "safe" therapist's place constitute? How is it properly constructed? How does it function in continuity amongst limitations of health insurance or its absence?

First, we consider the clinical concepts that help establish our stance, developed over many years by astute clinicians whose theoretical scaffolding we build upon. The techniques that flow from these concepts can open posttrauma configurations in the self and define the treatment alliance. The timing methods of identifying and exploring trauma-specific metaphors (TSM) involve ways of listening and responding on the part of the therapist which in turn rest on theoretical and clinical conceptual frames of reference. This particular set of inter-related theoretical positions are outlined in Table 6.1. The interventions associated with these positions are enumerated in Table 6.2. As such, they serve as working tables for the discussion in this chapter.

Theoretical and Conceptual Underpinnings for Clinical Techniques and Psychological Practice

We begin with the theoretical-clinical positions as orientation anchor points. We will follow with practical steps and then with concrete, specific cases to illustrate how the two work together in day-to-day clinical practice.

Trauma Metaphors, Condensation, and Depth Psychology

Appreciating metaphor as a site for deepening understanding is not new in dynamic approaches to psychotherapy. It is central to the work of traditional psychoanalytic psychotherapy and linguistic analysis. In dreams, parapraxes, neurotic symptoms or in ordinary language, the clinician is alert to, and intrigued by how, as in poetry, our minds condense, displace, make puns, symbolize, and transform personal dilemmas and conflicts.

Table 6.1 Complementary Theoretical Frames of Reference Useful in the Technical Management of Trauma-Specific Metaphors (TSM)

- Metaphor: Depth Psychology and Clinical Insight
- Metaphor and Linguistic Creativity Processes: Interpretive Process
- Metaphor as Portal to the Self: Ego-States, Identity and Personality Processes
- Metaphor: Trauma and Psychobiological Allostasis
- Metaphor and the Working Alliance in Psychotherapy and Healing: How it is Unique
- Metaphor and the Special Configurations of the Traumatic Event(s)
- Trauma Transference and Countertransference: TST, TSM: (trauma-specific transference and trauma-specific countertransference metaphors)
- The Trauma Therapist as Historian and Nurturing Guide (NG)
- The Hero's Return from the Abyss Experience (MHS and AE)
- Posttraumatic Ego-Alien States from in Trauma Ego-States
- The Shadow Self: The Unspoken Darkness from Trauma in the Self-Process and Identity
- Narcissistic Rage, Anger, Guilt and Retribution: Soul Searching
- Testimony and Bearing Witness: Historical Disclosures of Necessity and Reality
- Metaphor and Metonymy: Word Transformations and Meaning in Linguistic Pedagogy
- Empathy as the Key to Trauma Recovery Interaction Processes

It is one form of the traditional dictum to listen with the third ear. From this perspective, the therapist takes the patient deeper at points of linguistic and affective condensation. It is, in essence, a journey to inner spaces of the psyche; the exploration of the unconscious and unsaid of trauma experiences

Metaphors, Linguistic Creativity, and Innovations

Linguistic constructions call for special interest because of their multi-layered meanings, trauma metaphors demonstrate the remarkable human capacity to use word-play unconsciously in both opening and hiding intrapsychic conflict. The patient is initially unaware how a dream image such as "twisted steel" (see Chapter 4) cleverly opened a window into a self-structure and hidden trauma; how an enactment such as insisting the clinician accept a $10.00 tip paradoxically condensed a complex trauma story of traumatic betrayal; or how a spoken phrase such as "banging my head" against the wall dramatically brought trauma from Iraq into the clinician's office 4,000 miles away.

If the trauma clinician listens empathically and compassionately with respect for individual unconscious creativity he or she leaves himself open to being surprised, learning that unusual phrases may be road signs to hidden trauma. Metaphoric expressions are always trauma-specific transference revelations. TSM and TST are fraternal if not identical twins.

Delayed Grief Work

Exploring the content of trauma often reveals multi-leveled loss: the death of loved ones, friends, fellow soldiers, innocent bystanders, the loss of personal capacities via injury, and the loss of character traits such as innocence through abusive experiences. Metaphors like a "hole in my heart" capture such loss. Because such losses occurred amidst the chaos of overwhelming stress, there often was no time or ego-strength available to grieve at the time. Hence, even years later, as the task of mourning went underground at the time of loss, grief needs expression in the course of the trauma work.

Metaphor and the Working Alliance

Greenson (1967) used the term working alliance to refer to the manner in which the clinician calls the patient's attention to sometimes uncomfortable problems that nonetheless must be addressed. He called for a direct, collaborative, and respectful, therapeutic and dispositional orientation manner.

Exploring a trauma metaphor may enhance or put strain on the working relationship.

When Micky (the tunnel rat) said his Doc was down in the foxhole digging alongside him, it spoke of a strong alliance, affirming that the pace of exploration was on target. But when another patient dreamt the small plane he was in was about to crash while the pilot appeared unaware of the danger, it was a warning that re-living trauma was coming on too fast for the alliance to hold it.

Special Configurations of the Traumatic Event

Decoding the trauma metaphor is abstracting the essence of that unique shape, that repetitive fractal or configuration of the trauma and applying it to a wide variety of here and now experiences, including the relationship with the therapist. In essence, trauma metaphors are projective manifestations of unspoken, if not unconscious, realities of historical events.

Trauma Therapist as Historian and Keeper of Untold Stories

Therapists, in order to be open to their own associations in the field of trauma, have immersed themselves in the actual history of the events that their patients have experienced. After all, the traumas of our generation are part of a shared history, albeit often an underground one, that joins the life of survivor and therapist in a given age in time in history.

Inter-Subjectivity and Trauma

In using the therapist's own associations in forming the *word bridge* between the concrete and the metaphoric, we are leaning on current work in the *inter-subjective field* by Thomas Ogden (1997) where the therapist attends to the reveries stirred by the patient's words and attitudes. The therapist may visualize an explosion in a combat zone while the client's behavior may be explosive in response to danger along a civilian road. The therapist may experience an ominous sensation while the client is describing a walk on a sultry day in a city park. In this manner the therapist becomes aware of the link to a roadside IED in Iraq or walking point in Vietnam. Survivors may suppress just those important connections that the clinician's reverie includes.

Trauma-Specific Transference (TST) and Countertransference (TS-CTRs)

Once it becomes clear from the inter-subjective space that some aspect of the trauma has been engaged within the space of the therapist's office, the therapist considers the possibility that, for the patient, the doctor now represents a figure from within the trauma situation, much as in other types of treatment, he or she might be an important transference figure from early childhood in trauma-related ways or childhood transference reactions.

For example, in a trauma-specific transference the patient may see the therapist as a dangerous insurgent who has just killed one of the patient's comrades (see Bill below). In a complementary manner (in the same case), the therapist may, in the trauma countertransference, experience himself as if he were the Iraqi civilian about to be assaulted and possibly killed. As such, this would be a clear example of countertransference in a trauma specific form (TS-CTR).

The Hero's Return From the Abyss of Traumatic Life-Experiences

The trauma clinician builds an alliance with the survivor through judicious use of pacing, respect for defenses, and knowledge of the psycho-economic turbulence associated with uncovering trauma details. In Chapter 4, we learned how important to the alliance is the notion of the survivor's road toward home from his experience at the abyss in trauma and through this meta-metaphor gains an appreciation of the parallels with the role of Nurturing Guide (NG).

Ego-Alien Posttraumatic States

The very circumstances of disaster, war, and individual trauma expose individuals to sides of themselves, such as the capacity for cruelty (i.e., the shadow archetype, that they were barely in touch with and which under other circumstances would be regarded as ego-alien). In contemporary parlance, the metaphor, steeling a battle-mind, provides a sharp rationale for behavior in combat, but when applied unfiltered to civilian life constitutes ego-alien behavior.

Narcissistic Rage

Sudden and deeply sinister expressions in actions in character following trauma, may be usefully understood as having their origins in periods of anger and narcissistic rage.

The work of Kohut on narcissistic rage (1972) is pertinent here, where profound and sudden damage to the self, particularly in individuals vulnerable to it in specific situations and circumstances, creates reactionary fragmentation, in the self, loss of control and intense rage which far surpasses the usual experience of anger in response to psychological injury. Particularly troubling are long-lasting effects of fantasies and, under certain conditions, actions of murderous retaliation, revenge, and more. In this way, narcissistic rage joins ego-alien, posttraumatic complex states and the shadow archetype self in deforming character (Wilson, 2006).

Testimony and Bearing Witness

While much of working through of trauma conflicts involves understanding multiple layers of meaning, as in work with other forms of psychopathology, there are several shifts in stance that are worthy of note as the therapist engages with his trauma patient, that rest on separate theoretical buttresses.

The first of these is the matter of testimony and bearing witness. The survivor's narrative is not only the expression of subjective memory, it is testimony to a self in duress amidst a world gone awry and in crisis. It is one person's intimate struggle with that fractured world and the forces it releases within the self. The survivor gives testimony; the listener bears witness, i.e., the bond between narrator and listener becomes close, so that co-participation in both silence and newly constructed words and phrases is an intimate matter. Referring to work with Holocaust survivors, Laub and Felman (1992) comment,

> the listener . . . must listen to and hear the silence, speaking mutely in both silence and speech, both from behind and within the speech . . . The listener to trauma needs to know all this so as to be a guide and an explorer, a companion onto an uncharted land, a journey the survivor cannot traverse or return from alone.

Metaphor and Metonymy

The discovery that the survivor has created new language out of the concrete experiences born in the throes of trauma, is a major step in the healing process. It is part of the rediscovery that words can offer organization and meaning, especially through linguistic metaphors. Metonymy and metaphors are close cousins; they hug each other.

The special configuration of the traumatic event is often distorted by the mistaken notion that it is causation that connects intensely held sequential aspects of memory. As we learned in Chapter 2, we tend to replace metonymy, the neutral experience of having been next to, with the notion of cause.

Empathy in PTSD Treatment

Empathy for the trauma survivor is a central key in its treatment (Kohut, 1959; Wilson, 2006). But in trauma cases, empathy is often a complex matter, requiring the therapist to appreciate irony, paradox, contradiction, and ambivalence as well as to be in tune with the many affects of trauma as they emerge singly or in combination such as fear, rage, over-stimulation, guilt, and shame. These central and critical themes have been discussed extensively by Wilson and Thomas (2004) as to their essential relevance to therapeutic outcomes.

Theory and Relevant Technique Clinical to Understanding Case Illustrations

In the case illustrations below, we rely on the family of inter-related theoretical positions above to guide us as we follow three survivors with different types of trauma metaphors: The first, a verbal phrase along with identical behavior, offers a rapid dramatic course during a single clinical session. The second (i.e., a dream image) and third (i.e., a metaphor abstracted from an enactment) required months of work from the initial noticing of the metaphor to the deciphering of its meaning. The theoretical base for the clinical work conforms to Table 6.1; the specific steps in technique useful in all three cases are drawn from those outlined in Table 6.2.

Twenty Steps of Basic Consideration in Technical Activity

Table 6.2 outlines 20 steps in the technical activity of the trauma therapist working with trauma metaphors as the starting point. The therapist first notes a *behavioral pattern*, non-verbal gesture or charged word or phrase that is unusual and often intense. He or she underlines the patient's words, or co-constructs them, if they are not yet in verbal

Table 6.2 Clinical Procedures in Technical Management of PTSD Trauma Metaphors

1	Identify an unusual phrase, or behavior
2	Clarify the condensed overlapping and trauma related connotations of the phrase
3	Expand the phrase sequentially
4	Empathize with the affect states present in the trauma narrative
5	Map the phrase as possible trauma metaphor on to the present
6	Re-concretize the potential metaphor and map it concretely on to the traumatic past
7	De-code the trauma metaphor by linking it with the subjective trauma experience
8	State, and re-state as corrected by the survivor, the special configuration of the traumatic event and its expressions in metaphors
9	Explain how the trauma metaphor is the survivor's unique way of discovering new words to express the special configuration of the traumatic event
10	Explain how the trauma metaphor originates as event in the past while continuing to cast its shadow on to the present.
11	Expand the historical trauma map horizontally (what else was going on near-by that influenced the survivor's and other people's behavior?)
12	Expand the historical trauma map vertically (what else was going on in the authority structure in which the trauma was a part)
13	Alter crop lines as result of expansion above
14	Re-phrase special configurations of the traumatic event, in light of altered crop lines provided in an historical context.
15	Appreciate paradox, ambivalence, and contradiction
16	Empathize with more complex understandings of trauma than those accessed through the original configuration of the traumatic event, as presented by the patient
17	Hear the survivor's narrative as testimony and bear witness to it as therapist (place in context of civilized and merciful set of ethics)
18	Interpret and work through the metaphor (i.e., identifying patterns in multiple situations where perceptual distortions and similarities replicate elements in the trauma and lead to tendency to repeat, yet can be identified and distinguished from original trauma) so that a wider repertoire of defensive and problem-solving behaviors can be explored and found to be more adaptive
19	Monitor progress in the journey home from the Abyss Experience
20	Listen for changes in metaphor construction, meaning, and function (see Chapter 7)

form. He or she notes how the phrase overlaps with the trauma experience. He or she helps the survivor expand the phrase both horizontally in time sequence and vertically in terms of the hierarchical social matrix of which it is part. He empathizes with the survivor's dilemma within and after the trauma experience. The therapist then, tentatively, maps the trauma-generated metaphors onto the organization of the survivor's current life circumstances, particularly those aspects that are symptomatic. This is the special configuration of the traumatic event.

Having clarified this subjective truth about the trauma that has cast its shadow onto the present, the therapist helps the survivor consider sequential and hierarchical considerations that were outside his awareness as he originally construed the event. This leads to previous opportunities for the survivor and his Nurturing Guide (NG) to reframe the trauma anew, to appreciate contradiction, paradox, and irony. It is in this setting that the survivor gives testimony and the therapist bears witness to his experience. It is only then that the work of interpretation and working through can occur in earnest. It is then that transformations of the trauma metaphor may occur in the most existential and important manifestations.

Bill: Iraq Veteran

Bill is a 25-year-old currently unemployed Iraq veteran who served in the National Guard. He had tried on several occasions to receive help at emergency rooms where he entered in an angry, agitated state, and usually left before an adequate assessment could be made. Characteristically, he blamed the caregiver for his disarray.

Intervening Trauma Patients so as to Identify the Significance of an Unusual Phrase and Metaphor

Bill was late for his appointment at the OEF/OIF clinic.[4] He said he had no help in finding his way to the clinic and was immediately skeptical as to whether or not it was a mistake to come. He doubted anyone could help. Bill's tone and body language was agitated; it was as if he was entering the office in order to find someone to assault. The therapist was struck by an unusual phrase. Bill said he felt like banging (someone's) head against the wall. The phrase was unsettling. It also stood out because of non-verbal cues: a pause, an intense tone, a gesture and an oddly accented word. Bill accented the word "bang," giving it a sense of immediacy and proximity to action: I feel like BANG-ing (someone's) [inaudible] head against the wall. There was even a slight gesture with his neck as he said it that was threatening. It was as if the phrase was not being used as a common idiom, but rather the banging had some other more idiosyncratic meaning (potential for condensation within metaphor).

Clarifying the Unusual Verbal and Non-Verbal Metaphoric Expressions in Language Over Time

Depending on what he meant, Bill's phrase seemed to condense opposing thoughts and confusing pronouns. Whose head was he threatening? Was he angry at others or at

4 OEF Operation Enduring Freedom (Afghanistan) and OIF Operation Iraqi Freedom.

himself? Did he wish to unleash his anger, or was he frightened of his anger? Trying to untangle some of the confusion, the therapist brought attention and hopefully mutual curiosity to the phrase by repeating it in question form.

He asked, "banging (a) head against the wall?" He was underlining the ambiguity about wish and fear in the phrase and the confusion as to the pronoun Bill intended, i.e. whose head was it that he might bang against the wall? Bill clarified then that it was his own head that he had in mind to bang against the wall.

Contextualizing the Unusual Expression

Here the therapist repeated the unusual phrase, "you feel like banging your head against the wall." Then, pondering the phrase, he tried to contextualize it, empathically placing it in general psychological terms next to the events comprising what Bill had told him about his current situation. He reviewed the sequence of events that Bill had just explained. He recalled that Bill had been complaining that the signs to the new clinic, located in an area of active reconstruction, were confusing, that he had been given misinformation and as a result was late for his appointment. He saw that Bill was clearly agitated and upset with the apparent blocks to his arriving at his destination.

So, the therapist, narrating the sequence above, acknowledged, "I can see how these road-blocks to getting here might be personally frustrating."

Mapping the Unusual Phrase With Its Affective State on to the Present as Insufficient as It Is Rooted in the Traumatic Past

At this point in the clinical encounter a number of inter-related events occurred rapidly in the inter-subjective space between survivor and therapist. They centered on the fact that the intensity of affect alluded to in the unusual phrase was excessive, given the current situation. With Bill, the narcissistic rage incorporated in the phrase, "bang my head against the wall," did not fit well or map with the simple sequence of events just narrated. It was simply too intense. Nor did it make logical sense that Bill would want to bang his own head against a wall because others frustrated him. After all, the usual phrase about head banging is expressing anger at someone else. Something was missing. The therapist had become aware of more rather than less tension in the room as a result of the attempted empathy. He, the therapist, was also becoming aware that the scene he has just paraphrased, one of blocked roads, confusing signs, inaccurate information, active reconstruction, was reminiscent of circumstances in an urban warzone, one of re-enactment. The doctor's mind, immersed in narratives of the warzone in Iraq, had taken him from the present moment to a moment in urban warfare in a far distant part of the world.

The Trauma Link: Re-Concretizing the Potential Metaphor: Mapping the Concrete Phrase Onto the Traumatic Past

The therapist now had a strong hunch that the unusual phrase, in this case banging (someone's) head against the wall, belonged, concretely, in the war zone rather than in the present moment. He may have elected to offer this as a hypothesis to the survivor for him to consider and build on, if appropriate, or reject if inaccurate or if the timing was not correct. However, in this situation Bill continued to say he felt like banging his head against the wall, and in fact began to do so. These were not gentle taps against the wall, but violent thrusts of his head and neck that would quickly damage his skull and the wall.

With the clinical situation appearing to unravel before him, the therapist sensed that Bill was losing control. Whatever the trauma was, it had caused a fracture in Bill's sense of self; an allostatic state barely kept his sense of coherence and continuity in tact. It was possible that a dissociative reaction was starting to take form. So, in order to aim at re-cementing the rapidly fragmenting self, and in an effort to stabilize a working alliance, the therapist turned his idea into a statement rather than a question.

The therapist leaned forward and said gently and firmly to Bill, "in Iraq, something terrible happened involving a head being banged against a wall."

Decoding the Trauma Metaphor, Linking It With the Subjective Trauma Experiences to the Self and Its Constituent Processes

The matter of decoding the metaphor is the work of the survivor. The therapist reorients the survivor in time and place, taking him or her from the unusual phrase or action back to the scene of trauma, thereby reframing the issue at hand and providing a context for the survivor to narrate that part of his or her trauma experience that has until now been unspeakable.

The therapist does so by using the new words (linguistic creativity) the survivor has already created. When the fit is right, the survivor continues without hesitation as though this story were one he has always wanted to express, but has never felt he had the safe place to do it. Mutually decoding the metaphor serves multiple functions. First, it starkly interrupts a negative cycle, in this case an impending dissociative state, with understanding. It creates a potentially reflective space. The trauma survivor is startled at the ease with which he connects his current state of mind, via the metaphor, into the details of his traumatic experience. He is startled at how close to the surface the trauma really is. He is reminded how centrally his attention has been drawn to the trauma in everyday life despite his conscious efforts to deny and disavow its impact.

In Bill's case, he immediately settled down, stopped banging his head and began speaking. He and his fellow squad member had broken into an insurgent's home. They had cornered an unarmed Iraqi and began beating his head against the wall. They did so continuously and mercilessly until they heard and felt his skull crack, saw blood and tissue ooze from his head and watched him fall unconscious and presumably dead to the floor.

An unusual tone now crept into the room, a tone of testimony was present in Bill's unspeakable words. On the one hand Bill was narrating the terrible trauma of which he was part, including the excitement and power of the ability to have life and death control over another human being; on the other he was giving testimony to his actions; he was accusing himself of an unspeakable crime. In retrospect, the therapist wondered to himself if he was not, in the trauma-specific transference (TST), the Iraqi insurgent Bill assaulted. The metaphor Bill had created permitted him to convey that he wished to bang his head against the doctor's wall as punishment for his crime in Iraq. The doctor's role was to bear witness to this confession.

Identifying the Special Configuration of the Traumatic Event

The special configuration of the traumatic event (SCTE) is an existentially powerful and highly defended subjective memory, usually involving rage, disillusionment, guilt, or shame colored by anxiety, hypervigilence, or agitation whose impact has been so great as to mark a developmental arrest and to change subsequent character development (Lindy, 1985). The details of the special configuration are not evident from the usual reports of dangerous roles, in this case running missions to find and report mined sites in an urban area. Yet, once discovered, the SCTE seems to explain much. In Bill's case, the special configuration went far in accounting for his incessant drive to reach adrenaline-inducing experiences that might approximate the power of holding life and death over another human being, for Bill an ego-alien shadow side of himself unleashed in war. At the same time he was punishing himself mercilessly, behaving with suicidal abandon having recently run off the road with his vehicle and defeating all efforts to help him. It was as if his rage was free-flowing, ready to affix itself to the slightest frustration in the present, pressing for expression in action, to be followed by suicidal remorse. The concrete phrase, banging a head against a wall, finally understood as a trauma re-enactment, would soon function as a metaphor mapping the contours of the trauma onto events in the present and those yet to come.

Expanding the Trauma Map Horizontally

One of the reasons that the special configuration of the traumatic event (SCTE) is particularly shameful or guilt-ridden is that it is often remembered somewhat out of context. Like a film where a scene begins with certain action and fades out after certain sequential actions, the trauma survivor has psychically edited his trauma experience with a beginning point and an end point that often tell only part of the story. The task of extending the trauma narrative horizontally refers to inquiries regarding additional information as to what preceded and what followed the remembered trauma. For example, Bill focused exclusively on the out-of-control rage in which he smashed in the skull of an Iraqi insurgent. What he had neglected to point out was the sequence of events that preceded it. Bill's vehicle was behind several others as his column approached a potential mine position. As friends of his exited their vehicle to explore the situation, he and his squad mate saw an Iraqi civilian press what appeared to be a remote device, followed by an explosion in which his friend and many others were killed. He and his squad mate pursued the Iraqi to a house, forced entry and found him. They had no doubt (then) about his guilt and proceeded to kill him literally with their own hands.

Expanding the Trauma Map Vertically

Vertical geographical expansion of the trauma scene involves the levels of authority that bear on the trauma. In war trauma this involves the chain of command, the tactics, operations, strategies, and policy decisions that set the stage for this tragic encounter. In civilian disasters there are the roles of civic officers, those with warning functions, and those responsible for emergency crisis delivery systems.

Defensive Editing or "Re-Cropping" of the Trauma Scene as Experienced

The process of horizontal and vertical expansion of the dimensions of experienced trauma allows for new opportunities to crop and shape or edit the trauma scene. For example, the Sunni insurgency of 2003 was larger than Bill's experience of it. He was not the only soldier in Iraq to lose control as a result of witnessing an IED blow up his comrade. The boy, dressed in battle gear, was not able to discipline his rage when events contrary to the Order of the Stars (the death by mine explosion of his friend) suddenly overcame him. Interestingly, Bill, not long after the outpatient session outlined above, reported that he had submitted and won a photographic contest. The picture was one of himself in full battle gear, a picture he arranged to take of himself in the mirror. His cherubic face was striking; surrounded, as it were, by his shadow side, the uniform of death and evil destructiveness.

Appreciating Paradox, Ambivalence, Contradictions

Bill's photo was an expression of the paradox and contradictions of his experience. With barely the hint of a beard, Bill had been expected to carry out a man's duty. Reflecting the raw innocence of a child, he was in full battle gear with weapons of destruction all about him. On the one hand he was proud of his experiences in Iraq facing death and meting it out, while on the other, Bill felt guilty and sought punishment, literally, by banging his head against the wall.

Empathizing With Complex Understandings of Trauma: Beyond the Initial Trauma Configurations to a Wider Understanding

Elaborating the many levels of the war situation put Bill's act of killing in a number of perspectives, ones involving a questionable strategy of urban warfare, a questionable policy of nation-building in Iraq, some failures in the chain of command to reign in those tending to be overwhelmed by the demons of war, the appeal of superhuman power, and the devastation of losing a friend to a mine explosion. Many forces were at work to loosen Bill's hold on his rage. And in the aftermath a harsh moral judgment was pounding on his head with unmitigated condemnation. All of these levels would be available for empathy, some now, some later.

Hearing the Survivor's Narrative as Testimony and Bearing Witness to It as Nurturing Guide (NG)

Given sufficient time, the development of a safe therapeutic space and a true bond with a Nurturing Guide (NG), Bill would soon be in a position to tell his story in full, complete with its need for atonement and confession seeking absolution. In so doing he would be giving testimony to the combat soldier's experience of waging war in Iraq in the first part of the 21st century, its trials, accomplishments, conflicts, unspoken traumatic situations, and deathly confrontations, its pitfalls for revenge and need for atonement. His Nurturing Guide (NG) would then be in a position to bear witness to his trauma, to validate the testimony of his inner world of confusion and self-loathing arising from actions in a world gone awry.

The latter steps in the treatment process, interpreting and working through the metaphor so that a wider repertoire of defensive and problem-solving behaviors can be explored and found to be more adaptive, monitoring progress in the journey home from the Abyss Experience (AE), and listening for changes in metaphor construction, meaning, and function, would need to await further periods in the work.

In Bill's case, navigating the distance between the unusual phrase, identifying it as a trauma metaphor, and allowing it to uncover the special configuration of the traumatic event, took place quickly.

In the following cases, we present the road between these points as more circuitous, even though the same theoretical and technical considerations apply. With the unexpected twists and turns in the cases, the pattern was only recognizable in retrospect.

Whereas the case of Bill was one in which the nature of the trauma was immediately apparent in the directness of the trauma metaphor, the case of Pete, below, is more complex. Uncovering the trauma metaphor took place over many months of work, yet similar steps were followed.

The Case of Pete: Explosive Ordnance and Living

Pete's depression and PTSD following service as an EOD (explosive ordnance device or landmine specialist), in Vietnam, was severe and long-lasting (see case history in Chapter 4). Adaptation and failure to adapt had fused into an opaque and confused allostatic state. He was acutely and chronically suicidal in a predictable pathway. Despite this, his wife, a registered nurse, was a devoted partner, and like his son, a well-functioning young adult. The two of them would place Pete on 24-hour watch when he became suicidal. For many years he had been unsuccessful in finding a psychiatrist with whom he felt comfortable enough to work.

Difficulties in Elaborating and Contextualizing the Trauma Metaphor: A Dual Process for Survivor and Therapist

Pete reported a recurrent dream image that intruded as a waking image. It was the image of twisted steel. Pete was only able to connect the image to an impersonal sense of dread. His therapist became intrigued with the image, supposing that it might be a window into his life and trauma. But, when he carefully repeated the phrase in order to obtain associations to it, Pete had nothing to add. Suggesting to Pete that he might think of it as a creative drawing, Pete could only explain that the steel existed in an empty space, void of humans, void of vegetation or other material objects. Pete felt the image somehow belonged in Vietnam, but he was not certain about this. Extending the edge of the description led only to desolation. Pete tried to share his therapist's curiosity in the image, but it led nowhere. Unlike Bill's rich associations, Pete could come up with nothing. There were no people, there were no further events to follow; it was a kind of end stage, almost the end of the world. While it was clear that the affect in the image represented a self-state, whatever meanings were condensed into the image would have to wait.

After one tour of duty in the military police (MP), Pete discovered the EOD. It appealed to him as a patriotic and altruistic career for a young man. A film on how defusing bombs after World War II had saved children's lives appealed to his sense of adventure and sense of service. He was gifted in finding things others had lost, in finding his way three-dimensionally in repairing machines and in being calm under pressure. His would be a straight path to a successful military career in the EOD. Vietnam was a plum assignment to test his metal. And, in the beginning of his second tour, it appeared Pete had found his calling.

Pete's metaphor seemed to recede into the background. If it were to map anything, it seemed to represent only desolation, the absence of human life. Pete continued to experience the dream image but could make nothing of the twisted shape so the matter of linking the metaphor to aspects of his life seemed moot.

Identifying Overlapping and Condensed Meanings in the Trauma Context and Metaphors

At this point in the treatment, it was difficult to follow the nature of Pete's missions. Paradoxically, he was now speaking not of defusing bombs, but rather of making them. He talked about his black ops missions with the CIA. Having seen, up close, the effects on our people caught up in mine explosions, he had elected to go on missions where, rather than defuse bombs he was now creating clever devices and leaving them in areas where they would likely be picked up by enemy. Afterwards, when found, the device, such as an American watch seemingly lost on patrol, would explode in the enemy's face or otherwise maim the enemy. The image of twisted steel returned. This time Pete and his therapist could relate the image to the twisted steel of explosive devices that Pete had made, rather than defused, placing himself in the role of perpetrator rather than protector.

Thus the first reference to twisted steel occurred many months later in the treatment and referenced the result of his black ops work with metal explosive devices. Clandestine work is just that: secretive and non-disclosed.

Expanding the Metaphoric Phrase and Empathizing at Deeper Levels

In a second reference to the combat zone, Pete remembered the scene after his crew demolished a large cache of enemy weapons only to learn that their favorite Vietnamese child helper who collected casings of shells had been blown up in the explosion. Here Pete accessed another recurrent image: it was his carrying the Vietnamese boy, injured from the blast in his arms, to the safety of the medic station. This image, he later explained, was simply a fantasy, one of restoring to wholeness a child who had been blown apart. The therapist linked the fantasized wish (holding the injured but alive child as though he might be saved) to the actual trauma (death of the innocent child by his own explosive ordnance) with the original metaphor by repeating the word twisted. Pete had set aside the task of grieving for this child while in the combat zone. The irony of his death now needed to be mourned. By now the condensation, depth, irony, contradiction, and pain in Pete's image of twisted steel were all palpable. For Pete, the creativity of his image included its capacity to hide as well as reveal.

Overlapping Childhood Trauma and Adult Trauma: How Does It Work?

Soon, Pete's therapist was to learn of how the trauma metaphor of twisted steel related to Pete's life journey and to the inner drives of his psyche. These steps were not far away, but had an unexpected change in direction. Pete described his life course as one that was radically changed by his discharge from the military. Pete had chosen a career in the army; he loved his demolition work. But, he had ignored the details of a crucial event: after two tours, Pete had turned himself in for seriously considering the option of seducing a 10-year-old child. Given his excellent military record Pete was discharged honorably, but the end of his military career led to his first suicide attempt.

Complexities in Decoding Trauma Metaphors: Images, Memories, Metaphors, and Self-Reconfigurations

Perhaps the twisted steel was an image representing the turning force of pressing sexual urges toward children and an abrupt end to his ever-so-straight military path. Pete worked hard on this twist to his sexuality in the therapy, uncovering his own sexual abuse as a child, and the long hours in Vietnam after missions where he brought black market goods to orphanages there. Pete could not erase the possibility that he had solicited sexual favors from some of the children after particularly horrendous missions. He did not know whole periods of time were unaccounted for; he simply could not remember. What he could remember was the yearning for innocence, an innocence that might wash clean the destruction of the war and of his role in it. Somehow if he could connect with an innocent child he might reconnect with his own sense of innocence, regain continuity with a coherent self that was now broken and incoherent. Now, aware of such impulses, and the damage they would reap on a child, he resolved to execute himself if he were ever to give in to such yearnings. The dark periods of strong suicidal urges requiring 24-hour coverage from his wife and son were now clear.

While hidden from view for long periods, the metaphor of twisted steel now mapped onto his combat experience, his childhood, and his current life course. Pete's ambitions in life had run headlong into forces, both external and internal, that twisted his motivation into something destructive rather than creative. This was the special configuration of his numerous traumatic events.

Interestingly, as trust evolved in the treatment relationship and there was some working through of his traumatic experiences, it became possible to affix a transformed version of his metaphor to register progress. Here, Pete mentioned how he was productively working on making precise tools to mold metal into ingenious devices made for good: he was creating mechanical devices that would efficiently cool hot air and, as needed, reverse the process to create heat mechanically for third world countries in the Far East.

For Pete, it took many months to extend the metaphor, map it to his tours of combat (with his activity as perpetrator as well as rescuer), affix it to his current external world (with his activity in third world countries), and to his internal world (of twisted sexual arousal) and his childhood (sexual abuse). Pete's metaphor gave way to a complex trauma story, testimony to high, altruistic and military ambition, to trauma exposure, unforeseen twists and breakdowns in the ethics of his command structure and in himself, and a desperate sexualized self-destructive yearning for a lost innocence. All these paradoxes and contradictions were open for his therapist to understand, to appreciate, to empathize, and to bear witness.

Pete explained at the end of treatment that the words and feelings, the empathy that transpired in his treatment, was life-saving.

The Case of Lee: The Kiss of Death

Once more, with Lee, deciphering the multiple meanings of a trauma metaphor took place only over a long period of treatment. In this case, a ten-cent piece of paper money came to be a metaphor for both brotherly protection and deathly attachment. It condensed the paradoxical wish to take care of someone with the conviction that closeness is the kiss of death. Most important, tracking the metaphor, and its multiple associative directions, opened painful truths regarding betrayal that were crucial to understanding and bearing witness to Lee's Vietnam experience.

Metaphor as Unusual Behavior

There was something almost intimate in the way Lee placed the crumpled ten-dollar bill onto his therapist's desk at the end of the hour.

I don't trust those POGs (GI talk for bureaucrats or "pricks of government") (to pay you what you deserve for being here for me), Lee would say.

Overtly Lee was sealing his bond of trust with his doctor, while simultaneously distrusting the reimbursement system that designated the U.S. government payment for his treatment. But the amount, equaling only a fraction of the cost of the session, must have had some additional meaning. The therapist, under most circumstances, would have refused the gift. But he felt it represented something important, a behavioral metaphor representing some as yet unknown piece of a trauma experience. So he let the enactment stand, reasoning that there would be other ways to make sure the accounting system for his payment remained at its agreed upon level, and that Lee's extra gift found its way to charity. The gift was a creation of the survivor's unconscious, and seemed to be a marker of progress in the journey home. It was a metaphor linking the intersubjective space that the two would certainly return to as the treatment proceeded.

Delay in Clarifying and Expanding Metaphors

Lee valued loyalty and prided himself as protector of the weak. One of the examples of that loyalty was the special friendship he developed with a 12-year-old Vietnamese boy. And something had gone terribly wrong with these two values in Lee's experience with the boy, but Lee had not as yet divulged the details.

That Lee had participated in covert special operations during the war was well known to his therapist. At first, Lee would follow his trauma dreams about the assassination missions he was on with the statement, "Doc, if those dreams are true I have no choice but to execute myself."

Indeed they were true. He was assigned as squad leader to break into a village at night and assassinate certain Viet Cong-leaning elders. The attacks had been designed to look as if the Viet Cong had carried them out. It was part of a complex mind-game to win the village over to the United States.

But, in time, with the development of a non-judgmental and supportive alliance, he was able to tolerate that while these were indeed his assignments and actions, they were the actions of a young man who believed in the correctness of the American mission in Vietnam. Both he and his therapist took a historical interest in his activities. They researched the special operations activities in Vietnam, their relationship to the CIA, Special Forces Ops from Da Nang and the Origin of Delta Forces and the central role this counter-terrorism activity played (Operation Phoenix). His doctor was witness to the strategy and tactical assignments that placed Lee in the particular situation he was in, during this terrible war of horror, enacting a shadow side, an ego-alien part of himself as executioner.

The Special Configuration of the Traumatic Events

One day, Lee came to his session very agitated. He had learned through the grapevine that the government was pulling out of its commitment to fund the study that his doctor had been conducting. He was worried what would happen to his doctor, once the funding was gone.

His therapist wondered out loud about the configuration of the worry: You are worried about my being in danger that someone you care about will be suddenly cut-off by the government and that something terrible would happen, in ways like Vietnam.

Decoding Trauma Metaphors

Lee spontaneously remembered a situation in Vietnam during his second tour. He had occasion to return to the village that he had been advisor to during his first tour of duty, the village with the boy he had befriended. By the time in question, Lee was now active in special operations. He learned through the grapevine that the village had been wiped out by Americans. Our own forces intentionally killed the boy, the friend to whom he had promised safety. Only with the pain of this betrayal and death clearly in mind was Lee able to recall that when he had served as advisor to that village and befriended the boy, every time he left he gave the boy a ten-cent piece of paper American military money.

He told the boy he should keep it (i.e., money and connection), and should remember that his friend Lee was thinking of him while he was away and would return to protect him. Now Lee returned, an assassin in his second tour; the boy and his village, thought essential for U.S. tactical purposes only months before, was now dispensable and had been marked for destruction. The ten-cent piece of military paper money had been a metaphor, born in the conditions of war, and now transferred as his metaphoric bond to his therapist. The doctor had become, in the trauma transference, the boy whom Lee had vowed to protect. In Vietnam, our side's betrayal of the boy, Lee's turning of his protective impulses into murdering ones, the multiple contradictions that were part of American and enemy tactics and policies during the war: all were part of the ten-cent piece of military money. Now, he was learning once again that the person he was looking out for, this time his vulnerable doctor, was to be abandoned and at least symbolically killed by Lee's government.

Giving Dual Testimony and Bearing Witness: The Reciprocal Roles of Survivor and Nurturing Guide (NG)

The gift of military money was an unconscious creative act. Once understood, it condensed the special configuration of Lee's traumas in Vietnam. It was now a portal, opening the way for Lee's grief over the boy's death, his testimony to the despair at the center of his and others' war trauma. What Lee revealed now was more than narrating his trauma memory; it was the giving of testimony. In response to this testimony his therapist was bearing witness to Lee's dilemmas, and not only to the destruction of this village and the death of this boy, but to the betrayal of a generation of young Americans For Lee's therapist, empathizing meant understanding not only that in the transference he had been a helpless child, but owning that as a doctor in America, his own role as citizen in a democracy he had been unwitting party to the deadliest of disloyal actions.

Contradiction, Paradox, and Irony

Lee's confidence in the beneficial effects of his protective loyalty had turned to the notion that trusting him was the kiss of death. The central self-coherence of his character felt shattered. Yet the re-awakening of this trauma metaphor, this token of loyalty in the treatment, also had a hopeful side to it; that by laying out the dynamics in clear colors, Lee might reframe his trauma experiences, mourn the war, his youth, and the tragedy of his young friend, and begin in earnest finally to return home. Clear colors are like the beauty of spring, rebirth, new life, new colors for life's beauty.

The metaphor of the ten cents of military money became the first of several symbolic gifts, each of which demonstrated a gradual transformation of Lee's capacity for attachment, his recovering self, a story of his journey home that we shall return to in Chapter 7 when we examine in more detail the transformations of metaphors and their eventual integration within personality and self-processes.

7 Transforming Metaphors and Metaphoric Transformations of Trauma

In this chapter we explore how trauma metaphors change over time, carrying out new synthetic mental functions for the survivor and eventually reconnecting them with his or her culture. As we have throughout the book, we continue to examine how the clinician's recognizing and verbalizing trauma-specific metaphors (TSM) as creative expressions of the unsaid, unspeakable, have the potential to transform the survivor's sense of themselves in new and integrative, transformative ways.

Three Levels of Transforming Metaphors and Intrapsychic Dynamics (L-1 to L-3): Lysing Processes and Trauma Metaphors

Three Posttraumatic Levels of Transforming Metaphors (L-1 to L-3)

Spontaneous trauma metaphors occur at three levels. For simplicity's sake, we refer to the first level as concrete and trauma bound; the second level as figure of speech and metabolizing in cognitive function; and the third level as symbolic and culture-restoring in among other functions.

Co-discovering (with an NG) and decoding *primary trauma metaphors* (first level metaphor) can change how the survivor thinks of himself or herself. Permutations and transformations of new metaphor (second and third level) permit mastery and reconnection from the past to the present. Trauma metaphors, at each level, address the most difficult questions that arise from the trauma experience, the core of the trauma metaphors per se . . . its existential meaning and life-significance.

At the first level (L-1): "How can I find words for something unspeakable? How can these words convey to others what I experienced when they have never gone through anything like it? How did I protect myself from the worst of the trauma even as I was experiencing it?" What were the *central fracturing components* to the experience?

At the second level: "In what way can I draw on past experiences to offer models of how I might cope with its consequences? What has the experience meant to me personally, and to my view of the world?"

At the third level: "How has the trauma disconnected me from my own past? How have I become disconnected from the communities and cultures around me that matter?"

Levels of Metaphors and Their Clinical Expression

First Level Trauma Metaphors (L-1)

- Concrete and trauma bound
- Verbal or non-verbal allusions
- Unusual gestures or phrases or weird, unexpected expressions
- Unpleasant repetitive sensory and motor experiences
- Striking usually destructive interpersonal actions
- Subtle or obvious repetitions (i.e., compulsive re-enactments at unconscious levels).

Second Level Trauma Metaphors (L-2)

- Figures of speech
- Metabolizing in function of overwhelming trauma experiences
- Reduces overwhelming experience into digestible units, bit by bit, in emotionally disclosing ways
- Facilitates mastery of overwhelming trauma
- Transforms the survivor's sense of competence from helplessness, hopelessness to mastery and control.

Third Level Trauma Metaphors (L-3)

- Symbolic, representational movement toward integration
- Culture-restoring in function via rituals, treatment, therapy, etc.
- Marks the potential transformation of the fragmented traumatic self into a more integrated posttraumatic self: Gradual, holistic transformation
- Complement to sublimation: New pathways to life-change
- Metaphor at the third level answers the question of how reconnecting the survivor with a greater culture is possible, and how to grow and go beyond the strictures of trauma.

Three Levels of Transforming Metaphors: What Is Their Function and Purpose?

L-1

First level metaphors are initially, non-verbal, bodily-sensory based expressions. They come in the form of unusual gestures, unpleasant repetitive sensory experiences, and striking, usually destructive, interpersonal actions. When decoded into words, these concrete *somatic-perceptual sensations* or actions become recognizable as metaphors from *specific episodes* from the traumatic past that have been acting to organize current behavior. Understanding the original traumatic circumstances empathically provides insight as to how the survivor is unconsciously organizing much of his or her posttraumatic life, how the survivor's thinking and feeling about himself or herself in the present is a metaphor for their experience of the trauma. Creating and identifying these patterns with actual words and understandings change the survivor's view of life, giving organization to what he or she thought was chaotic or the edge of the absolute abyss. In this way the survivor recognizes that trauma has an extraordinary organizing hold on life. But, because he or she can now express the metaphor in words, the hold is less vicious and constricting. Finding the right words to express unsolved problems implies that at some future date the problem is capable of being mastered and resolved. The survivor's decoded behaviors may no longer be thought of as symptomatic evidence of shame and fragmentation but rather as testimony to the extraordinary circumstances of his or her trauma experience. An empathic understanding of the survivor's testimony, in turn, means that *the listener bears witness* to the extraordinary and thus offers an alternative self-attitude, namely respect.

L-2

Second level metaphors (L-2) take the form of *figures of speech.* They reduce the overwhelming experience of trauma into digestible units. They facilitate mastery and transform the survivor's sense of competence. At the second level, word-play offering variations in a given figure of speech occurs, each change accessing a different layer of dynamics to the same trauma experience, broadening and often reversing its subjective meaning to encompass paradox and ambivalence.

L-3

Finally, at the third level (L-3), *metaphors with symbolic overtones* weave individual experience with culture, marking the potential transformation of the fragmented traumatic self into a more integrated posttraumatic self. At this level metaphor is often a complement to sublimation, transforming the residue of traumatic energy into more productive and prosocial forms.

Taken together the survivor's spontaneous metaphors have the potential to mark and contribute to change: From shame to self-respect; from chaos to order; from feeling overwhelmed to mastery; from fragmentation to re-integration; from nihilism to self-direction and autonomy and the restoration of free will.

First Level Metaphors (L-1) and Their Clinical Expression

Somatic Expression and Bodily Language: The Sensory-Motor Perceptual Trauma Metaphors

It is in the state of increasing self-awareness trying to absorb a new and as yet unnamable experience, that the survivor unconsciously encodes trauma into body language or somatic expression. In earlier chapters we discussed dramatic examples of first level metaphor where unusual actions or bodily sensations carried a metaphor from the trauma itself. Here, we look at illustrations of how understanding these metaphors within the therapeutic dyad can lead to change and transformation.

Case Illustrations

Josh and His "Crushing Chest Pain"

Josh presented having traveled to numerous emergency rooms for a crushing chest pain, where medical work-ups, including EKGs, had been negative in outcome. Josh had served in Vietnam about 12 years earlier as a truck driver's assistant in a supply unit. His doctor was struck by the expression "crushing chest pain" and wondered if it might not refer to something in the war. Josh changed how he looked at himself when he learned that the crushing pain in his chest was not physical but rather a life and death psychological replay of a trauma from his war experience. The crushing pain in his chest fit exactly with the pain he imagined that a Vietnamese girl had, a girl whose chest he and his comrade had crushed when they ran over her with their truck at a potential ambush site. Once interpreted or decoded, the phrase "crushing chest pain" changed from a somatic symptom to a metaphor capable of expressing some aspect of Josh's unique and unconscious response to trauma.

Ursula: Fire Survivor

Ursula, a supper-club fire survivor, kept feeling as though her bladder was full and she needed to urinate, a reversal of the actual situation just before the Beverly Hills Supper Club fire when her friend asked her to join her in the ladies room. At that time Ursula had sensed no urgency from her bladder and had declined the invitation. Minutes later, lights went out and her friend, unable to escape the lavatory, burned to death. Meanwhile Ursula and her group had formed a human chain and escaped the fire unharmed. After negative medical work-ups, identifying the urinary symptom as a trauma metaphor allowed Ursula to be in contact with her own strong wish to reverse the tragedy of her friend's death by taking her place, to join her friend in the actions that would lead to their being together. The changes evoked in Ursula as a result of the decoding of the metaphor allowed grief work for her friend to come into focus.

Vietnam: Paul's "Picking at Cleats on His Boots" for a Long Time

Paul spent long periods with his therapist in silence as he picked at specks of dried mud on his boots. On one occasion, somewhat exasperated by this habit (and the mess it was making) his therapist asked, what is it that is so engaging about getting every particle off your boots?

Paul replied, it's his brains. Paul explained during one mission, he saw incoming fire hit, and went over to see how his friend had fared. He saw his friend's torso, mangled head, and then looking down discovered his friend's brains now adhered to his boots. When Paul and his therapist recognized the origins of his habit, it was as if the intimacy of the trauma invaded the office. But after the initial shock, a reflective cooperative space was born, one where Paul could for the first time remember and grieve the death of his combat buddy.

Tristan, the "Groggy Boxer"

Tristan was already an adult when he sought treatment. He described his current life as that of a groggy boxer, being barraged unexpectedly from his blind side. Over time his doctor learned that the traumatic antecedent of this metaphor was an experience in early childhood in which his sister left his side to cross a busy road, was struck by an oncoming vehicle and killed, thrown like a rag doll into the air. In this instance, Tristan realized that his doctor, working with the phrase groggy boxer, had uncovered his unconscious identification with his dead sister. It was now Tristan who was being hit again and again by life's forces, and behaving in his depression as though he were dead. It is as if his doctor had climbed back in time with him to that long repressed traumatic space (a fold in time) and was now with him so he could review the trauma's psychological impact in detail. Re-establishing the trauma space as one of reflection rather than repression made Tristan feel alive rather than dead.

Like Hollywood Movie Editing: Transpositions of Figures From the Trauma Scene Into Memory

It is important to note that the somatic expressions and non-verbal behaviors do not necessarily recapitulate the trauma unchanged but rather present a kind of compromise formation expressing a subjective truth about the self in the context of the trauma. For Josh, the trauma was one in which the girl experiences anguishing pain in the chest, while in the re-enactment, it is Josh who feels he is about to die. In the trauma, Ursula had no urge to urinate and therefore declined to join her friend in the lavatory whereas her current bodily sensation involves a transposition of figures in the trauma scene: it is she who experiences urinary urgency, as if to say I wish I had joined my friend in death. Tristan puts himself in the place of his killed rag doll sister.

As such, somatic enactments of trauma translate into something true about the present world and the world of the trauma and the posttraumatic world: for Ursula, "I wish I were still connected to my best friend"; for Josh and Tristan, "I am the one who should be dead."

This newly extracted subjective truth of the self in relation to the world of trauma arranges and organizes the present and casts its shadow on the foreseeable future since it is possible that the future will be repeat the failed resolution of the trauma itself. The somatic expression is the non-verbal form of a developing trauma metaphor. It condenses the subjective experiences of the trauma and now serves to map present and future experience. For the survivor, it is an unconscious working metaphor that he misapplies to everyday problem-solving. But how it interacts with the many stresses of ordinary life of the non-trauma world becomes a tragedy in itself.

First Level Metaphors (L-1): Their Place in the Hero/Survivor's Journey Home

In the therapeutic situation or the survivor's contact with the Nurturing Guide (NG), the manner in which *first level sensory-motor trauma metaphors* come to be recognized as having their basis within memories of the trauma itself, is a matter of co-construction, a joint enterprise. Once its origins are clear, the survivor finds himself saying out loud aspects of the trauma of which he has never previously before spoken. He has unexpectedly given testimony to hidden parts of a traumatic truth. That is: he has shed light on the human and inhuman behavior of himself and others both in a life and death circumstance and in an ethical context. As the therapist or Nurturing Guide (NG) listens, he or she quietly bears witness to the impossible choices and existential dilemmas with which the survivor continues to deal within unresolved complex ways in terms pre-traumatic personality dynamics (see Chapter 3).

Out of the testimony and the witness, the metaphor now gives way to empathy. In this way the metaphor serves to contain, organize, and offer empathic resonance with otherwise chaotic posttraumatic experience. The organizing linguistic feature of first level metaphor is transforming, in that, recognizing the metaphor, empathizing with the associated affective state, and bearing witness to its traumatic significance permits the survivor's psyche to move in the present from chaos toward order; from dysphoria toward wholeness. Identifying and honoring first level trauma metaphors suddenly offers room for reflection, at just the psychological site that had previously been one of imminent emotional dysregulation. Unlike worn out metaphors from a more naïve past, first level metaphors herald a capacity for new language, one ultimately capable of transforming self and relationship patterns in new directions. It is a portal to a new life.

Second Level Metaphors (L-2): Lysing Processes

While first level metaphors (L-1) bring the therapeutic dyad back to subjectively central, concrete details of the trauma, second level metaphors (L-2) introduce ways of breaking down trauma from an overwhelming whole into smaller coping segments. This is the lysing process mentality. Second level metaphors give shape to problem-solving cognitive activity. They do so in two ways: first by lysing the larger trauma into smaller manageable segments, and secondly, by identifying layers of meaning to the experience. Below we shall approach lysing and layering metaphors separately.

The second level lysing metaphor (L-2) is a phrase or figure of speech that breaks down the trauma into workable manageable bite-sized pieces in the service of metabolizing or working through its impact. Like enzymes, they break down or lyse the larger trauma molecule into smaller chains, turning something overwhelming into a familiar shape capable of being comprehended and metabolized. These metaphors take their cue from earlier experiences of mastery in the life of the survivor based on coping in the pre-traumatic years. In this book, the vignettes from the treatment of Tom, Judd, and Karen illustrate lysing metaphors.

The second level lysing metaphor (L-2) addresses further central questions for the survivor: confronting a trauma experience in many ways totally new, are there *any* past experiences that might serve as a model for coping in this new situation? The lysing metaphor transforms by giving the trauma a working definition and offers through language a new organizing or coping tool. Mapping this metaphor onto the present provides clues as to how to cope with the trauma's consequences. With this new tool in hand, the survivor changes; seeing his situation as one with the potential for mastery goes far in restoring a damaged self.

Second Level Layering Metaphors (L-2)

A *layering metaphor* is best distinguished by how it enables understanding of overlapping dynamics of the same trauma. For the survivor, it addresses the question, how is it possible to integrate multiple ways the trauma experience has changed the view of the world? Here a linguistic turn of a special metaphor, for example, a pun or a reversal of phrase, uncovers paradoxes that existed within the trauma and in the present existential reality of the victim/survivor. In adding layers of complexity, these metaphors undercut a premature one-dimensional understanding of the trauma situation, clarifying that there are multiple layers of truth each with its own definable level of meaning. The word-play inherent in the layering metaphors allows a deepening of understanding of the many ways, at times paradoxical and ironic, in which the trauma tends to re-play itself. It reminds the survivor that he is capable of unconsciously identifying with all of the participants in the traumatic experience.

Illustrations of Second Level Lysing Metaphors (L-2)

Tom and the "Game of Musical Chairs" in a Situation of Death as a Vietnam POW

Tom first dreamt of his Vietnam experience as a set of crusted yellow pages permanently stuck together. It was simply a yellow stain (of shame) never to be opened. At home, Tom removed the furnishings in his basement retreat, dressed in old fatigues, and sat up against the wall for hours. At other times he lay still on the basement floor. Still other moments he shouted indistinguishable sounds. With alcohol in hand, his movements and sounds increasingly frightened his wife, especially as she knew there were weapons in the basement as well. When fatigue-dressed Vet Center counselors appeared at her request, Tom held them at gunpoint for over 30 minutes. Tom could make no sense of his basement arrangement (i.e., hooch-like, Vietnam dwelling) or activity. He had no conscious knowledge of his behavior as a re-enactment (i.e., dissociation). The Viet Cong held him as prisoner-of-war (POW) in Vietnam for 13 days along with other American soldiers. Each day one of the Americans was executed (hung on the central flag pole of the VC camp until dead while the other Americans were forced to watch). It was a cruel and common game in which either he or his buddies would be killed. Every night he searched for clues as to how they chose the victim for the next day: But their game had no rules.

Tom explained in his therapy session that he had been most distressed when a simple activity at home occurred with his children. He was supervising a birthday party for one of his boys. Having set the cake on the kitchen table, Tom had inadvertently set one less chair than the number of kids. When he called them in for the cake, they scrambled for seats and one child was left out. Tom felt a welling up of excessive emotion. He excused himself and lay on his bed sobbing uncontrollably. His therapist, after waiting and trying to digest the experience, said, "like a game of musical chairs." The deaths in Vietnam were like a cruel game of musical chairs or Russian roulette. Mapping the metaphor, the one who stayed alive could be grateful only at the death of a buddy . . . a yellow stain for life. Tom cried in his doctor's office, quietly, for the first time since Vietnam, about his trauma and his losses, and allowed himself, again, for the first time, to feel empathy for his own experience.

The pages to the crusted yellow stain (the first metaphor) opened onto the complex re-enactments in his basement, finally condensed into a transforming metaphor, the childhood game of musical chairs. Trauma metaphors enabled movement from Level 1 to Level 2 and beyond.

Tom, an engineer by education, had shown interest since childhood in how things work, and in life, what one might call the "rules of the game." Musical chairs was a ready-made metaphor from childhood that he, together with his therapist, discovered applied to his prisoner-of-war (POW) experience in Vietnam.

For Tom and his therapist, mapping the old game of musical chairs onto the trauma experience shed a new light on it. Tom had been in the role of the guilty winner of the game, feeling he had only won at the cost of the deaths of his buddies. Now, in the moment in the kitchen, he was the unwitting organizer of the game, causing pain to the child who had no seat at the birthday table, a thought so unbearable that he broke down and sobbed in his bedroom, isolated from the party. He realized that for the Viet Cong such games were part of an overall strategy of random horror to defeat the American will to remain in their country.

Tom applied his new knowledge of how the trauma was repeating itself in new circumstances to solve the mystery of his anxiety in public places, especially where he did not have control of the exit possibilities. He now saw the logic in those special anxieties that repeated certain characteristics of the configurations in the POW hut. He applied his understanding of the interpersonal configuration of musical chairs to other situations in his life, such as the reason for his being temporarily laid off, as a logical recession policy rather than a random decision to hang him. As he did so, he noted a return of energy in the present.

Judd and the "Missed Hand-Off"

Judd found a way to reconfigure his complex trauma metaphor by way of an unconscious transference experiment. He would have his therapist put him on trial (first level [L-1] metaphor). It was simple in Judd's mind. He was responsible for 16 deaths because as flight controller he had missed the hand-off, the point at which one radar observer reports to the next as the flight tracking goes off one screen and on to the next. Judd's view about this was uncompromising and self-crushing.

The phrase, "missed hand-off" referred not only to the field of trauma but to a moment of shame in junior high school, when he missed the hand-off. He was going out for defensive back in football. There is, his coach insisted, no excuse for missing the hand-off, referring to the defensive job of seeing to whom the quarterback hands off the football.

Newspapers that described him as a hero only infuriated him further. He resigned his position, became depressed, put his life on hold, and sought out widowed spouses, volunteering his services to be certain that they received the death benefits they deserved.

A problem with Judd's self-evaluation was that the original radar screen was not within his range of vision. He was theoretically responsible yet had to rely on another for the information that the plane had veered off-course. Overtly he wanted the therapist to put him on trial for his offense so that he could receive the guilty sentence he deserved. In fact, an aviation board had acquitted him of responsibility and the press hailed him as hero for having saved even more lives after he brought the pilot in with his navigational instructions. During the therapy trial (he brought in evidence and argued vigorously against himself), another scene was going on off-stage. It was the story of his billing, which had been handed off from one third-party payer to another. Suddenly, he interrupted his narrative and accused the therapist of woeful disregard in the matter of following up on his payments for the treatment. He documented how the doctor had missed the hand-off regarding the payments. In this way he reconfigured the hand-off so that it was he who was the accuser and the doctor as the perpetrator. In its revised form, the doctor, cast in the role of perpetrator, was quite comfortable with the limits of his tending to the bill. It was not a crime; it was not a matter of self-denigration, the doctor was keeping his sights on his patient, and the excessive guilt and responsibility he had been experiencing. The missed hand-off was only a step away from keeping your eye on the ball, another metaphor, that opened the way for Judd to expand his current tunnel vision. Judd needed to keep his eye on the ball of his professional development, his previous as well as current relationships. Most importantly to ask himself how long he would need to keep his eye affixed to atonement for his excessively harsh judgment of his contribution to the crash.

Through the second level metaphor, Judd could more easily break down his current dilemmas into manageable units and begin to feel that he would, at some time, master his trauma, while the therapeutic space became the unconscious experimental field in which to test out his self-punishing views.

Karen and the "Unfair Wrestling Match"

For Karen, the phrase "unfair wrestling match" originated in a posttraumatic dream. It gave metaphoric form to her trauma. Karen was a strong and independent woman. She was skilled in martial arts. Running was an important avocation that reinforced her independence and strength. The way her rapist had taken her by surprise, tripped her in the rain, dragged her off the road, beat her with a blunt instrument breaking her maxillary bone and endangering an orbit of her eye, and forced her to submit holding broken glass next to her face, all seemed incomprehensible. It was a deathly fearful, shaming, enraging experience, and it felt as if it broke her character and sense of coherence. During her therapy she dreamt of a wrestling match with her older brother in which she was being pinned down. She protested that it was unfair, but no one stopped it. She associated the dream image to actual experiences from her childhood where her two-year-older twin brothers would wrestle her in a way that she thought was merciless but from which she could survive and even gain strength. Her trauma, an inchoate beating that was close to death, had drawn to it an accretion from childhood of lost wrestling matches with her brothers. While she felt enraged and humiliated at the time, she remembered father saying, yes the wrestling match is unfair, but in some way we grow from such matches. Redefining the rape as an unfair wrestling match gave definition to her experience and transformed it into something that Karen could eventually move beyond.

Layering Metaphors

Josh and "My Pained Heart"

In Josh's case subtle changes occurred to his original (L-1 first level metaphor) crushing chest pain, a pain he was sure would kill him, a sensation that unconsciously identified him with the Vietnamese child he and his friend had run over in Vietnam. Older truths came to adhere to the first level metaphor (L-1) like accretions from earlier metaphors onto a sensory-motor aspect of the trauma. While originally a physical crushing chest pain Josh's metaphor came to represent, as well, a pained heart. A pained heart referred to the emptiness and loss he experienced for years after the death of his mother as a child. It then applied to lost girlfriends who broke his heart and to unexpressed heartfelt grief for the many un-grieved losses in Vietnam from both the Vietnamese side and ours. It became the pained heart acknowledging loss of innocence, not only the innocent girl on the road, but also the innocence of fellow soldiers, and poignantly the loss of his own innocence in war.

Like a telescope collapsing in on itself (Kohut, 1971), Josh's chest pain found a linguistic antecedent, pain in one's heart, that linked him with dilemmas in his past. In his level 2 metaphor Josh and his therapist found numerous layers to the meaning of pained heart.

Ursula's "Pissyness" (Urinary Urgency)

Ursula's symptom, urinary urgency, captured the moment in which she sensed her own bladder not being full; a moment when she declined her best friend's invitation to join her in the lavatory, a refusal she came to believe had sealed her friend in a fiery tomb while Ursula walked to safety. It was later that the symptom of urinary urgency as primary metaphor lent itself to associational accretions from earlier in life. In fact, Ursula was quite capable of feeling pissy when upset. Indeed this affect surrounded her, set her off from others, and functioned as a defense against dealing with her grief. She could ultimately see that in her pissyness she continued the unconscious tie to her friend and avoided the painful work of grieving her.

Paul's "Picking"

For Paul, like Josh, and Ursula, level 2 metaphors evolved linguistically close to the first phrase, in this case, picking at his boots. Both he and his therapist observed how at times he was picking the brain of his therapist with annoying questions, or in the reverse direction, he feared a silence being pierced by the therapist's picking his brain. Now the word picking lent itself to word-play: he remembered being picked on as a child, and then later, picking on others, indeed it is this characteristic that seemed to describe his relationship with his buddy who died. Here the second level metaphor serves as a trope uncovering multiple layers of meaning to the relationship with the doctor and with the friend who died, layers that included contradiction and paradox.

Tristan's "Feeling Boxed In"

In the case of Tristan, in the first level metaphor, the groggy boxer, constantly getting into situations where he was blind-sided, transformed to an awareness of a more complex interpersonal pattern. Not only did the phrase derive linguistically from an embodied form of the original trauma, it also succinctly outlined the pattern of his adult life, in which he allowed himself to be boxed in by events and people. One pattern drew him to ephemeral nymph-like women (a quality reminiscent of his dead sister) but he was then blind-sided by actions he failed to predict.

We recognize second level metaphors (L-2) as more colloquial figures of speech, different linguistically from the idiosyncratic concrete first level metaphors (L-1). They involve a creative flow between trauma, past and present. They break trauma down into more manageable units (lysing metaphors) making coping with their aftermath possible.

They set parallel understandings next to each other (layering metaphors) allowing paradox and ambivalence to be integrated.

Third Level of Lysing Trauma Metaphors (L-3)

The co-construction of second level trauma metaphors marks progress on the survivor's road to recovery, with special emphasis on the re-establishing of a continuous sense of self.

Third level metaphors mark the survivor's reconnection with others and ultimately the culture of which he feels a part. They tend to be symbols rather than concrete aspects of the trauma or figures of speech. They are markers that there has been degrees of psychic re-integration, where lucky, at a new level posttrauma recovery, leading to a revised and more constructive identity, one broad enough to include past, the trauma, present, and future, one that accepts ambivalence and paradox. Often third level metaphors (L-3) encompass the vitality to sublimate some portion of the trauma experience into constructive current activity. Their symbolic character links the survivor with a group larger than himself. Taken together with the earlier parts of the journey from the abyss to recovery, level three metaphors reference the Hero myths of a given culture. Charting metaphor change gives an assessment of progress or regression on the journey toward recovery. L-1–L-3 is a clinical simplification of the Journey of the Hero (see Chapter 1, Figures 1.1 and 1.2).

The different levels of transforming metaphors are indicated in Figure 7.1 on the right side as L-1, L-2, and L-3.

Level 1

First level (L-1) metaphors present in the form of unusual gestures, unpleasant repetitive sensory experiences and striking, usually destructive interpersonal actions. As

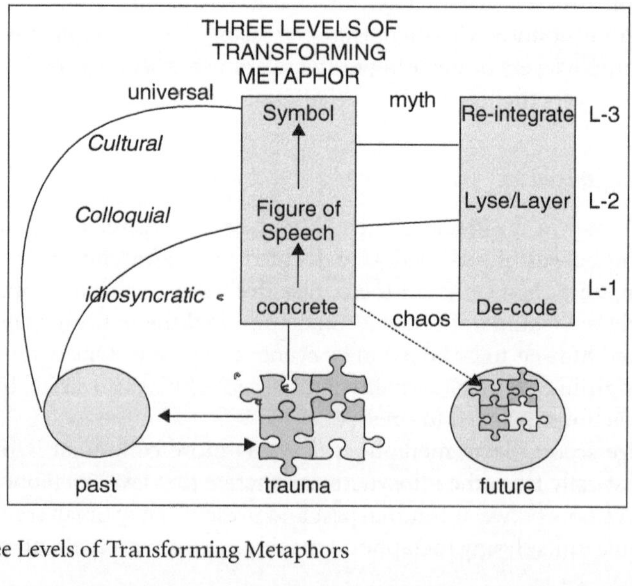

Figure 7.1 Three Levels of Transforming Metaphors

metaphors, when decoded into words these concrete sensations or actions become recognizable as specific episodes from the traumatic past that have been acting to organize current behavior. They manifest traumatic specific metaphors and more.

Level 2

Second level (L-2) metaphors take the form of figures of speech. They reduce the overwhelming experience of trauma into digestible units of encapsulated memories. They facilitate mastery and transform the survivor's sense of competence. At the second level, word-play offering variations in a given figure of speech occur, each change accessing a different layer of dynamics to the same trauma experience, broadening and sometimes reversing its subjective meaning to encompass paradox, ambivalence, and survivor guilt.

Level 3

Third level (L-3) metaphors are symbols. They weave individual experience with culture, marking the transformation of the fragmented posttraumatic self into a more integrated posttraumatic self. At this level metaphor may be a complement to sublimation.

At the bottom of the table, we denote two circles of experience or, in Lakoff's (1985) terms, source domains from which metaphor may arise: the world of the survivor's past, the world of the trauma itself, and the world of the posttraumatic present and foreseeable future.

The central vertical rectangle indicates the linguistic forms of metaphors at each level. Level 1 metaphors are concrete; level 2 are figures of speech; level 3 are symbolic. The vertical rectangle on the right side of Figure 7.1 indicates the mechanisms through which each level evokes change. The figure illustrates how the concrete trauma-based metaphor simply casts its dark shadow on the present and foreseeable future. But, as each element in this column indicates, first level metaphors can be transformative when decoded; second level when used to lyse or break down trauma into smaller units, and when multiple layers of meaning are understood, and third level metaphors are important markers for re-integrating a posttraumatic self. Listed on the left side of Figure 7.1 is a continuum of referent groups who might understand or use words in a way consistent with each metaphor moving from specific to general: from idiosyncratic, to colloquial, to ethnic, cultural, and universal. Listed on the right, between the two rectangles, is a continuum of organizing stories, from chaotic fragments of trauma to well delineated mythic narrative. The arrows indicate the direction of ideas and images from their source domain.

Linguistically, posttraumatic second and third level trauma metaphors adhere to earlier sensory-motor posttraumatic metaphors like connotative accretions (Josh's heart metaphors, Paul's picking metaphors, Karen's wrestling match, Tristan's boxes) or they can evolve freshly as in the case of Tom or Lee. Sequentially these more advanced metaphors have a common theme such as a unit of attachment, safety, responsibility, power or grief, categories that parallel core beliefs to the patient. In their idiosyncratic and unique form, the metaphors may reference competitive games, puzzles, repairable machines, even valued human qualities in shared myths, or shifting elements in ecological setting. They serve the function of reconfiguring the original subjective trauma so that earlier passive or displaced elements become active and a matter of direct responsibility in a manner relatively free of survivor guilt.

Case Examples: Third Layer Trauma Metaphors (L-3)

Lee's "Gifts"

We have examined previously the case of Lee, the Vietnam veteran whose gift to his therapist represented the ten cents in military money (piasters) that he gave his small Vietnamese friend when they would part for months at a time. Here we want to elaborate on how these gifts transformed over time, gaining symbolic significance and marking Lee's reconnection with the outside world and its cultures. In Vietnam he left the same small gift, a talisman, to keep the child safe in his absence. But once his assignment was changed during his second tour, Lee lost contact with the boy only to learn a year later that the U.S. army had wiped out his village and him as well.

At the beginning of his therapy, Lee pushed people away, believing that attachment to them was the kiss of death, especially, if there were to be separations between himself and someone to whom he was attached, mortal danger lurked for the other. He would therefore not permit separations from his wife or daughter for more than a few hours. It was understandable that unusual separations from his doctor were not easy.

During the course of the treatment, there were many occasions when Lee's therapist traveled out of town and sometimes abroad. Lee was uncanny in his hypersensitivity for picking up such travel and tracing down the destination. Under such circumstances Lee presented his medical doctor with a series of symbols to keep the doctor safe during their separation.

There was a St. Christopher's cross, capturing the story of the saint who carried a small boy to safety on his back across a raging torrent. Lee used to wear this when riding with a motorcycle gang. There was a white bird feather configuration that represented protection during absence for Native Americans. There was a two-sided metal pin, with a cross on one side and a star of David on the other. This was reference to the story of Abraham who needed to lie about his wife Sarah in order to pass safely through hostile territory. Each symbol directed itself to the issue of safety for those whom he needed to protect, repeating the configuration of the Vietnamese boy and the ten cents of military money.

At level 3 of metaphor transformation, several things were remarkable about this series of attachment gifts. First, the tokens became more subtle and capable of including paradox and irony. Second, the attachment gifts finally stopped, as Lee felt a more secure attachment to his doctor, and confidence that his new posttraumatic self no longer required magic gifts to prevent repetition of past trauma. Third, the gifts represented different strands of Lee's new posttraumatic identity, one that he was forging out of the different heritages that were part of his past.

His paternal grandfather had been a Scandinavian craftsman, a role model that he had endorsed in his masonry and carpentry work even before his military service. His paternal grandmother was a deeply religious Catholic who told him stories of the saints. His maternal grandfather was Native American, a strand of his DNA that he felt saved him on numerous occasions in the bush in Vietnam and whose spirituality included the life in all natural beings. His maternal grandmother was Jewish, a tradition he respected for its common-sense wisdom, craftiness, and appreciation of community. The different attachment-safety gifts represented the four heritages and composed together the different strands of Lee's postwar identity. Keeping each strand alive, he strove to take on carpentry jobs and a life of disciplined ethical rigor. He psychologically refueled himself through lengthy camping trips in the wild, and invested in the future by purchasing and fixing up a house. Taken together these third level metaphors, each a symbol of a different strand of Lee and his working through of attachment issues, began to form into a new more integrated posttraumatic self.

Josh's the "Heart to Go On"

For Josh the many transformations of second level metaphors relating to heart altered once again as it reached a third level. This time it gained the meaning layer of having (rather than crushing) heart. In this sense Josh noted his own courage to endure, to live, and to love in the present. During his follow-up interview after treatment he explained to the research physician that the doctor could not possibly understand how much the treatment had meant to him as the doctor's hands were too smooth. They did not have the calluses he and his brothers had; they were not the hands of tobacco farmers like himself. This past spring he and his brothers had planted tobacco, and this autumn he had harvested the small crop. It had always been a love of his, one he had stopped for 12 years after Vietnam, one possible only when he had once again regained heart. At the third level, Josh had reconnected with his family, the land, and his rural Appalachian heritage. He had the heart to come home and they had their wisdom to welcome the "Hero" from his journey (see Chapter 1).

Tom's "Rubik's Cube"

Tom chose an intriguing symbol to illustrate his reconnection to the culture of mechanics. It was the parting gift of a Rubik's cube complete with an engineer's drawing explaining to his therapist how the outer squares were connected to two rotating axes within the cube. It all made sense. Within the theme that life is a puzzle potentially capable of being deciphered, Tom's Rubik's cube was symbolic of his feeling a part of a larger community of the world of engineering. He was now resuming his work, engaged in his marriage and the role of father. A sense of coherence, continuity, vitality, autonomy, and integration were now re-integrated in his ego-identity at L-3 transformations.

Tristan's "Boxing Day"

Tristan's therapist observed that, as he healed, his happiest day of the year was when he visited his nieces and nephews on the day after Christmas. He gave them gifts and they showed with pride the gifts they had received. In his English tradition, this day is called Boxing Day, a third level metaphor (L-3). In carrying out his new practice, Tristan was departing from his previous isolated role in life and participating pleasurably in the cultural life of his family and community. In this sense, trauma transformation.

Karen's "Women Running Together"

Karen was ultimately able to sublimate her rape trauma by founding a community-wide organization that helped women to be able to escape without fear of predators. In doing so she elaborated on her level two metaphor, unfair wrestling match, by re-loading the odds. Her new organization saw to it that women escaped in groups, so that together they would not be targets for the potential rapist. Karen saw to it that women could exert their athletic prowess publicly on streets that were now safe. The icon for the new group involved symbolic representations of women holding hands while running. Karen was now able to move on with her own life including running, marriage, profession, and motherhood.

Linguistic Threads, Metaphors, and Ongoing Posttraumatic Processes

Transformations of metaphor for a particular survivor may or may not be linked by a common linguistic thread. For Josh, linguistic elements relating to heart pain remained constant, the central thread to his metaphoric transformations: first as a damaged vital organ and later as a symbol for love attachment and loss.

Also, for Karen some type of wrestling match remained constant. Originally her trauma pitted a strong woman against an even stronger, more devious raping and weapon-wielding man. In her dream she transformed the original image of hopeless struggle to an unfair wrestling match from childhood. In the metaphor's final form Karen founded a new organization that helped women run safely. Similarly for Tristan the word boxing was a constant: originally a somatic state of mind the groggy boxer, then the lysing metaphor, being boxed in, and finally, enjoyment at a symbolic level of interactions with his nieces and nephews on the day after Christmas, or Boxing Day.

In other instances the second (L-2) and third (L-3) level metaphors may have no clear linguistic relation to the first, taking off from different roots. Tom, the original trauma metaphor, a closed book with congealed and unopened pages tainted yellow, represented the unsuccessful effort to repress trauma. Once the repeated trauma burst on the scene, a new metaphor emerged, at a second level (L-2); it took another shape, a deadly sadistic game of musical chairs. In its final form his metaphors continued the game or puzzle theme: figuring out the trauma's impact is like knowing how the rotating axes of the Rubik's cube work, so that whatever point you begin it is possible to find a solution.

In retrospect, Tom was always interested in the rules of the game. Part of the chaotic nature of the traumatic deaths of his fellow soldiers was an unresolved puzzle: Tom's recovery hinged on discerning the rules that the Viet Cong were playing by: the unsettling answer of none.

Mythic Dimensions of the Trauma Metaphor

Metaphoric transformation in the survivors and wounded warriors above, underscore many cultural and symbolic universals of the trauma experiences. Josh's and the child's crushed and pained heart reference the universal human condition of lost innocence and love; Tom's independent search to find the rules of chaos are the stuff of myth. Ursula's metaphors remind us that the bodily functions of urinating and defecating rid us, as humans, of unmetabolized poison. We are reminded of gods and goddesses who poison each other for eternity for breaking cultural codes. Karen's wrestling with the gods is archetypal. As in Jacob's wrestling with the angel, when the match pairs a human fighting with the powers of fate, the story touches on the universal. Thus each of the metaphors that patients spontaneously create, such as the heart in pain, the rules of chaos, the expelling of poison, the wrestling with the more powerful, all blend into myth. When the Nurturing Guide (NG) and the Western therapist attend to the many dimensions of the trauma metaphor, they appreciate how intensely personal stories interact with the Hero myths of culture, and point the way to recovery.

Summary: Levels 1, 2, and 3 of Transformation of Trauma Metaphors

First level metaphors are idiosyncratic and concrete. They may be somatic, non-verbal, or interactive. They arise directly from the field of traumatic experience. They intrude spontaneously into the world of the present and foreseeable future because something in the present has acted as a trigger for the traumatic event. They disrupt healthy functioning in the present and confine the survivor and his personality to the emergency defense field of trauma. Sensory-motor aspects of the trauma itself, when accurately decoded into language, become transformative metaphors, in that they inform the survivor as to the meaning of his symptoms: that they are not the end products of a deranged mind, but rather a truth about the trauma being transferred onto current experience. Decoding the metaphor often reveals an implicit reworking of the subjective trauma experience in dynamic terms such as survivor guilt.

Second level trauma metaphors are colloquial figures of speech that refer both to the present and to the traumatic past. They may be linguistic modifications of the first level metaphor. Alternatively the figure of speech may have arisen as an interplay between reflections on the trauma and past experience. Second level metaphors transform by serving one of two functions: they break down or lyse a complex and inchoate experience into a definable and digestible unit; or they rearrange themselves into linguistically connected metaphors, each one accessing a new layer of meaning to the trauma. The first mechanism permits metabolism of trauma, the second permits new layers of meaning allowing paradox and ambivalence to be part of a more complex understanding of what happened and what it has meant.

Third level metaphors make use of symbols. They express the re-integration of the survivor to a new posttraumatic identity, one that finds renewed vitality in the present, neither negating the trauma nor remaining a prisoner within it (Wilson, 2006). They may arise via a complex interaction of the trauma, the past, and the culturally relevant as for example Lee's symbols of safe separation, or they may arise as a simple variant of a second level metaphor, as when Josh began to think less of the pain in his heart, and more of himself as having heart, the courage to go on. Survivors who reach the third level metaphor are ones who have re-engaged their present phase in life. In short, they transform the past stressful trauma in their own ways of recovery and transformation in the new posttraumatic self (Wilson, 2006). The Journey of the Hero, per se, begins anew, with vigor and new energy.

8 New Configurations

Trauma Metaphors and Cognitive Behavioral Therapies (CBT)

Using actual CBT case material with trauma survivors, we wish to examine what sometimes happens to spontaneous metaphoric expressions in the presence of protocol-driven therapies and contrast this with an altered perspective where the clinician listens for such verbal metaphorical expressions and attempts to make use of them for therapeutic purpose.

Listening for a Metaphor in a CBT Group: What Is TSM or TST?[5] How Do These Clinicians Know?

The Participant Patients Try to Name Their Problems

As an invited and silent guest, one of us (JL) had the opportunity of sitting in on a residential CBT group for male war veterans with PTSD throughout much of a 12-session twice-weekly format. During this time, because of scheduling conflicts, Dr. Lindy (JL) was present for the odd numbered sessions only, enough for significant observations.

He (JL) found himself resonating with the powerful phrases these men were finding to describe their current war-related and personal experiences, feelings and dilemmas, phrases or trauma metaphors similar to those described elsewhere in this book: "gun-shy, break him in half, stabbing people in the face, people shot in the head, crash and burn, at the edge of blowing up, etc." It seemed to him that these phrases were powerful expressions of how they felt in the present and likely metaphors from the field of combat that continued to define their current lives. He was also curious about how the patients were expressing with metaphors from the different wars they had fought to describe their states of mind and how highly trained CBT group therapists would respond to such language.

In the session that preceded the one we shall describe below, the emotional tone of the check-in had been quite tense, colored by phrases such as the ones mentioned above. After several minutes of spontaneous discussion, the leader explained to the group members, "OK, we need to change (the topic of discussion) over to self-management." One of the group participants said, in response, "(No) we need to do something about our over-steamed selves." Jack (JL) was struck by this creative use of language. The patient, Antonio, condensed esteem with steam, forming a new word, "over-steamed." As

5 TSM = Trauma-Specific Metaphors; TST = Trauma-Specific Transference.

if to say the anger that has built up in us (Iraq veterans), our steam is too intense, needing some form of release, but we fear that in its current form, this anger will spill over into unwise action; this is the source of our self-esteem problems. Jack (JL) was disappointed that the group leaders chose to ignore Antonio's neologism, failing to appreciate him and his metaphor. This lack of recognition by the group leader led to a dampening of the group's meeting; they grew quiet and felt unheard. In effect, they all quit and detached from the group therapy for that session. So what happens next after that dampening, closed-off therapeutic response?

The Eleventh Session

What follows comes from technical notes (JL) and thoughts largely focused on the following session with contributions from the senior author (JPW) of this book. This occurred in the final week of the six-week residential program and was the eleventh of 12 sessions.

The group session followed a milieu event in which several veterans in the group had formally requested that they continue to have access to showers during day-time hours, a habit that was objected to by permanent residents of the domiciliary which housed the in-patient setting. The group leader had announced that their request was denied. It was also one week prior to the end of the time-limited CBT program, so that anxieties about the end of the program and the return to civilian life were at the fore of the veterans' attention.

As the leader was late, the co-leader began the group meeting asking each person to check-in by describing how he was feeling and whether or not he wanted the group's attention to talk about a specific problem he was having. To begin, let us select three responses.

Jerry said, "I feel crushed, smashed."

Homer said, "No one wants to listen to what really happened."

Antonio said, "I'm a fucking penis."

Later, in this chapter, we shall discuss some other responses as well. The co-leader, listening to the first two comments, tried to universalize and therefore contain the metaphors. He said to Jerry that he must be feeling frustrated, and to Homer, that he was struggling with disturbing thoughts. The choice of these more neutral phrases was not accidental since group and individual work had been around management of frustration and disturbing thoughts. At this point the leader came in and, sensing the high tension in the room, said that she too had had a hard day and that managing things is not always an easy task, even for her.

Antonio's check-in phrase, "I'm a fucking penis," occurred after she had entered the room. At this point she interjected that the language was not acceptable in the group as it crossed a boundary. She knew that Antonio was working on trying to control offensive language, and she reminded the group that there were limits to kinds of offensive language they could use. The group responded with some decrease in tension and assumed a more work-like clinical atmosphere. Antonio apologized, but the tension persisted. Why he said what he said was not explored.

While the situation was quite tense, it seemed that the co-leaders were staying on message regarding the work that their patients were doing. For Jerry, managing anger was central and connected to his belief that every time he got angry he destroyed something. Homer was having great difficulty with his nightmares, ever since writing his trauma narrative. There was risk of flooding his cognition, so the leader tried to confine the overwhelming nature of intrusive phenomena by calling it disturbing thoughts. The leader was in no mood to deal with generalized disruption from the group or the offensive nature of Antonio's "in your face obscenity." To categorize the comment as out-of-bounds was in keeping with the overall plan with this veteran whose barroom behavior had already landed him in jail.

Remaining on task with their educational protocol for the eleventh of 12 group sessions, the leaders directed further discussion to the task of revisions of core beliefs that group members, as a result of their work in the program, no longer felt to be true. It was Antonio, the group member whose obscene language had just been the center of the group's attention, who offered case material for the group to discuss that centered on his stuck point, a belief around safety, namely that letting my guard down unleashes all kinds of hell.

Neither Jerry nor Homer requested special time from the group. The group turned irretrievably away from Jerry's feeling crushed, smashed, from Homer's complaint that no one wants to listen to what really happened, or to Antonio's original thought that he felt like a fucking penis. None of them experienced a leader simply reflecting those troubling words, or showing curiosity in them or suggesting that special time in some context be found to explore these feelings further. As it turned out, Antonio sought the special time anyway.

For understandable reasons the co-leaders focused on frustration, disturbing thoughts, and crossed boundaries. These indeed were target symptoms and potentially measurable variables that related to trauma beliefs that they hoped were in the midst of changing.

Jack (JL) wondered what might have transpired if the leaders' sensitivities were, instead, drawn to the metaphoric language of the three military veterans. For Jerry, the words crushed and smashed may well have had special meaning. He wondered if Jerry's history might not have paralleled the veteran whom we have called Josh earlier in this book. If so, the phrases would carry the implicit impact on him of having run over and crushed a child with his truck, and would have lent a poignancy to the words crushed (what happened to the child) and smashed (what he did). Something about the milieu events of the day or the upcoming end of the in-patient experience may have precipitated this posttraumatic state. Jerry felt he was in a dangerous situation. It was like Iraq in that he felt as if he had no alternative, approaching a potential ambush site, but to drive very fast, to exit the program, to return home. If, on the other hand, he expressed his anger at the milieu frustration, someone, perhaps himself, would be crushed, and he would remain the guilty smasher. All of his significant self-schema and trauma beliefs based on the impact of his trauma narrative might have been right on the line, with an opportunity to reflect on his tendency and in fact to behave quite differently.

Homer's metaphor is hidden (i.e., the unsaid trauma memories) because the intrusions (what really happened) do not seem to be of interest to anyone. Homer is complaining that the focus of his treatment has been on faulty beliefs arising from an experience that no one can bear to hear. It is a case in which offering his testimony is hardly possible, and the opportunity that a wise elder might bear witness to his horrendous experience seems impossible.

Jack (JL) thought that Homer was thinking, "How can I learn to think differently about my horrendous trauma when no one is able to bear listening to it?" We can only imagine his pain. Listening carefully to his words Homer did not say that he was stuck and isolated with disturbing thoughts and images he could not share, as the leader implied, rather, he said, no one wanted to listen.

Antonio's imagery, a "fucking penis," is disturbing to hear for the female group leader. It conjures up naked rape-like aggression, especially when directed, as it was, at a female therapist. We shall return to discuss some possible meanings of the phrase shortly. It obviously has unmetabolized unconscious components and trauma with distressing memories of the "unsaid" types.

Lessons of the Day: Changing Core Beliefs in War Veterans

Antonio: Iraq Veteran

The group leaders redirected attention to the study question of the day: How does one go about making revisions in beliefs about the world and about the self after one realizes that the original beliefs are impaired by faulty cognitions such as overgeneralization, jumping to conclusion, faulty logic, unreliable history, distorted memories, or denial process of cognitive encoding?

Here Antonio volunteered to be the "fall guy" to demonstrate how he became aware of a faulty belief, how it worked in his mind, while the leaders garnered evidence to point out ways in which this or any belief about one's trauma memory can be challenged. Antonio is a veteran of the war in Iraq who nearly lost his life and in fact lost consciousness in an IED explosion. He believes that if it were not for the fact that he let his guard down, the trauma would not have occurred. In fact he believes that letting his guard down always leads to catastrophe. The leader actively found situations in Antonio's life (outside combat) where being relaxed or sleeping was not followed by catastrophe so that she could challenge the belief that letting his guard down is always dangerous. The leader makes the point that Antonio has over-extended and generalized this belief in the form of incorrect thinking rather than a fact. She argues that since he believes it to be always true but it is not always so, the belief is based on habitual modes of analysis rather than fact. Hence, Antonio exhibited a faulty cognition, a fault in reasoning that can be corrected by cognitive restructuring processes.

Second, the CPT[6] clinician points out that, having been stunned and knocked unconscious by the IED blow, especially with apparent retrograde amnesia, Antonio is not a good source of accurate information regarding what he was or was not doing during the moment preceding the explosion, that his belief about what took place is not factual, is not real, and not causative. Third, she clarifies that the central affect in this connection is guilt, a feeling state that is not a primary, basic, or true affect such as mad, glad, sad, or scared. But rather it is a manufactured affect, one not basic to the human condition and therefore falsely constructed and potentially replaceable. Like a legal prosecutor, her three-pronged case rests on: (1) the source of information is unreliable; (2) the belief statement is not true (i.e., factual); and (3) the interfering emotions are

6 Staff and patients in this group tended to use CBT cognitive behavioral therapy synonymously with CPT cognitive processing therapy.

manufactured ones. With these three arguments, the therapist attempts to batter down Antonio's wall of faulty beliefs and thinking processes.

As time was running out in the group there was not much opportunity to explore the new, more reliable factual beliefs, namely, that at times Antonio believes that sometimes his letting his guard down (i.e., his hyperarousal/hypervigilance) may lead to negative consequences. With that change in belief, Antonio now has permission to replace it with another belief that, in safe settings, it may be possible for Antonio to relax (i.e., in non-hyperarousal states).

Listening to this interchange in the group Jack (JL) could not help but think of the phrase "letting my guard down" as an interesting and spontaneous body-centered metaphor. He thought of how a small child's muscles relax as he falls asleep in a parent's arms, but how violent the muscle contractions might be if this same child were to be suddenly exposed to domestic violence after having fallen asleep. Jack (JL) wondered if, as a youth, Antonio did not receive good advice from a boxing coach regarding how to conduct himself in a fighting situation; he even wondered about an older brother punching him on the arm and then blaming him because his guard was not up: Lindy thought about combat advice from a first sergeant and how his muscles may have felt upon regaining consciousness after the IED explosion in Iraq. Then, Lindy thought of Antonio's current situation and the danger he felt about the coming end of the treatment program as he prepared to re-enter the world outside which he anticipated being unsafe. Don't let your guard down had taken on important mapping functions for understanding difficulties in his current posttrauma life. He must be on alert (i.e., hypervigilant) as the potentially dangerous situation of discharge from the safe setting in the hospital was approaching.

Were there alternatives to Platonic debate with Antonio over his faulty reasoning based on our understandings of trauma metaphor and metonymy? Yes, very much so!

First, "don't let your guard down" served a coping purpose in the warzone. And even today, the metaphor serves the temporarily adaptive function of turning passive into active. In this way Antonio's hypervigilance and excessive responsibility serve as a defense against helplessness. Of course the conviction that letting his guard down might constitute a complete and causative explanation for why things go so badly for him, is irrational, but by its intimate association with trauma, it is also highly personal and meaningful as are all defenses. For Antonio, letting his guard down identified the place next to the trauma, the metonymy from which he views the trauma, which he mistakenly identified as causative (see Chapter 2). Letting Antonio know that we understand these universal responses to trauma may allow him more comfort as he exposes his trauma beliefs to a critical eye.

Lindy was tempted to consider the later group interactions, the more cooperative and banter-like discussion about letting his guard down, between Antonio and the female therapist-leader, as a more sublimated response to his earlier obscene phrase, that he feels like a "fucking penis," and her response, that the remark was out of bounds. Using Antonio's own contribution to the rest of the group session as associations to this first uninhibited phrase suggests that dropping his guard exposes him to helplessness and damage to his manliness. His rage, in response, is the reversal of powerlessness, the kind of rage seen in rape. One might be tempted to understand him as saying the experience of this treatment program challenging his beliefs about his trauma has been very unsettling, in fact it strips him naked, and humiliates him, stirring a vengeful unbridled aggression with a sexual overtone that was released in the warzone and he fears will be released again.

In this metaphor he is his "penis/weapon"; and he will use it to destroy and abuse others. Sadly, on occasion in the environment of war, such references actually refer on the one hand to rape and on the other to bodily mutilations to our side or theirs after bloody battles with terrible losses. Contrarily, synonyms for penis, like prick, often connote underhanded meanness and retaliatory isolation. "I'm a prick" has such self-connotation. So, the current masculine strength understanding for Antonio may contain a paradox, a self-perception of meanness and isolation. His state of combativeness in the therapeutic situation called for structure, respecting boundaries, but Antonio's unusual choice of words also challenges the clinician and the group with questions about the meanings of such bodily metaphors to describe himself, his war trauma and PTSD, challenges that are screaming to be heard.

Other Group Members and Their Problems

We return now to other veterans in the group, and the phrases they used to describe themselves. In Table 8.1 we list the phrases along with the niches where the co-leaders placed them.

The group participants, nearly all, offered unusual word phrases, quite consistent with the metaphors we have been describing in this book, to describe their current feelings. Several of these seemed to have clear military and war-related antecedents (i.e., TSMs).

For example, one group member chose a single word to express his current feeling state: assassinate, a word so foreign to usual feeling states in civilian life that it cries out for exploration. Such a self-state is immersed in a world of kill-or-be-killed, of extreme adrenaline rush fused with challenge, danger, demand for competence, yet co-existing

Table 8.1 Trauma Metaphors and the Generic Bins in Which We Place Them

TRAUMA SURVIVOR'S PHRASES	*THERAPIST WORDS*
Blah	Avoidant
Calm and comical	Less anxious
Not calm	Anxious
Can't slip up behind me	Suspicious, hypervigilant, guarded
Fuck it, who cares	Withdrawn and angry
Assassinate	Angry and rageful
Don't beg on someone	Guilt, loyalty
Feel crushed, smashed	Frustrated, diminished
Broken	Hopeless, loss of connection
Like I've been dumped on	Sad, angry, abandoned
A fucking penis	Crossed boundary, intrusiveness
Fucking crazy	Disturbing thoughts, confusion
Plagued with thoughts that keep going through my head	Disturbing thoughts and intrusive images
No one wants to listen	Disturbing thoughts and intrusive images
At the edge, ready to explode	Angry, tense, irritable

with existential despair and shame. For those specialized war veterans who served or acted as assassins, and survived, is tantamount to feeling like a God, with the power to take life, to experience aggressive omnipotence. To assassinate is to judge and eliminate the other or the self before the journey home is complete and is a powerful warning to the Nurturing Guide (NG) that the survivor is in grave danger upon re-entry at homecoming.

Another group member described his current feeling state as, "Can't slip up behind me," a sensory-motor configuration that maps the silent moves of invisible danger onto the present. It refers to a paranoid and hypervigilant state of mind. The adverbial modifier, "can't," suggests that he feels some safety that his alerted or signaled vigilance can protect him from danger. Such an ego is constantly at work, often leaving little energy for current and future problem-solving. Perhaps, the bodily trauma metaphor refers literally to danger from behind, even as some bantering in the group indicated, as for example exposure to sniper attack while defecating.

"Can't slip up behind me," as a metaphor, may also reflect a mistrust of someone or some group in the therapeutic milieu. One might wonder if the therapist-leader is temporarily, in transference terms, in the place of enemy, that is threatening to slip up behind and endanger by confrontation, disclosure, or embarrassment.

A final example, "blah," is a word that is not truly a vocabulary word but a sound that connotes disengaged nonsense or non-attention or indifference. It might refer to a self-state with no vital energy or resilience, an ego-preference for dismissive or passive responses to stress. Trauma may have occurred originally during a period of let-down. It might even convey a hostile response to educational instructions which sound like blah, blah, blah, whatever, what do I care.

The opportunity to explore spontaneous metaphors that refer in unusual ways to the expression of a state of mind did not occur in this CBT group, so that focus could remain on the educational objective as outlined in the protocol for the eleventh group meeting. Had there been follow-up work with the group members giving room to explore their interesting spontaneous phrases, these phrases might have served as insights regarding self, personality, ego-processes, actual trauma experiences, and situations on homecoming. Their relevance to the upcoming end of the in-patient program and their discharge would have become more striking. The metaphors could lead the clinician to a position of empathy with the current stressors and with the existentially despairing and shameful aspect of the trauma, permitting a bearing of witness and honoring survival amidst horrendous happenings.

The Veteran PTSD Patient Group and Its Family of Metaphors

In addition to its connection with trauma, the language used by patients and staff in the group sessions presented above reference several families of metaphors. One such family is the treatment program as school. There are assignments, homework, ABCs; they check attendance, ask for rewrites, and speak of tutorials, texts, packets, and binders. Clients in the same groups refer to the leader as teacher, the group meeting as class; and both refer to graduation.

In a slightly more specific manner, veterans compare this school to military courses or briefings that taught them to perform in their military roles (i.e., MOS[7] education)

7 MOS military occupation specialty.

and briefed them regarding military situations once they were in combat. Regarding hand-outs and instructions, they say don't make no sense; just do what they tell you; don't rock the boat; they don't really know the terrain. Don't question them; don't challenge too much; keep your mouth shut.

Clients in the group in this chapter also compared their in-patient unit to a military platoon: they spoke of orders from higher-ups, another unit is getting the good stuff, if you want a pass you'd better go through proper channels, it's dangerous here, the leaders don't understand, we're all in this together. Specific problems on the minds of group members were frictions over living spaces, use of equipment, group loyalty, access to proper medical care.

The families of metaphors prepare the clinician for unconscious frames of reference that may easily be transferred from the original context to the present one. For example in the group-as-school metaphor, participants were concerned that graduation might come before they were fully prepared. They felt badly that there were assignments they had not completed. They were ashamed that they had not done a conscientious enough job. Therapists attuned to this metaphor family might have commented that some in the group feared they would get a graduation certificate but not feel truly prepared for what was next in their lives.

In the military training family of metaphors, participants were condescending of paper and pencil activities in training camp that could not possibly prepare one for combat. An attuned therapist might have teased that this time perhaps the course would be more useful than were some of the courses in basic training.

In the pre-combat briefing metaphor they were fearful that return to real life outside the hospital would be like combat and the consequences were life and death. The attuned CBT therapist might have drawn the comparison between the life and death intensity of the metaphors in the group and the briefings before actual life and death situations in war, pointing out that this time there was the potential opportunity to change.

In metaphors that described the group as if it were "a platoon," the group members had specific gripes with their leaders: failure to be able to override higher headquarters, seeming favoritism to other units, and disappointment that their leaders did not advocate sufficiently for them. In war, they had reacted with alienation, disillusionment, and despair, how were they going to respond now, in newer situations where they were learning new coping strategies. In the form of trauma-specific transference (TST), the group leader-therapist was like the military officer with power of authority in trauma-specific metaphorical ways (TSM). The attuned therapist might have owned some of this hostility as being aimed at them, having let them down as their leaders in this platoon, demonstrating by their actions the present need not to repeat the past.

Being aware of these metaphors and having the flexibility to use them might have opened-up therapeutic opportunities. Failing to pursue metaphors in the service of following the protocol limits therapeutic opportunity in very important ways.

We believe that engaging the salient, authentic, but painful aspects of the survivor–clinician relationship by exploring the trauma metaphors above would have offered these patients in this group a better opportunity to absorb the ideas presented by the group leaders: to repair the faulty cognitions, the jumping to conclusions and overgeneralizations that lead to faulty core beliefs in PTSD. The two positions, addressing trauma metaphors and finding new solutions to the problems of PTSD, complement each other.

Clearly, the veteran is more prepared to risk thinking differently about himself if he feels that the therapist, in the foxhole with him, has earned his trust and is not afraid of his wishes and fears.

When clinicians attend to the spontaneous words and phrases of patients and become aware of the families of metaphors used in our daily work with clients we are better prepared to listen to their communications on multiple levels and to expand our vision of the domains in which they are addressing their stuck points and posttraumatic beliefs.

A CBT Coping Strategy Group With an "Eye" on Trauma Metaphors

What occurs when CBT trained therapists keep their eyes open-wide for the metaphors their patients use? How do these expressions give glimpses to damaged ego-processes, self-states, and personality processes? How do they resonate with knowledge in the field of trauma, and become part and parcel of the experience-near vocabulary of change?

This second CBT group was conducted in an outpatient clinic within months of the first group. Participants were veterans of the Vietnam war with PTSD, who many decades after their combat were all graduates of earlier therapeutic efforts. Each was in an individual treatment that felt stalled, each was reacting to adverse events in their current lives and each was searching for more useful coping strategies. It was the latter goal, coping strategies, that was to be the center of this CBT oriented group.

Hal, a taciturn previously divorced veteran, was alluding to suicidal thoughts as he dealt with his current wife's decision to leave him. His speech was halting and eerily death-like. "I feel like digging a hole and putting a sock over me." (Flashing back to Vietnam) "I need to free myself of this ghost." "It (Vietnam) never goes away." (Returning to the present situation) "Sounds put me in a bad mood. I snap when I should be careful, watch my back . . . I have to get into a corner . . ." Fellow group members reacted:

Spike responded spontaneously, "I got your back covered."

Hal was quiet and then teared up.

Spike continued, "No, I mean it, I've got you covered." Later Spike insisted that Hal take his phone number and call if he thought of doing something drastic. All members of the group exchanged telephone numbers, promising to support one another.

The group leaders returned to this interchange as they spoke of coping strategies, pointing out that in Vietnam, to cover the other guy's back was an act of protecting life, the 180 degrees he could not see. That way of helping each other still applied in today's world, and turned an ominous situation (Hal's dilemma) into one in which there was hope (group members could help).

During a second session, Ted, speaking of attending a life-cycle event with his wife, felt he could not sit in the confined space in the middle of the aisle he was assigned, and decided to stand at the back of the church. His wife, having already taken a seat, was furious, seeing it as an affront that he did not sit with her. Ted disclosed that:

- She attacked him verbally.
- Ted explained, I was really burned.
- Ted alluded to feeling like drinking (alcohol).

The metaphor of burning remained on the therapist's mind and Ted's mind as well.

Several minutes later, the leader underlined the word burned as she responded to another group member's talking of a situation of injury and anger.

Ted then blurted out, almost as a non sequitur, "yeah, burning's bad; we had to leave the Swift boat, had to find comrades, they were set on fire by enemy, they were from our unit, had to return the bodies whole, for proper disposal."

Ted sighed and then commented that the lieutenant passed alcohol around to all the men after the mission to calm down and relax. "Yeah," Spike commented, "Jack Daniels was my best friend and still is today."

Further discussion revealed that all the men had gotten into trouble in their marriages when, after an angry confrontation, they started drinking heavily and became confrontational.

Here the group leaders were able to point out that while some coping strategies that had their origins in the combat experience, like covering your back, were useful in the present, other coping mechanisms, like alcohol and drugs, had only caused more trouble upon return.

In the two examples above, the clinicians paid careful attention to first level metaphors, "got your back covered" and "burned," allowing expression of them including associated memories, and were thereby able to respond more poignantly to the group members, validating their expressive language, helping the group to bear witness to their experiences, and using this vantage point as a useful one to introduce ideas about efforts to improve coping strategies today.

On the final regularly scheduled weekly meeting before this group would move to monthly meetings, all members arrived in attire that contained some Harley Davidson motorcycle reference (T-shirts, hats, boots, etc.) as though they had found a common uniform, one that followed combat yet referenced the complex journey home. The coping strategy under discussion from the protocol for the group was the topic of gratitude. As each member contributed to a common pool of positive remembrances, the leader returned to the motorcycle metaphor implicitly in the room. She added, each of you is storing up a reserve tank, memories you can access when things get tough out there and you might get low on gas.

It was the leaders' perception (and mine (JL) as well) that the group's supportive, coping, behavioral objectives were well served by attention to trauma and trauma-specific metaphors.

Metaphor and CBT Literature

Metaphor is well within the standard vocabulary of cognitive processing therapists. Walser and Westrup (2007) give multiple examples of metaphor that CBT clinicians might use to help patients with PTSD. Metaphors may help the patient move out of a stuck position where they are fighting and resisting against their trauma-related problems. In the "quicksand metaphor" the patient is encouraged to stop struggling, an act that gets him ever deeper in the quicksand, but rather spread out his whole body in a relaxed fashion to minimize weight on a single contact point; in the "person-in-a-hole metaphor" the patient is asked to consider that if he has only one tool, a shovel, he will only go deeper in the hole; or the Chinese finger trap analogy, in which more force only ensnares one's finger further. In fact, in this metaphor, the "first person to let go and relax the tension is released." The authors recommend this metaphor as an approach to conflict and to life itself; when to hold on versus letting go, a psychosocial modality described in detail by Wilson (2006).

Other metaphors are directional, such as being value-centered or future-oriented like a compass. When the patient maps these stories onto his current dilemmas, they open new possibilities.

Often these metaphors are stories, from a Zen Buddhist or mindfulness perspective. The relevant metaphor is a fragment of a larger story or parable. And the story is intended to offer advice, guidance, or wisdom. Indeed these are most useful contributions to the healing of the trauma survivor by the wise Nurturing Guide (NG).

For example, one metaphor intentionally introduced by the leaders in the first CBT group, discussed above, was the image of "feeding the fire." This refers to specific ways in which ruminating about certain thoughts initiate self-generated feelings into a consuming fire of downwardly spiraling depression.

These metaphors are introduced by authors or leaders as allegorical stories used by the counselor or clinician in order to teach. They are not the spontaneous phrases of the individual trauma survivor. They do not follow the unique process of new metaphor creation by the survivor during the recovery process that we are tracing in this book (see Chapters 3–6). Nurturing Guides in many cultures use parables in an attuned manner as such stories can be of great help as sources of illumination.

We believe there is then no inherent incompatibility between attention to metaphor and the different modalities of treatment for PTSD, be that EMDR, prolonged exposure (PE), CBT, or Cognitive Processing Therapy (CPT). In each mode of psychotherapy, the client is looking for words to express dilemmas; some of those words will inevitably be in the form of metaphor, especially sensory-motor ones. In each treatment we recognize that as humans we understand the present in terms of creatively rearranging experiences and symbols of the past. In each treatment, where therapist-generated metaphors may help, it is the survivor's own search for useful metaphor that is so indispensable in his recovery.

CBT Stuck Points, Pathological Beliefs, and Metaphor

To some extent the cognitive behavioral term "stuck point" relates both to the vocabulary of psychoanalytic mastery theory as articulated by Weiss and Sampson (1986), and their use of the term pathogenic belief, and to the vocabulary we are offering in this book, namely trauma metaphor. A given survivor might remain fixed at the level of the trauma metaphor. Rather than experiencing it as the first phase of mastery, namely naming and identifying the problem, it remains in its concrete form in which its symbolic meanings are overlooked. It spreads as a way of seeing the present: e.g., "all human relations pain my heart." It confines the boundaries of living: I can't risk endangering my already pained heart. It gains the adverbs never and always, and becomes the articulated words of a constricted ego in the midst of posttraumatic decline. As such, it is now a stuck point, an attitude about the self that does not lend itself to critical evaluation, and becomes a rationalization for a downward spiral. We might think of CPT or PE as directing its efficacy at that downward spiral. It is a way that education can produce new rational alternatives to the stuck point.

Both the psychodynamic therapist and the CPT therapist see it as being within their role to interfere with the spread of this malignant pathological belief. Keeping the veteran's own choice of words, his metaphors, increases specificity, and limits and qualifies the trauma context, easing the challenge to change generalizations in the present.

Specificity, Metonymy, and Causation

The linguistic idea of metonymy is a great asset for the patient's grasping the idea that he has substituted a random activity, sensation, or experience, as though it were causative of the trauma and avoids this part of life in order to prevent recurrence of the trauma in the present. According to Jakobson (1970) we, as humans, associate the state we were in just prior to, or as we were beside a trauma, with the trauma itself. This indeed is one pathway for remembering, equally as important as remembering by similarity. The memory association between action that is next to trauma is so sharp that it feels as if it were causative. Such an idea is conveyed in films when the camera pans in or out of an incidental detail that is adjacent to the traumatic event, a sunset, or bright light, or wallpaper pattern, or a beautiful woman's necklace. The adjacent item takes on the symbolic meaning of the trauma itself, but, in fact, it has no causative connection. Understanding and communicating this phenomenon to the client aids the therapist, whatever his perspective, in explaining how certain apparent trauma precipitants are incorrect predictors of a damaging belief in the present.

Treatment Modalities and Their Families of Metaphors in Daily Work

In this chapter we have explored how the words, phrases, and metaphors we use to describe our work, words that offer insight, words that describe how we perceive ourselves, words that describe how clients perceive us, words that capture the way we work, actually construct distinct families of metaphors. Within each family we find hidden assumptions that affect how each of us thinks and behaves in the particular setting in which we choose to work. Becoming aware of the families of metaphors that we, and our clients, accept as givens in the vocabulary of our work, underlines assumptions we have about a given psychic therapeutic modality, what brings about change, and how we are supposed to work together. But these same metaphors, when unexamined, provide places to hide, conceptual blind alleys where collusion may encumber progress.

We have previously described how CBT therapists and their patients use a language of ABCs or school. Inherent assumptions in the treatment setting as school include many positives, such as, studying hard enables one to learn new things. Taking notes helps. Respecting one's teacher aids learning. Asking questions is useful. But some assumptions may be detrimental. Such as schools react to students within a formal hierarchy; it is a non-intimate place where one dare not share too much, especially vulnerability; peer norms are powerful.

Dynamically-oriented psychotherapists speak of in-depth therapy, the mind as layered, peeling the onion, going deeper, covering over, striking a hidden vein, or staying on the surface. Their patients say, an interpretation was too deep, or it really hit something hidden, or I have to guard against going there. Their metaphors speak of developmental perspectives to psychological difficulties: fixation points from early childhood, attachment, autonomy and competitive difficulties, relationships often in the context of the early parent–child relationships. And their patients pick up these references by calling themselves childlike, dependent, obstinate, or independent.

The metaphoric vocabulary of the dynamic therapist promotes reflection, intimate self-awareness, and the simultaneous presence of multiple layers of meaning. But dynamic treatments can seem to have no end to them, minimize specific guidance or advice, or attribute emotional pain to early childhood rather than adult trauma.

Medical Physicians and Metaphorical Analogies

Therapists who are physicians often use medical and biological analogies. They speak of pathology, malignant processes, healing and recovery, pathogen, pathogenesis, allostasis, homeostasis, fight/flight response, stress response, latency, over-shooting responses, return to baseline, feedback loops, brain functioning, molecular configuration, enzymes, digestion, metabolizing. On their part patients report bodily symptoms, look for pills to heal them, refer to themselves as ill with all the advantages (notes from the doctor) and disadvantages (stigmatization) that come with that.

Awareness of these families of metaphors helps the therapist pick out allusions to the work, frustrations with a particular modality, and pitfalls that stand in the way of recovery. It instructs us that we, humans who dwell in the world of words, and convey much of how we understand the world around us, and the traumas that interrupt that world, in the metaphors we use unconsciously. We choose to surround ourselves with words that make order out of disorder, much as our patients invent words to give testimony of their intimate exposure to personal trauma in a world gone awry. Thus, the task of trauma transformation and integration into the wholeness of personality.

9 Traumatic Stress Disorder Pedagogy

Teaching the Complexity of Posttraumatic Intrapsychic Processes, Trauma Metaphors, and Adaptive Mechanisms in Psychotherapy

Critical Pedagogical Issues in Psychotherapy, Psychiatric, and Psychological Clinical Training Programs

How do mental health professionals, medical practitioners, and psychotherapists of various "stripes," clinical robes, credentials, licensure, certifications, and diplomas come to an *experiential basis* of the clinical and complex nature of properly understanding the intricate posttraumatic effects and the onset of PTSD to the body and psyche of the patient/survivor?

In this sense of learned and evolved compassionate understanding, we ask: are providers properly educated and knowledgeable enough in their clinical and medical training as to the significance of TSM (trauma-specific metaphors) for overwhelming, taxing, if not potentially devastating, work with trauma patients, trauma experiences, trauma-specific transference (TST) and PTSD re-enactments in treatment (see Wilson & Lindy, 1994; Wilson, Friedman, & Lindy, 2004; Wilson & Thomas, 2004)? In fact, how do the new and younger providers learn possible portals of entry (POE) into the psychological world of the trauma survivor (see Chapter 1)? If so, how? What are the critical psychological, medical-psychiatric, diagnostic portals of entry into the world of the vulnerable trauma patient? What is their phenomenological existential reality of life on a daily basis? How does the treatment provider discover these emotional realities?

Do medical residents (especially in psychiatric residency or clinical psychology, social work services, addiction specialists, nurses and others) receive adequate training and knowledge about trauma metaphors and PTSD, their meaning and processes of transformation in body and spirit? How do mental health providers utilize the information contained in such trauma-specific metaphors (TSM) or other linguistic expressions reflective of trauma – embedded in powerful stressor experiences of all sorts and dimensions stored in various levels of consciousness? How to understand the basic cognitive processes associated with the encoding, storage, intellectual metabolizing and memories of trauma and their expressions in language, especially metaphors, dream symbols, and complex ego-functions of an adaptive or maladaptive nature?

Trauma-Specific Metaphor (TSM): Relevance and Relation to Trauma-Specific Transference (TST): Trauma-Specific Data Transmission (TSD) in New Perspectives of Understanding PTSD

What does traumatic stress pedagogy mean and what is its relevance to posttraumatic stress states and disorders (PTSD)? These are, clearly, essential and central issues to be a focus of concern and considerations in the development of an educational curriculum and training practicum at professional levels. We will, in the interest of space constraints and directed focus, limit our discussions to the central concerns and clinically essential implications for finding ways to enter the inner sanctum of portals of entry to the interior psychic spaces of PTSD (Wilson, Friedman, & Lindy, 2004) and its internal identity and self-configurations (see Chapters 1 and 3). *PTSD is not only a prolonged stress syndrome, it is a complex posttraumatic amalgamation of personality traits, self-processes, and identity structures, all woven together in the fabric of the posttraumatic self* (see Wilson, 2004, for an extended discussion).

Pathways to the truths of life are exactly that: pathways to a location of profound importance in human experiences of a life-changing nature. Traumatic disclosures in a proper clinical setting express the heart and soul of the victim/survivor. Through empathic attunement, the therapist unleashes or simply opens doors to trauma encoded metaphors and other distressing memories of life challenges, existence itself and loss of others in bad, horrible, and overwhelming traumatic situations. To unleash or facilitate the expressions of trauma metaphors stored in posttraumatic memory states requires a true and genuine sustained empathic attunement (Wilson & Thomas, 2004). The Nurturing Guide (NG) is then confronted with the past of the victims' journey and their own, at the same time. That moment is often a junction of destiny. A surreal meeting of two persons in body, soul, and spirit, all merged together in one spiritual moment. It is a dual process of discovery and proper therapeutic facilitation. At that critical moment, both therapist and patient struggle together in the journey. In essence, this is the NG encounter with a soul survivor and fellow human spirit (see Chapter 1, Figure 1.1).

In Table 9.1, we examine ten critical clinical considerations regarding the importance of understanding and decoding trauma's impact to the self, ego-processes, identity configurations, and the well-being of the PTSD survivor. We consider these concerns as a foundational and a minimal beginning of a basis of trauma pedagogy and curricular development, beyond learning and understanding DSM-V diagnostic symptom clusters and their clinical meanings in the treatment processes.

The Journey of the Survivor

As mental health professionals, how do we teach these psychological challenges to clinical-psychological, medical or psychiatric residents or others in professional training? What are the trauma survivors' journeys and what can they teach us? What are their trauma narratives, stories, emotional pains, and disruptions in the life journey (see Figure 1.1 in Chapter 1 for an overview). What do these profound human experiences inform us about living life fully and with love and compassion? What do they (patients) need therapeutically to be whole again?

Table 9.1 identifies at least ten fundamental considerations in trauma/PTSD education. For purposes of this book, while we believe that there may be many more critical

Table 9.1 Posttraumatic Stress Disorder Pedagogy

Critical Issues in Psychotherapy Education Relative to Trauma, PTSD, and Metaphors

1 Teaching how to best educate and train professional students as to posttraumatic intrapsychic processes (e.g., trauma specific transference (TST), empathic strains, trauma specific cues, trauma specific data transmissions in self-presentations, and *trauma specific metaphors* that reflect unmetabolized internal psychological states).

2 How do mental health professionals and psychotherapists of all types learn how to decode the trauma specific or generic metaphors reflective of intrapsychic states following trauma, the onset of PTSD or alternations in dimensions of the self-structure?

3 It is important to educate about Abyss and transcendent trauma experiences as the unconscious vault self-reinvention, reconstruction and structuring. It is important to explain the vicissitudes of self-reconfiguring following traumatic experience (Wilson, 2006).

4 How to educate psychotherapists and mental health professionals as to how to use the Portals of Entry (POE) into the traumatized ego-state of the patient. The need for clear case presents actions goes here (Wilson, Friedman, & Lindy, 2004). How do clinical case presentations illustrate the complex dynamics of intrapsychic mechanisms?

5 Clinical-Theoretical Considerations: Are trauma metaphors reflective of intrapsychic states and trauma specific transference reactions (TST), the purest form of experience of internal self-schema and altered ego-states and self-processes.

6 In terms of psycho-educational and training, should future mental health professionals be required to learn about cross-cultural and anthropological knowledge concerning the diversity of ways to treat traumatized persons? Would cross-cultural case examples illustrate and broaden intellectual information as to how to understand the universal pathway to healing? The journey of the Hero (see Chapter 1).

7 How did different cultures develop ways to treat and heal traumatized persons? What specific forms of medicine (healing), treatments (rituals), or social-psychological processes did they evolve to address the issue of wounded humankind of the kinship group, culture or nature?

8 The issue of how cultures deal with its traumatized survivors intersects with the present of how cultures and societies deal with social denial, cultural control over normal behavior and those who, because of political oppression of systems that fight against the government power. In terms of educational objectives and training of mental health professionals, this exercise of critical analogies would be extraordinarily valuable and easily incorporated into training modules.

9 It is important, educationally, for professionals in training to learn how to differentiate the critically important concepts as part of the intrinsic nature of psychotherapy in a traditional sense.

10 In the educational training of trauma therapists, each candidate should be able through case presentation to identify and explain all of the clinical processes associated with metaphors.

factors, these are an important beginning point. In the future, educators and clinical faculty will refine and further delineate what constitutes core sets of knowledge, clinical insights, and acquired skill sets necessary to a certified competent posttraumatic professional specialist.

PTSD and Trauma Metaphor Pedagogy: A Portal to the Inner World of the Trauma Survivor

In Chapter 1, we identified and briefly discussed the five portals of entry into the inner-psychic configurations of traumatic states and PTSD (see also Wilson, Friedman, & Lindy, 2004, for an extended discussion). Table 9.1 summarizes the importance of teaching and educational clinical training of trauma metaphors in professional education rendering assistance to trauma victims. Based on our experiences, TSM principles are universal and cross-cultural in nature and scope. But, TSM are inextricably interlinked with all other PTSD dynamic processes at all levels of organismic functioning (Wilson, 2006).

While a much larger discussion is warranted, page limitations allow us at this point to make relevant core-summary points: We regard these as fundamental considerations for curriculum of teaching about trauma and posttraumatic states of multiple and complex dimensions. In the future, we hope that they will multiply in a valley of PTSD fruit across the earth in all nations or countries of the world. In short, a world globalization of shared research and knowledge of traumatic stress syndromes.

Basic Core Considerations of a Trauma-Based Pedagogy

- First, what is the best way to teach *trauma-specific pedagogy* (TSP) concerning the relevance of metaphors for trauma victims and survivors? What about teaching the whole phenomenological spectrum of insights, emotions, and behavioral patterns that accompany such expressions in therapy? How to define, codify, and classify them and understand their dynamic structural processes? Do they conform to the diagnostic DSM-V PTSD criteria or psychodynamic clinical wisdom? If not, why not?
- How do medical faculty, university professors, teachers, and educators learn how to transmit knowledge of the following trauma-related critical processes: (1) trauma-specific metaphors (TSM); (2) trauma-specific transference (TST) processes; (3) trauma-specific cues and stimuli (TSC); (4) trauma-specific countertransference reactions (TS-CTRs); (5) the use of the matrix concept to identify and understand changes from pre- to posttraumatic psychological states and psychological functioning (see Wilson, 1989; Wilson & Moran, 2004); (6) the relation of PTSD states to all forms of psychosocial and anti-social behaviors, including drug abuse and high-risk behaviors; (7) proper and scientific differential diagnosis; (8) the effects of trauma on aging and life-span development; (9) changes in worldview, morality, ethics, spirituality and life-orientation; (10) brain–body health connections for illness; (11) effects on family and loved ones; (12) effects on sexuality and intimacy; (13) transgenerational effects; (14) impacts to treatment providers; (15) teaching resilience and healthy coping; and (16) other relevant topics and issues.
- Mental health professionals and medical personnel, where possible, are always seeking new ways to assist their patients' recovery and healing. Educationally informed curricula can provide unique information and insights as to how to do this. It should rest on a solid, sophisticated, clinical, evidence-based and academic

knowledge of the complexity of trauma and PTSD amongst diverse trauma populations.

- We believe that it is important to broaden the educational relevance of mythology, anthropology, philosophy, archaeology, literature, theories of personality, psychiatric nosology and more, to the educational application of their wonderfully astute insights to analyzing the significance of various forms of trauma experiences in the life-cycle. As noted by Wilson (2006), trauma complexes and trauma archetypes are universal in nature and form across the world's cultures. What do they tell us? Simply, we must learn to listen and interpret in culturally-specific forms, and realize, if not recognize, ourselves in them. Ultimately, we are all spiritual and soul survivors. It is confrontation with truth, processes of denial or the face of self-dissolution in the aftermath of significant trauma that makes a difference in the question of life quality and existential meaning of life itself.
- In a world of rapid change we now live in an age of uncertainty and unpredictability on a globalized basis because of instantaneous worldwide communications and capacities. Recently, traumatic events in Japan (e.g., 2010 tsunami and nuclear crisis); the war in Afghanistan (2011); record historical levels of natural disasters by tornadoes in the United States (2011); and brutal political and upheavals and turmoil in Egypt, Syria, Libya, Yemen and elsewhere (2011), only underscore the fact that these important and worldwide events can have huge, if not long-range consequences, to ordinary people trying to live basic lives with structure, security, and a sense of a hopeful future. These examples could be further illustrated and detailed as punctuation points for our current times and concerns for the victims and survivors but also the future generations long after this book is published.

A Globalized Trauma Psychology Curriculum Regarding Traumatic Stress

In the most encompassing, passionate, envisioned way, how do we develop state-of-the-art curriculums all over the world, in all cultures (someday, perhaps, in a universal, systematic, integrated curricula and methodology) for the betterment of the human race regarding psychic trauma? It is no longer just a necessary task, but an *imperative mission* for the entire world concerned with the broad sweep of trauma's impacts. To wit, it is a part of everyday life in our modern times for everyone.

In Table 9.1 we made an initial attempt at identifying and explicating the fundamental pedagogical concerns for students, medical trainees, and other professionals who want to improve their knowledge and clinically-essential and research-based information concerning traumatic stress reactions, PTSD, posttraumatic personality alterations and more. In fact, as we presented earlier (see Chapter 3), how does trauma impact the existing self- and personality structure (see Wilson, 2006)? Therefore, how do educators focus on the central objectives of their obligated coursework in this area of traumatic stress studies? For example, what would constitute a trauma/PTSD coursework curriculum to address the issues presented in Table 9.1? What would their course syllabi look like?

In Table 9.2 we construct an abbreviated list to speak of trauma-specific metaphors (TSM) and their ultimate relevance to essential pedagogical needs and eventual curriculum development.

Trauma Pedagogy: Curricular Core Essentials

Table 9.2 is a template as to how trauma metaphors are critical to posttraumatic and medical education for the roles of trauma metaphors in resident education in medicine, psychiatry, and psychology. How does the resident, clinical trainee become more comfortable with their work with trauma and PTSD patients? When do they really learn what they should have learned under proper circumstances? When will they have enough "hands on" clinical experience to know what is what?

What is the Future Necessity for Training and Education in Trauma Studies and PTSD?

Table 9.2 presents critical needs for pedagogical education and curricular development:

- The entrance to the inner space of psychological trauma in all of its potential complexities and mental organizations is enormous. The components and psychological structures need to be undisturbed but discovered. What are the most effective pathways?
- The sensitive and properly educated psychotherapist will be able to identify trauma-specific transference (TST) and trauma-specific metaphors (TSM) immediately in conversation, traditional psychotherapy, or just being a friend or Nurturing Guide (NG). The focal point is simply that these responsible licensed and certified mental health providers realize that they have a difficult, if not frightening, or overwhelming, client to deal with in a clinical setting or situation. What are the appropriate treatment modalities or ways of being a Nurturing Guide (NG), whether professionally trained or not?

Table 9.2 Trauma Pedagogy and Metaphors: Critical Educational Needs

1	Knowledge of TSM and their complexities
2	Attuning therapist sensitivity to TSM
3	Recognizing TST processes and their relativity to TSM
4	Moving beyond CPT manualized PTSD protocols
5	Learning the language of the trauma survivors' experience
6	Understanding transference and countertransference through the portals of entry and metaphors (TST, CTRs, etc.)
7	An open, non-defensive therapeutic posture to explore TSM, TST and other verbal (linguistic) clues to intrapsychic processes
8	The willingness to have a receptive, open-mindedness as to unexpectable and potentially overwhelming disclosure of trauma encounters, including atrocities
9	The willingness to inform the therapist of self-healing by reading ancient and modern history for knowledge of trauma-related experiences and their impact to the self
10	To be willing to have a clinical flexibility to incorporate multimodal approaches to PTSD treatment

Cognitive Behavioral Paradigms and Beyond: Where Do We Go From Here? What Does the Future Hold?

Cognitive behavioral therapy (CBT) and its variant foci have many empirical studies to support its useful efficacy in the short-term treatment of PTSD (see Chapter 8). Nevertheless, we must ask, from a complex PTSD dynamic understanding, what are the limitations and stopping points of CBT/CPT prolonged exposure therapy regimes and protocols? How does the war veteran, for example, respond to such treatment? Is it useful and successful in reducing associated PTSD hyperarousal behaviors and symptoms (e.g., alcohol abuse, proneness to aggression and erratic behaviors)? *Does the CBT and related protocols miss the critical importance of trauma-specific metaphors (TSM) and trauma-specific transference (TST) among other important intrapsychic and interpersonal processes?* We think so and therefore the careful in-depth exploration of the trauma narrative may be missing and unexplained. Upon recognition of TSM and TST, could CBT protocols be modified accordingly to increase effectiveness? Yes, of course (see the clinical illustrations in Chapter 8).

Trauma Speak: Learning to "Talk the Trauma-Specific Talk"

As part of the pedagogical process, we think that it is important for mental health professionals to learn "trauma speak" which specifically refers to the patient's own words or shared words with the Nurturing Guide (NG) for the immersion into traumatic memories and events. For example, Vietnam veterans, during the active war period (1964–1973), adopted and expressed such phrases as "Victor Charlie" (VC) for the enemy Viet Cong, mama-san (Vietnamese woman), slicks, gooks, gunships, medevacs, hooches, dust-offs, puff-the-magic-dragon, and so much more for aircraft, enemy, and villages. These were words of specific references and importance to unit cohesion and successful functioning and daily personal experiences in unit operations. Indeed, how would an outsider, non-combatant in a warzone understand such words as "incoming mortars," RPGs, Punji, or IEDs?

To be an effective posttraumatic therapist, one must learn the nuances and specifics of linguistic references within a cultural-posttraumatic context. Stated somewhat differently, all traumas are different in their specific effects to the victim/survivor, language and memory expressions, their idiosyncratic nuances and differences. Without therapeutic sensitivity to these linguistic verbalizations and anomalies, the helper will not perceive the intrapsychic conflicts and posttraumatic battles being waged in identity consciousness and complex self-processes (Wilson, 2006). Therefore, language is the key to the inner world of the trauma patient. A fine-tuned therapeutic "ear" equals potential efficacy in the treatment process.

The Core Psychic Processes: Understanding the Relation of Trauma-Specific Transference (TST) and Trauma-Specific Metaphors (TSM)

In posttraumatic psychotherapy, transference and countertransference are inevitably present and quite readily detectable (see Chapter 8). Patients suffering posttraumatic after-effects universally manifest trauma-specific transference (TST) and trauma-specific metaphors (TSM). These common and indigenous reactive processes should be recognized and understood by the care provider, as they provide portals of entry (POE) into intrapsychic spaces where the residual effects of trauma exist as a psychic repository of a special sort. In this regard, this critical investigation requires an open non-defensive therapeutic posture critically essential to explore TSMs, TSTs and other linguistic clues to internal cognitive schemas of posttraumatic mental processes. This, of course, includes the willingness of the therapist to be non-judgmental and prepared to hear unimagined trauma narratives (e.g., the unsaid secret non-spoken horrors). As such, it may demand multi-modal treatment approaches and the exploration of mythologies and literature from many diverse liberal disciplines. Understanding TSMs requires more than basic counseling skills. It requires informed knowledge of the Hero's Journey in the wisest humanistic-clinical sense of life's journey itself (see Chapter 1) (see Wilson & Lindy, 1994, for a detailed discussion).

Pedagogical Foci and Curricular Considerations

It is a fact that traumatic experiences and life-events are ubiquitous in nations, cultures, and societies throughout the world (Wilson, Friedman, & Lindy, 2004). In the past and our current times, unfortunately, they are everyday life-events. So, how do we awaken the Nurturing Guide (NG) who wears various uniforms, responsibilities, or efforts to do his or her role-related job to comfort and deal with traumatized persons? Among other questions of direct relevance: Did the essential medical, psychiatric, psychological training efforts properly equip them to professionally treat or deal with psychological trauma and PTSD? Did their formal training include specific courses in acute psychic trauma management, PTSD, trauma effects, compassion fatigue, and trauma dynamics specific to the program of treatment of stress-related disorders? If so, how? If not, why?

These broad considerations raise many issues about pedagogy regarding trauma and PTSD. In essence, there is an important, if not urgent and critical, national need for mental health specialists to understand trauma metaphors (TSM), trauma-specific processes, the processes of posttraumatic transference (TST) and much more about posttraumatic psychotherapy (see Wilson & Lindy, 1994). In short, there is a rich harvest awaiting collection and use in improving healthcare services in the areas of trauma care delivery. There are, at a minimum, two sets of necessary and conflicting needs. To have a more qualified and competent treatment provider to care for PTSD patients. Second, to properly recognize in an epidemiological sense the scope and severity of the problem especially for Iraqi and Afghani war veterans.

How Do Mental Health Professionals Learn How to Decode Trauma-Specific Metaphors (TSM) and Trauma-Specific Transference (TST) Relations With Patients?

As previously noted, Table 9.1 presents ten critical issues in psychotherapy/psychiatric education relative to trauma, PTSD, and traumatic stress studies. These initial understandings potentially provide considerations for more inclusive and comprehensive educational curricula on these and more important clinical-educational treatment programs for traumatized victims, especially U.S. war veterans from Iraq and Afghanistan as well as refugees and victims of genocides in Africa in our current times (2011).

In this book we have presented 67 case histories to illustrate some of our knowledge and insights about trauma-specific metaphors (TSM) and the dynamic intrapsychic processes of PTSD. These PTSD/trauma clinical cases have demonstrated the relevance and importance of the therapist learning how to *decode trauma-specific metaphors* (TSM) as among the other major portals of entry to internal self-configurations of trauma-encoding in mental states and psychodynamic-psychoformative processes (Wilson, Friedman, & Lindy, 2004).

An important component of pedagogical curricula for medical-psychological students or residents in training is to learn *how to decode trauma-specific metaphors (TSM), trauma-specific transference processes (TST), and other unique aspects of helping trauma survivors metabolize difficult life-experiences.* How do we educate the next generation to learn to listen empathically and sensitively in this specific culturally and historically valuable way?

While it seems overtly evident and transparent, the student in medical or psychological training needs to be cognizant of the complex nature of the Abyss Experience (AE) (Wilson, 2006) and be able to explore the patients' involvement in such traumatizing experiences, i.e., what it means to confront the Abyss Experience (AE) and the specter of one's own death in traumatic experience.

For the trauma patient, there are clearly expectable changes in themselves and views of life and a posttraumatic cross-cultural views of the nature of living things. Simply focused, how do cross-cultural factors and anthropological knowledge bear on the linguistic expressions of trauma metaphors and clinical presentations, especially in non-Western nations? If they are different; how so? If they are similar, how so? Are these archetypal manifestations of posttraumatic and human adaptive processes? If yes, in what specific ways?

In terms of cross-cultural anthropological incorporations into the clinical training of mental health professionals, why should they not be educated in a cross-cultural, globalized, knowledge of healing and treatment approaches on a worldwide basis (see Wilson & Tang, 2007)? For example, what does traditional Chinese medicine (TCM) offer? Native American rituals and traditions (Wilson, 1989)? Responders to the 2002 tsunami disaster in Sri Lanka or Thailand and elsewhere? What posttraumatic interventions were successful and which ones were not? How to assess, evaluate, and comprehend these prosocial humanitarian efforts? How do we collect empirical or clinical knowledge on what was effective, therapeutic, healing or not (see Wilson & Tang, 2007)? What is the empirical–clinical based evidence and how best to evaluate it and by what set of appropriate cultural criteria?

The Future Lies Ahead for Posttraumatic Pedagogy

In an era of rapid globalization, posttraumatic educational pedagogy must move to the very specific understanding of different cultures and socio-political governmental processes and cultural regulations (Wilson & Tang, 2007). How are cultural policies shaping or governing programs to respond to disasters?

A trauma survivor is a victim, somewhere in the world, of good or bad human beings or good or bad situations, nations, or cultures. A traumatized person is always unique, painful, and suffers in their recovery process. How do we bring them "home again?"

What, if any, are the limits to this process of recovery? What cultural mechanisms will facilitate their recovery in salutary ways?

The professional resident in psychiatry, psychology, or social work needs to be educated about the special conditions of victimization. For example, being a victim of raping camps in Bosnia, murder by hacking the skulls of children and others in Rwanda, electro-shock torture to female genitalia in Chile; the witnessing of father-daughter rape in El Salvador; and more (see Wilson & Thomas, 2004; Drozdek & Wilson, 2007).

The resident who chooses to work with PTSD patients, especially war and political torture victims, must learn of the experiences of veterans and others, where possible, in the same "vet" language and proper, insightful metaphors. It is clear that without such knowledge and functions they will be significantly limited in effectiveness despite CPT, CBT, manualized protocols, and medical treatments (see Chapter 8).

Insights and Lessons Learned

The specific issues of how different cultures find their own ways of curing, nurturing, or treating trauma victims is an especially interesting one that we have explored earlier (Wilson, 1989; Wilson & Tang, 2007). While space limitations do not allow us a more complete presentation, we can make the following tentative conclusions and observations here: (1) every culture of indigenous peoples have evolved specific forms to help victims of trauma. These are "culture-specific" forms of rituals, interventions, and healing that are rooted in geographical and culture-based presentations in complex and creative ways. In general, they are non-exportable, indigenously based phenomena (Wilson & Tang, 2007). They are therapeutically successful *within culture-specific contexts.*

The issue of understanding cultural nuances, political or cultural ethnocentricity functions, extends to how professional resident trainees learn the "bigger picture" for political oppression, torture, sex abuse, disintegration of cultures, and other forms of societal dissolution. It is a fact that nations, cultures, and individual societies dissolve and their inevitable traumatic consequences encompass a totality of the whole population of survivors. For example, generating refugees, asylum seekers, and others. In this journey, finding exit visas, resources to support families facing arrest and torture by political oppression, or when lucky, the opportunity to immigrate to a host country in the European Union (EU) or the United States of America (USA).

In short focus, the resident-trainee medical doctors need to learn about these refugee-immigrant patients and the context of what they experienced. It cannot be assumed that Western traditional medical approaches will be most effective for their posttraumatic concerns.

These soon-to-be licensed professionals need to know that many asylum-seeking persons fake and lie about their trauma-experience (Drozdek & Wilson, 2007). Most others, of course, do not fabricate and cannot even express the unsaid traumas and horrific experiences (see Chapter 1). Therefore, how to diagnose the fake from the authentic can be understood in a good trauma pedagogy program (see Drozdek & Wilson, 2007; Wilson & Moran, 2004).

A comprehensive, professional curriculum should incorporate all contemporary knowledge for PTSD treatments in psychotherapeutic tools in the valued, necessary treasure chest that includes, obviously, all CBT/CPT techniques of dealing with PTSD.

However, beyond these important evolved and verified evidenced-based behavioral approaches, exists the psychodynamic and, perhaps, broader cross-cultural perspectives of how trauma is encoded in consciousness at various levels of awareness (see Drozdek & Wilson, 2007).

We believe that in a very critical sense, trauma-specific metaphor experiences (TSM), trauma-specific transference processes (TST), trauma-specific traumatic metaphoric transmissions and Type I and Type II countertransference reactions are active manifestations in ongoing therapeutic efforts of all types (Type I and Type II CTRs) (Wilson & Lindy, 1994). All of these interrelated, educational-clinical processes are germane and of utmost concern in the treatment of trauma and PTSD patients.

Therapists, physicians, and mental health professionals know all of this instinctively and through personal professional journeys. It is a simple tribute to their efforts and endurance to go further and find portals of entrance to the unsaid, unspeakable secrets of trauma. The PTSD vault in the unconscious is limitless. The more the therapist has to work within their knowledge base of PTSD and traumatic processes, the greater will be their efficacy, compassion, and capacity for genuine empathy.

Changes in Educational Focus: Architectural Themes of the Book

Two themes underlie every chapter of this book: improving the listening skills of those who work clinically with trauma survivors and expanding the context in which this empathic listening takes place to include the culture of the survivor.

Specifically, (1) we call for increased attention to trauma metaphors, the survivors' unique invention of *new language to contain trauma narrative* and to promote recovery. And, (2) we call for increased appreciation of interruption in the trauma story or trauma-induced disruptions in metonymy.

We call for placing the trauma survivors' current dilemma as a way-station of the Hero's journey, and we wish to expand the Western therapists' vision to include an awareness of the crucial role of the Nurturing Guide (NG) in the recovery process.

We intend this renewed interest in proper empathic listening as an antidote to the current learning atmosphere heavily weighted toward protocol-based interventions with trauma survivors. We fear that the current climate for our students risks dampening their appreciating the unique experience of each trauma survivor, undervaluing the role of empathy in recovery, foreshortening the discovery of multiple levels of meaning in trauma, and bypassing the crucial roles of giving testimony and bearing witness in healing work with trauma survivors.

Pedagogy in the Clinical Years of Training on Trauma

With the above curriculum considerations potentially in place, trauma educators will be in a better position to move their students into the clinical years where rotations at emergency rooms, community and student health centers, psychiatric hospitals, particularly the Veterans Administration (VA) hospital system, will expose them to the effects of rape, incest, war, and civilian trauma, if not more.

Educators must then function as role models, as supervisors and case conference leaders. In each role the educator will find the concepts in the book useful.

Professional Students, Residents, and Others

Students watch their teachers carefully and often model themselves consciously and unconsciously after them. With this in mind, the teacher, as clinical interviewer who is observed by students as part of the curriculum, improves the quality of that model by the following activities:

1. Shows genuine interest in the trauma narrative, noting empathically its interruptions and exploring respectfully potential trauma metaphors (TSM and TST).
2. Demonstrates respect for giving testimony and bearing witness.
3. Demonstrates attitudes consistent with the Nurturing Guide (NG), especially by placing existential despair of trauma into a larger humanitarian and ethical context.
4. Is open to how the trauma survivor is responding to the interviewer, especially when there are inadvertent negative reactions.
5. Demonstrates credible interest in and background knowledge of the circumstances of traumatic situations.
6. Completes the interview with the patient feeling that at least some of his existential despair and struggles with his journey home have been understood.

Faculty and Supervisors: Roles and Functions

As supervisor, the educator working in a one-to-one relationship with the student who presents specific sessions from a specific trauma survivor, seeks similar goals through slightly different methods:

1. Encourages the students' intuition and empathy in the process of gathering history.
2. Encourages learning background information on circumstances of the traumatic situation.
3. Encourages diligence in understanding the patient's current life dilemmas and the unusual phrases or possible trauma metaphors he uses to describe them.
4. Encourages exploration and expansion of trauma metaphors and traumatic specific transference.
5. Encourages a safe, respectful, and ethical space in the consultation room.
6. Encourages self-reflection on the part of the student clinician.
7. Encourages respect for stabilizing defenses as much as for truth.

Case Conference Leader: Seminars of Discovery

Finally, as case conference leader, the educator commenting on the work of one student in the presence of 6–12 students at a time, adds to the above activities the following:

1. Asks each participant to, first, put himself into the chair occupied by the trauma survivor.
2. Encourages associations to trauma metaphors.
3. Identifies points of empathic strain in the therapeutic encounter.
4. Keeps the discussion in the here and now, attending to nuances of the real encounter.

5 Encourages the attitudes of a Nurturing Guide (NG) within which the interventions of a specific form of treatment take place.

Thus, the specific recommendations to improve pedagogy in the clinical years return the focus of the student clinician to expanding his capacity for empathic listening, to the development and maintenance of an ethical space, and to the continued growth not only of the recovering survivor but of the clinician who takes on this incredibly important task as well.

Summary

In focus, TSM, TST, TSD, Empathic Modalities I–IV (Wilson & Lindy, 1994), etc., are germane and among the many essential psychodynamic processes that reveal the complex encoded states of intricate processes of traumatic recovery in posttraumatic therapies. These traumatic memories are always there and occur in one form or another every day. One goal of this book is to illustrate, by clinical and conceptual analysis, that gaining deep clinical knowledge from various trauma-specific dynamic processes will be an important and critical pathway to the interior of posttraumatic states; i.e., how they are encoded in memory and how they affect cognition, emotions, and behavioral dispositions. In the end, they are ultimately "just there," in one form or another, organismically based expressions of trauma states. In that sense, they await a Nurturing Guide (NG) for discovery and chances for transformation and integration.

10 Future Implications

Metaphors of Trauma and Where Do We Go From Here?

Changes in Educational and Future Research Orientations

Beginning in Chapter 1, we presented an encompassing perspective of the direct relationship of trauma experiences to the incipient development of trauma metaphors in linguistic forms across cultures in the world. Our initial foray and preliminary exploration revealed that, in the most basic ways, psychological trauma is encoded in a consistent pattern of psychic states of a socially encoded, sequential dynamic nature amongst cultures (see Figure 1.1 and Table 1.1). Stated simply, the internal cognitive processing and encoding mechanisms are humanly universal but culturally shaped by language and culture systems and traditions of socio-emotional processes. *Trauma-encoded metaphors transform over time from emotionally encoded memories to existential and spiritual representations in everyday language.* It is a process of transformation with many pathways to integration. As we have discussed elsewhere, trauma archetypes and trauma complexes are cross-culturally universal in nature (Wilson, 2006). In the most fundamental way, understanding trauma metaphors is just another portal of entry (POE, see Chapter 1) into PTSD intrapsychic, configurational space in conscious and unconscious posttraumatic processes. How does the therapist find these portals of entry (POE)?

Two central or major themes consistently underline every chapter of this book: (1) improving the empathic listening skills of those who work clinically with trauma survivors, and (2) expanding the context in which this listening takes place to include the culture of the survivor.

We now call, specifically, for increased attention to trauma metaphors, the survivors' invention of new language forms of representation of internal states. Trauma metaphors enable the survivor and the Nurturing Guide (NG) to see how details of the experience map onto the present and future. They open doorways to multiple levels of meaning and hidden trauma. They lyse and metabolize overwhelming experiences into manageable parts and thereby contain the trauma narrative through words; their appreciation promotes discovery and recovery of the unspoken and unsaid and yet undiscovered or disclosed.

For the listeners (i.e., shaman, native healer, therapist, priest, psychotherapist, physician, counselor, etc.), the survivors' unique language forms categories of metaphors that in turn reference paradigms that expand the clinician's body of awareness, stretch his capacity for empathy and enable growth as well as healing for therapist and client. While we believe that this is essential, it requires specific knowledge and education of professionals about trauma-specific encoding of linguistic representation of traumatic states (e.g., see TSM, TST, TSC, etc.).

We call for increased appreciation of interruption in the trauma story as a necessary and expectable set of steps in the recovery of painful memory. Trauma-induced disruptions in metonymy (see Chapter 2) are as much part of the survivors' narrative as are the unique metaphors he or she creates. Lexical "leakage" is most revealing of unconscious mental states, including death (Spence & Breznitz, 1983). Trauma-specific metaphors are a form of "lexical leakage" and demand attention and interpretation as to prevalent mental states and processes.

Disruptions in the course of treatment and psychotherapy occur for good reason: dissociation, as an adaptive defensive process, first and foremost, protects the victim/survivor. Finding the safe distance from overwhelming events that allows the survivor to place them into a perspective that integrates rather than distorts, is a process that takes time, patience, and trust.

We call for placing the trauma survivors' current dilemma as a way-station of the Hero's journey (see Chapter 1) and we wish to expand the Western therapists' vision to include an awareness of the crucial role of the Nurturing Guide (NG) in recovery (see Chapters 1 and 5).

Rather than cast the patient with PTSD as a person suffering from a list of symptoms, only vaguely and often incorrectly connected with his trauma experience, we prefer to see the trauma survivor as an injured human Hero/Survivor, flawed to be sure, but nonetheless one who has faced the Abyss Experience (AE) and returned from it a changed person (see Figure 1.1). As such, we must attend to his or her preparation or lack of it, her commitment to an ideal or responsibility greater than herself or her disillusionment in or with it, her mentoring or leadership or its absence, her loyalty to others confronting the same monster or the deterioration in morale, his confronting the monstrousness of evil and chaos, or retreat from it, and his multi-step journey home with wise advisors or their absence, protection from further trauma or vulnerability to it, and integration of newly transformed self into the fabric of her ongoing life or the fixation in earlier stages of the Hero's journey, delaying the development of the new self.

Rather than cast the clinician in a stereotyped role such as medicine prescriber or an advocate for cognitive change limited to protocol-defined actions of treatment (CBT/CPT) and interventions, we prefer to see the Western clinician expand his or her range of activity to include many of those of the Nurturing Guide (NG): abilities, gifts, talents, and God-given gifts of compassion. Insight regarding trauma metaphors, clarifying how trauma has induced changes in self and personality, developing a healing relationship that includes advice, wisdom, protection, soothing, and most importantly the roles of listening to the survivors giving testimony and the activity of bearing witness. In short, to have the courage to become a Nurturing Guide (NG) in the fullest sense of our understanding.

In this book, we have chronicled how the recovery processes overwhelm psychic injury. Trauma overloads psychological and somatic pathways. Coping with the repetitions of these processes, set off secondarily by relatively neutral stimuli, damages personality on many levels and alters self-structures as well (Wilson, 2006). Efforts to narrate such experiences and the changes they have caused often take a *wordless form.* The beginning narrative may be decipherable only in metaphoric enactments of the trauma as in Paul's picking at his boots or Josh's crushing chest pain or Tristan's feeling like a "groggy boxer." Such metaphoric enactments accurately reflect a damaged post-traumatic self as one who walks on his dead friend's brains, or who ran over a child's heart, or who watches his sister get tossed like a rag doll by an oncoming car.

This use of words is the beginning of a metabolic process that links language to core dimensions of personality and the posttraumatic self (Wilson, 2006). These trauma metaphors encode that part of intrapsychic structure and cognitive processes that are damaged and clarify how they are affecting everyday life. It is this activity, the finding of words and phrases that capture critical aspects of the trauma experience (e.g., trauma-specific metaphor), that begins to locate the trauma in the survivor's past and foreshadows an emergent posttraumatic self who will survive.

Transformation and Integration

As transformed, these metaphors "break down" or delineate the trauma into manageable pieces or configurations, as for example, the discovery that Tom's prisoner-of-war (POW) experience was each day, like a horrific game of musical chairs, or Karen's discovery that being overpowered by her rapist was like the childhood experience of an unfair wrestling match, or Josh's understanding that he suffered from a broken heart, or Tristan's understanding that life continually boxed him in. Manageable and readily understandable segments lead the way to mastery experiences when exposed to the threat of repetition rather than the breakdown of psychic structure. And new mastery activity restores psychic structure and forms a bridge to self-integration. Finally, metaphor as a symbol reconnects the trauma survivor with his culture and the hero myths embodied within it as in Lee's feather from an Indian headdress, and his St. Christopher medal.

We intend this renewed interest in listening as an antidote to the current learning atmosphere heavily weighted toward protocol-based interventions with trauma survivors. This position, unfortunately, can create an atmosphere that, with empirical evidence to back us up, it is we, the clinicians, who have the answers to their problems, while our trauma patients seem to suffer only because they are guilty of cognitive distortions that should change simply because we convince the survivor of their irrationality. We fear that the current climate for our students risks dampening their appreciating the unique experience of each trauma survivor, undervaluing the role of empathy in recovery, foreshortening the discovery of multiple levels of meaning in trauma and bypassing the crucial roles of giving testimony and bearing witness in healing work with trauma survivors.

The attitude we encourage is, rather, one where it is the trauma survivor who has so much to teach us. Here are a few ideas for the future.

New Directions for Scientific Research on PTSD and Clinical Studies: Beyond What the Funding Agencies Want and Fund

The concepts and many clinical illustrations in this book have been organized in such a way as to promote future research. Below we present eight working hypotheses that grew from our work and appear to be ready for empirical testing.

1. PTSD patients and other trauma survivors use unexpected or foreign, trauma-specific expressions or gestures in a measurably different manner from non-PTSD patients and from the ordinary population (e.g., TSMs, TST, etc.).
2. Many of the unusual words and linguistic phrases are used metaphorically, *accurately mapping onto current feelings or adaptational states*, often at unconscious and symbolic levels.
3. The unusual words or phrases accurately reflect an important element of the trauma experience (i.e., what happened?).
4. Exploratory efforts to test for the presence of steps 2 and 3 above, during treatment, increase the patient's subjective feeling of being understood and of increased self-awareness. Increased empathic attunement.
5. PTSD patients and other survivors speak with more spontaneous interruptions in their attempts to converse about both current dilemmas and trauma narratives than non-PTSD patients and the ordinary population.
6. Such interruptions occur as the survivor nears some part of the narrative that reminds him of the trauma or represents symbolic equivalents (TSMs as resistance).
7. Respectful attention to these interruptions in a climate of trust promotes recall and disclosure. Interruptions in the narrative are a clue to defensive protection.
8. CBT/CPT groups structured to allow explorations of potential trauma metaphors result in improvements in standard measures of positive psychotherapy outcomes and increases in subjective measures of meaningfulness both for patients and group leaders. This quantitative data does not mean the patient is healthier, recovered, or has resolved their trauma-related issues.

Future Research Orientations and Considerations

While it will be up to the next generation of investigators to craft these studies in detail, we suggest that the above hypotheses lend themselves to at least three distinct research formats and orientations.

1. In the first format, individuals in three categories are interviewed individually and videotaped by researchers using common structured interview techniques. Gestures, words, and phrases that relate to their current feelings and adaptive states are examined to ascertain their comparative normal versus uniqueness in semantic expression and word choice. Inter-rater reliability is established so that word phrases may be placed into the expectable range or the unexpected range. Quantitative summaries for the two groups are then compared statistically.
2. In the second format (see hypotheses 2, 3, and 4 above), the design sample is limited to patients with current symptoms. Interviewers systematically explore unusual words, phrases, and gestures to clarify whether or not these words accurately reflect the patient's current feeling or adaptive states. They then explore if these same words or phrases map onto the trauma experience in a significant way. Finally, they ask the patient if the above explorations in step 2 and step 3 lead to an increase in feeling understood and increase in self-awareness. In a variant of this format, interviewers systematically attend to the breaks in continuity of the story.

3 In the third format, two CBT/CPT groups are compared. The first minimizes check-in time at the beginning of the group session with the leaders paraphrasing patient reports by linking each to a general CBT concept or goal such as disturbing thoughts, anger, control, or distrust, suggesting that these issues will be addressed in another setting. The second group agrees to spend from one-third to one-half of the time of the group focusing on the check-in. Where these brief comments contain a potential trauma metaphor the leader along with other group members takes time to explore and expand the meanings of such phrases together with the identified patient. Summary evaluations of the two types of groups look at overall measures of improvement and subjective measures of meaningfulness.

Summary

Our initial goal for this book was to lay out useful, practical, and clinically-relevant bases for *Trauma, Culture, and Metaphor: Pathways of Transformation and Integration.* In Chapters 1 through 9, we presented a full range of investigations starting with universal myths of the Trauma Hero (MTH), to how traumatic experiences get encoded in verbal forms and are cross-culturally universal in nature. As such, they not only reveal purely linguistic encoding in verbal memory and expression but provide portals of entry (POE) into psychic trauma space. So, once identified and recognized, these realities enlighten insight into the ultimate journey of the trauma survivor. What will they endure and survive? How will they transform their lives?

There is no doubt that the Journey of the Survivor takes many paths and vicissitudes. There is no clear or certain path for the Hero/Survivor, as Joseph Campbell illustrated. It is a journey of a complicated life that they could not expect, yet it happened and produced unwanted consequences for their life, well-being, and future existence. How could they know what was coming for them in the future? The Journey of the Hero in Mythology is just that: a truth of the human condition and the life vicissitudes they will face, encounter, and overcome. The final issue, per se, is whether or not traditional, culturally bound cultures and societies will evoke effective, universal, but diverse treatments and rituals. We believe that the globalized world is on the cusp of sure discovery of a profound scientific-humanistic realization of highest (transcendent) and lowest (trauma and despair) aspects of what it means to be human.

Bibliography

American Psychiatric Association (APA) (1980). *Diagnostic and statistical manual of mental disorders* (3rd ed.). Washington, DC: Author.

Barker, P. (1985). *Using metaphors in psychotherapy.* New York: Brunner/Mazel.

Breuer, J., & Freud, S. (1955). *Studies on hysteria (1895 [1893–1895]): Complete psychological works* (2nd ed.). London: Hogarth Press.

Busch, F. (1996). The ego and its significance in analytic interventions. *Journal of the American Psychoanalytic Association,* 44, 1073–1099.

Campbell, J. (1949). *Hero with a thousand faces.* New York: Penguin Books.

Campbell, J. (1992). *Pathways to bliss.* New York: Harper.

Davoine, F., & Gaudilleire, J.M. (2004). *History beyond trauma: Whereof one cannot speak, thereof one cannot stay silent.* New York: Other Press.

Eitinger, L., & Strom, A. (1973). *Mortality and morbidity after excessive stress.* New York: Humanities Press.

Erikson, E. (1968). *Identity, youth & crisis.* New York: Norton.

French, T. (1958). The art and science of psychoanalysis. *Journal of the American Psychoanalytic Association,* 6, 187–214.

Freud, S. (1895). Project for a scientific psychology. In *Standard edition, 1* (pp. 27–42). London: Hogarth Press.

Freud, S. (1900). Interpretation of dreams. In *The complete works of Sigmund Freud, Vol. IV.* London: Hogarth Press.

Freud, S. (1901). Psychopathology of everyday life. In *The complete works of Sigmund Freud, Vol. VI.* London: Hogarth Press.

Freud, S. (1905). Jokes and their relation to the unconscious. In *The complete works of Sigmund Freud, Vol.VIII.* London: Hogarth Press.

Freud, S. (1923). Ego and the id. In *Standard Edition, 19.* London: Hogarth Press.

Freud, S., & Breuer, J. (1895). *Studies on hysteria.* New York: Avon Press.

Gill, M. (1982). Analysis of transference, Vol. I. In *Psychological Issues Monograph, 53,* (pp. 59–84). New York: International Universities Press.

Gray, P. (1994). *The ego and analysis of defense.* Northvale, NJ: Jason Aronson.

Greenson, R. (1967). *The technique and practice of psychoanalysis, Vol. 1* (pp. 190–216). New York: International University Press.

Hagengimana, Athanase (1992). Ihahamuka, *Internal Journal of the Cincinnati Psychoanalytic Institute,* III, 12–16.

Halle, M. (1956). The two aspects of language and two types of aphasia disturbances. In R. Jakobson (Ed.), *Fundamentals of language.* The Hague: Mouton.

Horowitz, M. (1976). *Stress response syndromes.* New York: J. Aronson.

Horowitz, M. (1986). *Stress response syndromes.* New York: J. Aronson.

Ingram, D. (1996). The vigor of metaphor in clinical practice. *American Journal of Psychoanalysis*, 56(1), 17–26.

Ingram, D. (1996). How words mean in analytic psychotherapy. *The Journal of the American Academy of Psychoanalysis and Dynamic Psychiatry*, 527–541.

Jakobson, R. (1956). Two apects of language and two types of aphasia disturbances. In R. Jakobson and M. Halle (Eds.), *Fundamentals of language* (pp. 96–128). The Hague: Mouton.

Jakobson, R. (1970). *Main trends in the science of language*. New York: Harper & Row.

Janet, P. (1900). *L'automatisure psychologiqene*. Paris: Balliere.

Jung, C.G. (1912). The collected works (Bollingen series XX, 20 vols.). Trans. R.F.C. Hull. In H. Read, M. Fordham, & G. Adler (Eds.), *The theory of psychoanalysis* (CW 4). Princeton, NJ: Princeton University Press.

Jung, C.G. (1929). The collected works (Bollingen series XX, 20 vols.). Trans. R.F.C. Hull. In H. Read, M. Fordham, & G. Adler (Eds.), *The therapeutic value of abreaction* (CW 16). Princeton, NJ: Princeton University Press.

Jung, C.G. (1933). *Modern man in search of a soul*. New York: Harcourt, Brace, Jovanovich.

Jung, C.G. (1934). The collected works (Bollingen series XX, 20 vols.). Trans. R.F.C. Hull. In H. Read, M. Fordham, & G. Adler (Eds.), *A review of psychological complexes* (CW 8). Princeton, NJ: Princeton University Press.

Jung, C.G. (1950). The collected works (Bollingen series XX, 20 vols.). Trans. R.F.C. Hull. In H. Read, M. Fordham, & G. Adler (Eds.), *Four archetypes* (CW 8). Princeton, NJ: Princeton University Press.

Jung, C.G. (1957, 1972). The collected works (Bollingen series XX, 20 vols.). Trans. R.F.C. Hull. In H. Read, M. Fordham, & G. Adler (Eds.), *Recent thoughts on schizophrenia* (CW 3). Princeton, NJ: Princeton University Press.

Jung, C.G. (1959, 1968). The collected works (Bollingen series XX, 20 vols.). Trans. R.F.C. Hull. In H. Read, M. Fordham, & G. Adler (Eds.), *The archetypes and the collective unconscious* (CW 9i). Princeton, NJ: Princeton University Press.

Jung, C.G. (1960). The collected works (Bollingen series XX, 20 vols.). Trans. R.F.C. Hull. In H. Read, M. Fordham, & G. Adler (Eds.), *The psychogenesis of mental disease* (CW 3). Princeton, NJ: Princeton University Press.

Jung, C.G. (1960, 1969). The collected works (Bollingen series XX, 20 vols.). Trans. R.F.C. Hull. In H. Read, M. Fordham, & G. Adler (Eds.), *The structure and dynamics of the psyche* (CW 8). Princeton, NJ: Princeton University Press.

Jung, C.G. (1963). *Memories, dreams and reflections*. New York: Vintage Books.

Jung, C.G. (1963). The collected works (Bollingen series XX, 20 vols.). Trans. R.F.C. Hull. In H. Read, M. Fordham, & G. Adler (Eds.), *Civilization in transition* (CW 10). Princeton, NJ: Princeton University Press.

Jung, C.G. (1971). The collected works (Bollingen series XX, 20 vols.). Trans. R.F.C. Hull. In H. Read, M. Fordham, & G. Adler (Eds.), *Psychological types* (CW 6). Princeton, NJ: Princeton University Press.

Jung, C.G. (1972). The structure and dynamics of the psyche. The collected works (Bollingen series XX, 20 vols.). Trans. R.F.C. Hull. In H. Read, M. Fordham, & G. Adler (Eds.), *Psychological types* (CW 8). Princeton, NJ: Princeton University Press.

Jung, C.G. (1992). *Four archetypes: Mother/rebirth/spirit/trickster*. Princeton, NJ: Princeton University Press.

Kohut, H. (1959). Introspection, empathy and psychoanalysis. *Journal of American Psychoanalytic Association, 7*, 459–483.

Kohut, H. (1971). *The analysis of the self*. New York: International Universities Press.

Kohut, H. (1972). Thoughts on narcissism and narcissistic rage. *Psychoanalytic Study of the Child, 27*, 360–400.

Kohut, H., & Seitz, P.F.D. (1978). Concepts and theories of pyshchooanalysis. In J. Wepman & R. Heine (Eds.), *Concepts of personality* (pp. 113–141). Chicago: Aldine Publishing.

Lakoff, G. (2004). *Don't think of an elephant.* White River Junction: Chelsea Green.

Lakoff, G., & Johnson, M. (1980). *Metaphors we live by.* Chicago: University of Chicago Press.

Lakoff, G., & Johnson, M. (1999). *Philosophy in the flesh.* New York: Basic Books.

Laub, D., & Felman, S. (1992). *Testimony, crises of witnessing in literature, psychoanalysis, and history.* New York: Routledge.

Lifton, R.J. (1967). *Death in life: The survivors of Hiroshima.* New York: Simon & Schuster.

Lifton, R.J. (1976). *The life of the self.* New York: Simon & Schuster.

Lindemann, E. (1944). Symptomatology and management of acute grief. *American Journal of Psychiatry,* 101, 141–148.

Lindy, J.D. (1985) The trauma membrane and other concepts derived from psychotherapeutic work with survivors of natural disaster. *Psychiatric Annals, 15*(3), 153–160.

Lindy, J.D. (1987). *Vietnam: A casebook.* New York: Brunner/Mazel.

Lindy, J.D. (1990). *Long term follow-up of children exposed to disaster at Buffalo Creek: A comparison of types of long term outcome.* Presentation at the Annual American Psychiatric Meeting, New York.

Lindy, J.D. (2005). Mutative transference and the restoration of the posttraumatic self. In J. P. Wilson (Ed.), *The posttraumatic seslf: Restoring meaning and wholeness to personality* (pp. 295–331). New York: Brunner-Routledge.

McEwen, B.S. (1998). Seminars of the Beth Israel Deaconess Medical Center: Protective and damaging effects of stress mediators. *New England Journal of Medicine, 338*(3), 171–179.

Miller, J.G. (1978). *Living systems.* New York: McGraw-Hill.

Nmembamuka, Athanase, personal communication, July 1992, during summer fellowship co-sponsored by University of Cincinnati Department of Psychiatry and Cincinnati Psychoanalytic Institute.

Ogden, T. (1997). Reverie and metaphor. *International Journal of Psychoanalysis, 78,* 719–732.

Oppenheim, H. (1889). *Die traumatischen neurosen nach den in der nervenklink der charit'e in den letzten 5.* Jarhen gesammelten Beobachtungen.

The Oxford English Dictionary (2nd ed.). Oxford: Clarendon Press.

Pynoos, R., Frederick C., Calvin, J.M., Nader, K., Arroyo, W., Steinberg, A., Eth, S., Nunez, F., & Fairbanks, L. (1987). Life threat and post traumatic stress. *Archives of General Psychiatry,* 44(12), 1057–1063.

Reich, T. (1948). *Listening with the third ear.* New York: Farrar, Strauss.

Rizzuto, A.M. (2001). Metaphors of a bodily mind. *Journal of the American Psychoanalytic Association,* 49(2), 535–568.

Rosenheck, R.L. (1985). Malignant post-Vietnam stress syndrome. *American Journal of Orthopsychiatry,* 55, 166–176.

Schlessinger, H.J. (1994). How the analyst listens: The pre-stages of interpretation. *International Journal of Psychoanalysis, 75,* 31–37.

Schlessinger, N., & Robbins, F. (1975). The psychoanalytic process: Recurrent patterns of conflict and changes in ego functions. *Journal of the American Psychoanalytic Association, 6,* 197–214.

Schnurr, P., & Green, B. (2004). *Trauma and health: Physical consequences of exposure to extreme stress.* Washington, DC: American Psychological Association.

Seitz, P., Wepman, J., & Heine, R. (n.d.). Concepts and theories of psychoanalysis. In H. Kohut (Ed.), *Concepts of personality.* Chicago: Aldine Publishing.

Sharpe, E. (1949). *Dream analysis.* London: Hogarth Press.

Siegelman, E. (1990). *Metaphor and meaning in psychotherapy.* New York: Guilford Press.

Smith, M., Lin, M.K., & Mendoza, R. (1993). Non biological issues affecting psychopharmacology: Cultural considerations. In K.M. Lin, R.E. Poland, & G. Nalcasali (Eds.), *Psychopharmacology and psychobiology of ethnicity* (pp. 37–58). Washington, DC: American Psychiatric Press, Inc.

Spence, D., & Breznitz, S. (1983). The paradox of denial. In *The denial of stress* (pp. 103–185). New York: International Universities Press.

Titchner, J., & Kapp, F. (1978). *Post traumatic decline.* Unpublished paper presented at the Annual Meeting of the American Psychiatric Association.

Walser, R., & Westrup, D. (2007). *Acceptance and commitment therapy for the treatment of post-traumatic stress disorder.* Oakland, CA: New Harbinger Publications.

Weiss, J., & Sampson, H. (1986). Testing alternative psychoanalytic explanations of the therapeutic process. In J. Masling (Ed.), *Empirical studies of psychoanalytic theories* (Vol. II) (pp. 68–83). Hillsdale, NJ: Analytic Free Press.

Wilson, J.P. (1989) *Trauma, transformation and healing: An integration approach to theory, research and posttraumatic theory.* New York: Brunner/Mazel.

Wilson, J.P. (2001). An overview of clinical considerations and principles in the treatment of PTSD. In J.P. Wilson, M.J. Friedman, & J.D. Lindy (Eds.), *Treating psychological trauma and PTSD* (pp. 59–94). New York: Guilford Publications.

Wilson, J.P. (2004a). Broken spirits. In J.P. Wilson & B. Drozdek (Eds.), *Broken spirits: The treatment of traumatized asylum seekers, refugees and war and torture victims* (pp. 141–173). New York: Brunner-Routledge.

Wilson, J.P. (2004b). The broken spirit: Posttraumatic damage to the self. In J.P. Wilson & B. Drozdek (Eds.), *Broken spirits: Treating traumatized asylum seekers, refugees, war and torture victims* (pp. 107–155). NewYork: Brunner-Routledge.

Wilson, J.P. (2004c). Empathic strain, compassion fatigue and countertransference in the treatment of trauma and PTSD. In D. Knafo (Ed.), *Living with terror, working with trauma: A clinician's handbook* (pp. 121–143). Northvale: Jason Aaronson.

Wilson, J.P. (2004d). Empathy strain, trauma transmission and countertransference in the treatment of PTSD. In J.P. Wilson & B. Drozdek (Eds.), *Broken spirits: Treating traumatized asylum seekers, refugees, war and torture victims* (pp. 275–314). NewYork: Brunner-Routledge.

Wilson, J.P. (2004e). PTSD and complex PTSD: Symptoms, syndromes and diagnoses. In J.P. Wilson & T.M. Keane (Eds.), *Assessing psychological trauma and PTSD* (pp. 7–44). New York: Guilford Press.

Wilson, J.P. (2004f). The abyss experience and the trauma complex: A Jungian perspective of PTSD and dissociation. *Journal of Trauma in Dissociation, 5*(3), 43–68.

Wilson, J.P. (2005). The abyss experience and the archetype of trauma. In J.P. Wilson (Ed.), *The posttraumatic self: Restoring meaning and wholeness to personality.* New York: Brunner-Routledge.

Wilson, J. P. (2005). Trauma and the epigenesis of identity. In J.P. Wilson (Ed.), *The posttraumatic self: restoring meaning and wholeness to personality.* New York: Brunner-Routledge.

Wilson, J. P. (2005). Trauma, peak experiences and dissociative states: A continuum of altered states of consciousness and integrative psychological experiences. In J. P. Wilson (Ed.), *The posttraumatic self: Restoring meaning and wholeness to personality.* New York. Brunner-Routledge.

Wilson, J. P. (2006). *The posttraumatic self: Restoring meaning and wholeness to personality.* New York: Brunner-Routledge.

Wilson, J.P., Friedman, M., & Lindy, J. (2001). *Treating psychological trauma and PTSD.* New York: Guilford Press.

Wilson, J.P., & Lindy, J. (Eds.). (1994). Empathic stress and countertransference. In *Countertransference in the treatment of PTSD.* New York: Guilford Press.

Wilson, J.P., & Moran, T.M. (2004). Assessing PTSD in legal settings. In J.P. Wilson & T.M. Keane (Eds.), *Assessing psychological trauma and PTSD* (pp. 603–645). New York: Guilford Press.

Wilson, J.P., & Thomas, R. (2004). *Empathy in the treatment of trauma and PTSD.* New York: Brunner/Routledge.

Index